Southern History

Volume 32 2010

Southern History is a peer reviewed academic year book published by the Southern History Society covering the historic counties of Cornwall, Devon, Somerset, Gloucester, Wiltshire, Dorset, Hampshire, Oxford, Buckingham, Berkshire, Surrey, Sussex and Kent. It contains articles and reviews. Prospective authors are requested to email the editor for copies of Notes for Contributors. Outlines of proposed submissions are welcome and articles should be submitted in electronic form.

Southern History Society

Officers and Committee for 2009–10

Hon President:
Professor John Rule, Dept of History, University of Southampton, SO17 1BJ.

Officers:
Chairman: Dr John Chapman, Department of Geography, University of Portsmouth. PO1 2UP (email: john.chapman@port.ac.uk)
Hon. Secretary: Dr Jean Morrin, Department of History, University of Winchester. SO22 4NR (email: jean.morrin@winchester.ac.uk)
Hon. Membership Secretary: Dr Cindy Wood, History Dept, University of Winchester. SO22 4NR (email: cindy.wood@winchester.ac.uk)
Hon. Treasurer: Mr George Tatham, Higher Clapton College, Maperton, Wincanton, Somerset. BA9 8EB (email: george.tatham@btinternet.com)
Hon. Editor: Professor Andrew Spicer, Department of History, Oxford Brookes University, Oxford. OX3 0BP (email: aspicer@brookes.ac.uk)
Hon. Reviews Editor: Professor Michael Hicks, Department of History, University of Winchester. SO22 4NR (email: michael.hicks@winchester.ac.uk)

Committee:
Professor Ralph Houlbrooke, Department of History, University of Reading, Whiteknights, Reading. RG6 2AH (email: r.a.houlbrooke@reading.ac.uk)
Miss Sarah Lewin, Hampshire County Record Office, Winchester. SO23 8TH (email: sarah.lewin@hants.gov.uk)
Dr Steve Poole, School of History, University of the West of England, Bristol. BS16 1QY (email Steve.Poole@uwe.ac.uk)
Ms Karen Robson, Hartley Library, University of Southampton, Highfield, Southampton. SO17 1BJ (email k.robson@soton.ac.uk)
Mrs Pearl Romans, Hartley Library, University of Southampton, Highfield, Southampton. SO17 1BJ (email pma1@soton.ac.uk)
Dr Mark Smith, Department of Continuing Education, University of Oxford, Oxford. OX1 2JA (email Mark.smith@conted.ox.ac.uk)

Subscription Rates: Individuals, £18; Institutions, £30; Agents, £24: Individual subscribers in arrears, £24. Non-members £18 per volume. Details and back numbers available from the Hon. Secretary.

Further information about the Society, membership and conferences can be found on our website at http://www.winchester.ac.uk/?page=7578

SOUTHERN HISTORY

Captain Swing Reconsidered:
Forty Years of Rural History from Below

Volume 32 2010

Hon. Editors

Steve Poole
UWE Bristol

and

Andrew Spicer
Oxford Brookes University

SOUTHERN HISTORY SOCIETY

© Copyright Southern History Society
All rights reserved. No part of this publication may be reproduced, stored in a retrieval system, or transmitted, in any form or by any means, electronic, mechanical, photocopying, recording or otherwise without the permission of the publishers

First published in Great Britain in 2010

The Southern History Society is an educational charity, registered by the Charity Commissioners.

ISBN 978-0-9565545-0-5

ISSN 0142–4688

Produced by 4word Ltd, Bristol

Contents

Forty Years of Rural History from Below: Captain Swing and the Historians   1
    Steve Poole

'The Mystery of the Fires': 'Captain Swing' as Incendiarist   21
    Carl J. Griffin

'The Luddism of the Poor': *Captain Swing*, Machine breaking and Popular Protest   41
    Adrian Randall

The Diffusion of Contentious Gatherings in the Captain Swing Uprising   62
    Daniel J. Myers and Jamie L. Przybysz

'Two steps forward; six steps back': the Dissipated Legacy of Captain Swing   85
    Iain Robertson

The True Life and History of Captain Swing. Rhetorical Construction and Metonymy in a time of Reform   101
    Peter Jones

'The Owslebury Lads'   117
    Alun Howkins

Tumult, Riot and Disturbance: Perspectives on Central and Local Government's Roles in the Management of the 1830 'Captain Swing Riots' in Berkshire and adjoining districts   139
    Margaret Escott

'We do not come here … to inquire into grievances; we come here to decide law': Prosecuting Swing in Norfolk and Somerset 1829–1832   159
    Rose Wallis

The Immediate Reaction to the Swing Riots in Surrey 1832–1834   176
Judith Hill

Select Bibliography   201

Index   205

List of Contributors

Margaret Escott is Honorary Research Fellow of the History of Parliament and Swansea University and teaches at the University of Oxford. She contributed to D.R. Fisher (ed.), *The House of Commons, 1820–1832* (Cambridge, 2009) and her recent publications include essays on parliamentary representation, and the philanthropist Robert Owen. She has edited a collection of papers on the Swing Riots for Berkshire Record Society and has written on this theme for J. Dils (ed.), *Berkshire Historical Atlas* (forthcoming).

Carl J. Griffin is a Lecturer in Human Geography at Queen's University, Belfast. His research embraces studies of popular protest, as well as cultures of unemployment, human-environment interactions, and the history of political economy. He has published papers in, amongst other places, *Rural History*, *Journal of Historical Geography*, *International Review of Social History*, *Transactions of the Institute of British Geographers*, with a paper examining the use of violence in Swing forthcoming in *Past & Present*. As well as finishing a book on Swing, he is starting a British Academy-funded project on labour regulation and proto trade unionism in the early nineteenth century English west.

Peter Jones is currently Lecturer in the History of Medicine at Oxford Brookes University. He has published widely on popular protest, poor relief and social relations in the rural south of England in the early nineteenth century, most recently 'Finding Captain Swing: Protest, Parish Relations and the State of the Public Mind in 1830', *International Review of Social History* 54 (2009). He is currently working on a book exploring the 'moral economy' of the poor in the nineteenth century.

Judith Hill taught at the University of Surrey, where she completed her doctorate in 2006 on poverty and unrest in Surrey 1815–1834. She contributed M. Holland (ed.) *Swing Unmasked. The Agricultural Riots of 1830 to 1832 and their Wider Implications* (Milton Keynes, 2005). Recent research on poverty and welfare in early nineteenth century Britain, has led to an essay in M. Holland, G. Gill, and S. Burrell (eds), *Cholera and Conflict. 19th century Cholera in Britain and its Social consequences* (Leeds,

2009) and articles for *Family and Community History* 7 (2004) and *Southern History* 30 (2008) on rural poverty and emigration.

Alun Howkins is Professor Emeritus of Social History at the University of Sussex. He has written extensively on the social history of rural England during the nineteenth and twentieth centuries and besides the Swing riots is currently interested in the history of enclosure after 1845.

Daniel Myers is Professor of Sociology, Associate for Research, Centers, and the Social Sciences, and Fellow of the Kroc Institute for International Peace Studies at the University of Notre Dame. He is currently studying structural conditions, diffusion patterns, and media coverage related to U.S. racial rioting in the 1960s. Recent publications include *Social Psychology* (London, 2004) and *Identity Work in Social Movements* (Minneapolis, 2008).

Steve Poole is Principal Lecturer in Social and Cultural History at UWE Bristol, and the author of various works on popular politics and protest. These include most recently '"A lasting and salutary warning": Incendiarism, rural order and England's last scene of crime execution', *Rural History* 19 (2008) and (ed.) *John Thelwall: Radical Romantic and Acquitted Felon* (London, 2009).

Jamie Przybysz is a Ph.D. candidate in the Department of Sociology at the University of Notre Dame. She studies participation in the disability rights movement in the United States.

Adrian Randall is Professor of English Social History at the University of Birmingham. He is the author of *Riotous Assemblies: Popular Protest in Hanoverian England* (Oxford, 2006).

Iain Robertson is Senior Lecturer in Humanities at the University of Gloucestershire and has published extensively on land agitation in the Scottish Highlands in the twentieth century. More recently, he has returned to his earlier research interest of eighteenth- and nineteenth-century Gloucestershire.

Rose Wallis is currently conducting doctoral research within the School of History at the University of the West of England, Bristol. Her thesis investigates the relationship between magistrates and their communities between 1790 and 1834, focusing on the decline of judicial paternalism. Her work is a comparative study addressing phases of social unrest in Norfolk and Somerset.

Forty Years of Rural History from Below: Captain Swing and the Historians

Steve Poole

Four decades have now passed since the first appearance of Eric Hobsbawm and George Rudé's ground-breaking study of the agricultural labourers' rebellion of 1830, *Captain Swing*. As an addition to the newly developing literature of 'history from below', the book complemented E.P. Thompson's earlier *The Making of the English Working Class* (1963), but arose more directly from Rudé's existing interest in crowd studies and Hobsbawm's with the insurgencies of 'primitive rebels'. It was an important corrective. Even after revisiting his short chapter on field labourers for the 1968 second edition of *The Making of the English Working Class*, to 'clarify the argument', Thompson's engagement with Swing came and went in less than four pages and he was quite prepared to admit that the chapter remained 'inadequate to its theme'.[1] In 1969 then, Hobsbawm and Rudé were the first to adapt the agency-driven methodology of the new social history to events in rural England. In this special edition of *Southern History*, we re-assess the book's influence and importance.

The Swing rebellion had attracted little previous attention from any historian, but as they quickly acknowledged, one solitary 'classic of modern social history', originally published in 1911, stood out as an exception. This was J.L. and Barbara Hammonds' *The Village Labourer*, a deeply sympathetic account of English agricultural workers between the mid-eighteenth century and the passing of the Great Reform Act. While the Hammonds had done much to rescue village labourers from historical obscurity however, devoting two full chapters to Swing in the process, their analysis of its cause, its extent and its nature was comparatively thin and the book's undisguised indignation at the labourers' lot sat uneasily

---

1 E.P. Thompson, *The Making of the English Working Class* (London, 1968), p. 916.

with its scholarship. The background against which the great drama of Swing was enacted was, in the Hammonds' hands, one in which the complexities of under-employment, poor law dependency, rising crime, plummeting wages and social degradation were collapsed into the neat shorthand terminologies of 'Speenhamland' and 'enclosure'. Hobsbawm and Rudé were neither the first nor the last to find fault with that, and certainly many of *The Village Labourer*'s rhetorical flourishes lack objectivity, but we should perhaps remember that the Hammonds wrote at a time when the conservative complacency of much academic history permitted similarly partisan outbursts from their critics to appear reasonable. *The Journal of the Royal Statistical Society*, for example, disliked their account of the punishments meted out by the Swing Special Commissions, not because it lacked detail but because 'the barbarity of the penalties which the law then authorised for comparatively trivial offences is insisted on as if it were a special terror of the landowning system, instead of being a manifestation of the brutal spirit of the day, developed in a desperately mistaken, but still sincere, theory of the punishment and prevention of crime'.[2]

Whatever its shortcomings, Hobsbawm and Rudé were fully conscious of writing in *The Village Labourer*'s shadow. 'Virtually all subsequent references to the rising in general historical works are based on the Hammonds', they wrote, 'and what little is known of it by the general public is what is known of their book'. Moreover, they acknowledged a methodological debt. For beyond attempting a thorough and rigorous record of the events themselves, *Captain Swing* was driven by an objective 'which nowadays – and rightly – tempts many social historians, of reconstructing the mental world of an anonymous and undocumented body of people in order to understand their movements, themselves only sketchily documented'. It was as pioneers and practitioners in the new social history 'from below' that Hobsbawm and Rudé noted the insights acquired by the Hammonds' 'fairly systematic use of the then neglected Home Office papers in the Public Record Office which remain to this day the major source for our knowledge of early nineteenth century social

---

2   J. L. Hammond and Barbara Hammond, *The Village Labourer, 1760–1832: A Study in the Government of England before the Reform Bill* (London 1911); R.H.R., Review of 'The Village Labourer', *Journal of the Royal Statistical Society* 75 (1912), 440. The book's geographical conservatism led to its being dubbed by Andrew Charlesworth, 'The Southern English Village Labourer', its legacy an agricultural history 'shot through with southern English insularity': 'An Agenda for Historical Studies of Rural Protest in Britain, 1750–1850', *Rural History* 2 (1991), 238.

agitations'. Indeed, as one anonymous review of the *Village Labourer* noted in 1912, the authoritative detail with which the Hammonds approached Swing was due in no small part to their use of 'Home Office papers, now drawn upon for the first time'.[3]

To Marxist historians, the Hammonds' shortcomings lay in their Edwardian 'Liberal radicalism', and a discourse shaped by what Hobsbawm would elsewhere call 'moral and other non-material territories'. Essentially, in taking too static a view of class divisions, they had failed to address 'the interaction between the social-economic base and the ideology of various social strata'. By contrast, Hobsbawm and Rudé noted the degraded condition of many small farmers and craft producers and were unsurprised to find them playing an often prominent role in Swing crowds. Although a simple three-class model of landowners, tenant farmers and labourers had been established in much of the countryside since at least the middle of the eighteenth century, the severe depression of the years following the close of the Napoleonic War fractured this traditional model into a more complex triumvirate: landowners, bourgeois capitalist farmers, and then the rest, including small farmers and labourers, whose social and economic marginalism now permitted the discovery of common cause. Swing was therefore to be read as a moment of importance in the 'making' of class at a transformative moment in productive relations. During the early nineteenth century, they argued, the labourer was effectively proletarianised, stripped of his customary rights, under-employed and pauperised while, crucially, 'the nature of his labour and the rural society in which he lived and starved, deprived him even of the relative freedom of the urban and industrial poor' to organise effective resistance. If the Hammonds irritated Tawney for 'writing at times as though the fall of man occurred during the reign of George III', Hobsbawm and Rudé's revisionism was credited by several early reviewers for wearing its anticipated Marxism lightly. They approached *Captain Swing* without hyperbole, avoided reductionist explanatory models based loosely upon enclosure and the poor law, and embraced the systematic collection of quantitative data, which formed its empirical core. By these means, for

---

3   E.J. Hobsbawm and G. Rudé, *Captain Swing* (London 1969), pp. 13–14. All subsequent references to this book refer to the original 1969 edition unless otherwise stated; E.P., Review of 'The Village Labourer', *The American Political Science Review* 6 (1912), 296. Hobsbawm would later dedicate an essay, 'On History from Below' to Rudé as a 'distinguished pioneer' in the discipline in F. Kantz (ed.), *History from Below: Studies on Popular Protest and Popular Ideology* (Oxford, 1988).

example, they were able dispassionately to show that roughly half of those parishes in the sample that had been recently enclosed had not, in fact, taken any part in Swing.[4]

Understanding collective resistance to proletarianisation in 1830 as backward looking and obstructed by an absence of ideology, was not, however, to deny agency. The consequent emphasis placed in *Captain Swing* upon the agency of the rural poor, so vital to the working out of the new history from below, irritated and alarmed some early reviewers. Gertrude Himmelfarb, a practiced critic of social history in all its forms, was worried that in Hobsbawm and Rudé's hands, 'the victims of history have become its principal agents and actors', a potentially distorting process in which 'Village Labourers' became magically transformed into rather less neutral 'rebels' and 'crowds'. Less equivocally, E.L. Jones thought they had 'subordinated the mechanical but compelling facts of population pressure and sluggish industrial growth too much to the purely social decisions which made for rural under-employment and poverty', while G.E. Mingay complained at the 'exaggerated emphasis (given) to the symptoms of the problem' and a 'neglect of the underlying causes' (low wages and a superabundance of labour).[5] Further, if the proletarianisation thesis in *Captain Swing* has been taken up and developed by some recent historians, chiefly Roger Wells, it has been criticised by others, such as Alun Howkins, for simply substituting one over-simplification with another, particularly for its assumed corollary, a 'proletarian consciousness', distinct from the world view of the rural elite.[6] Debates over rural proletarianisation and its relationship to consciousness and ideology may seem less cogent today than they did in 1969, but we should remember that Hobsbawm and Rudé were also contributing to theoretical arguments ongoing at the time in English Marxism. It was a function of the quantitative nature of the methodology driving Captain Swing that many of these criticisms arose in the first place, and certainly the broad-brush analyses that flowed from it did not come to define the new history from below in later years. In *Captain Swing*, thought Patricia Hollis, 'we have a fine and definitive anatomy of

---

4   Hobsbawm and Rudé, *Captain Swing*, pp. 13–19, 180; R.H. Tawney, *J. L. Hammond, 1872–1949* (London, 1961), p. 13. For Hobsbawm's critique of the Hammonds' 'feeble' defence of pessimistic accounts of industrialization against the potsitivism of J.H. Clapham and others, see his *Labouring Men: Studies in the history of labour* (London 1964), p. 68.
5   G. Himmelfarb, 'The Writing of Social History: Recent Studies of 19th Century England', *Journal of British Studies* 11 (1971), 149; E.L. Jones, *Economic History Review* 22 (1969), 354–55; G.E. Mingay, Review of 'Captain Swing', *English Historical Review* 85 (1970), 810–14.

the riots, but we still know very little about the rural poor'. In 1969, the extent to which a strong structural and sociological framework would guide the methodologies of either the new social history or history from below remained uncertain, but as John Brewer has recently suggested, signs of an 'uneasy tension' between *Annales* and micro approaches had been discernible from at least 1966.[7] With hindsight, we may conclude that history from below has developed more substantively as a qualitative discipline, distrustful of statistical analysis as a tool for exploring popular *mentalités* and quotidian life. Significantly, E.P. Thompson's admiration for Captain Swing was qualified by a concern that its dispassionate analytical rigour left readers to view events only 'through a slight haze and at a great distance'.[8] We might argue indeed that it was Thompson rather than Hobsbawm and Rudé who inherited most from the qualitative polemic of the Hammonds. In its profound suspicion of both theory with a capital 'T' and of quantitative econometrics, as much as in its compensatory fascination with the cultural turn, Thompson's work, thought Raphael Samuel, might best 'be seen as a vast elaboration of their original insights'. Indeed, Thompson had made his hostility to quantitative approaches to the history of labour perfectly clear in a benchmark manifesto for history from below published in the *Times Literary Supplement* three years earlier.[9] Nevertheless, *Captain Swing* remains a foundation text in the development of history from below and, for that matter, the replacement of old 'plough and cow' agricultural histories by the new rural history, with its greater emphasis upon the social, the folkloric, and the regional.[10]

6 R. Wells, 'The Development of the English Rural Proletariat and Social Protest, 1700–1850', *Journal of Peasant Studies* 6 (1979); A. Howkins, 'Labour History and the Rural Poor', *Rural History* 1 (1990), 117–18.
7 John Brewer, 'Microhistories and the Histories of Everyday Life', *Cultural and Social History* 7 (2010), 89–90.
8 Hobsbawm and Rudé, *Captain Swing* (Harmondsworth, 1972), p. xv; P. Hollis, Review of 'Captain Swing', *History* 54 (1969), 434.
9 For Samuel's comment see the excellent appraisal of the Hammonds' work in David Sutton, 'Radical Liberalism, Fabianism, and social history' in R. Johnson, G. McLennan, B. Schwarz and D. Sutton (eds), *Making Histories: Studies in History Writing and Politics* (Minnesota, 1982). E.P. Thompson, 'History from below', *Times Literary Supplement*, 7 April 1966.
10 On the new rural history, see L. Bellamy, K.D.M. Snell and T. Williamson, 'Rural History: the Prospect Before Us', *Rural History* 1 (1990), 1. In this sense, rural history has inherited the concerns of the now not-so-new social history; 'the history of social relationships and the culture and of the culture which informs them', as Keith Wrightson expressed it in the same edition of that journal, in 'The Enclosure of English Social History', 73.

For all their quantitative imprecision, the Hammonds had identified sufficient Swing incidents to note the unprecedented scale of the revolt, and they devoted the final quarter of their book to an analysis of its significance. However, by attempting, for the first time, a comprehensive count of Swing incidents as well as the creation of a typology of protest, Hobsbawm and Rudé undoubtedly advanced our understanding of the rising's significance and exposed the relative conservatism of previous scholarship. They re-counted incidents and re-mapped the geography, for even Thompson had realised that Swing 'extended more widely into East Anglia and the Midlands, as well as the southern counties, and lasted longer than is apparent from the Hammonds' account'. Yet, as Barry Reay has recently pointed out, Hobsbawm and Rudé 'underestimated its sheer scale' too, in terms of both its incidence and its spread. This observation was borne out by the findings of the Family and Community History Research Society's (FACHRS) exhaustive survey in 2005, which almost doubled *Captain Swing*'s tally of incidents by increasing it from 1475 to 3283.[11] Arguments over the ways and means of counting and measuring Swing have been a constant feature of research over the last forty years and they show little sign of abating yet. Moreover, even without going into the difficulties presented firstly by the patchy nature of the historical record, and secondly by uncertainties over the definition of a 'Swing incident', a necessary subsidiary discussion about the relevance of counting things *per se* has been unavoidable. Has further digging and retrieving significantly enhanced what we know about Swing's epicentres, its spatial diffusion, or its social impact? As Gordon Mingay noted in 1969, the Hammonds' survey revealed a 'rising' which began in Kent in November 1830, spread into Sussex and parts of Surrey in the same month, then moved outwards by way of Berkshire, Hampshire and Wiltshire, 'westward to Dorset and Gloucestershire and northward to Bucks', before infecting parts of Oxfordshire, Norfolk, Suffolk, Essex, Cambridgeshire, Northamptonshire and the North: 'Hayricks began to blaze as far north as Carlisle'. Their estimation of incidence may have been crude and incomplete, but for all their 'neglect of the serious outbreaks of unrest in Norfolk, Lincolnshire and Huntingdonshire', wrote Mingay, 'the new statistics show that they were not unsound in stressing the dominant role of the southernmost counties'. And despite demonstrating a considerably more generous scattering of incidents into

11 Thompson, *The Making of the English Working Class*, pp.250–51; Barry Reay, *Rural Englands: Labouring Lives in the Nineteenth Century* (Basingstoke, 2004), p. 149; M. Holland, (ed.), *Swing Unmasked: The Agricultural Riots of 1830 to 1832 and their Wider Implications* (Milton Keynes, 2005), p. 5.

the midland and northern counties, even the revised Swing map produced by the FACHRS shows the highest concentration to fall south of a line drawn between Hampshire and the Wash.[12]

Hobsbawm and Rudé's quantificatory turn brought immediate approval in some quarters, most notably perhaps from hard-nosed economic historians dismissive of the Hammonds' emotive 'guestimates'. For E.L. Jones for example, the Hammonds had relied too heavily upon 'polemic or microscopic local studies purporting to convey the feel of events which are in truth beyond reliable recall'. Yet many of the problems we continue to rehearse today over quantitative studies, were also noticed at the time, and not least by Jones himself. No sooner had Richard Cobb confidently declared, 'It is unlikely that any village in which there was any activity at all that could be even vaguely associated with Swing has been omitted', than Jones cheerfully pointed out the omission of at least two incidents at Chilbolton in Hampshire.[13]

More theoretical difficulties were raised by Richard Hawkins, Gertrude Himmelfarb and the hyper-critical Mingay. Of concern to Hawkins were the unavoidable generalisations that arose from any analysis of so disparate and vast a body of data. No book could contain sufficient pages to adequately explore each incident for causal and typological distinctions, yet the particular parochial circumstances that surrounded most Swing events made such explorations essential. In the broad strokes of Captain Swing's analysis, local and regional nuances were all but lost. 'The disposition of a parish to riot in 1830 seems, as one might expect, to have been determined by local factors', he noted, 'of which we shall almost certainly remain ignorant, and which hardly lend themselves to generalization'.[14] And the broader the brush strokes, the more Swing began (perhaps too conveniently) to resemble a coherent social 'movement'. This greatly troubled Himmelfarb. George Rudé's determination 'to assign precise figures where the Hammonds made do with adjectives unwittingly gives the impression of greater activity on the part of greater numbers', she suggested.[15] Mingay, on the other hand, virtually inferred that Hobsbawm and Rudé had massaged their own figures by counting as a separate incident every appearance of a crowd in

---

12 Hammond and Hammond, *Village Labourer*, pp. 258, 268–69; G.E. Mingay, Review of 'Captain Swing', *English Historical Review* 85 (1970), 810–14; Holland (ed.), *Swing Unmasked*, p. 6.
13 R. Cobb, 'A Very English Rising', *Times Literary Supplement*, 11 September 1969; E.L. Jones, *Economic History Review* 22 (1969), 354–55
14 R. Hawkins, Review of 'Captain Swing', *Historical Journal* 12 (1969), 716–17.
15 Himmelfarb, 'The Writing of Social History', 149.

a village, even though it may have been a single crowd, on a single day, visiting a variety of locations. By these means, a village might be identified as a centre of discontent, whatever the origins of the crowd. Further, a single crowd might, in the course of a day, enact several incidents, of more than one 'type', thereby increasing the number of incidents but not the number of perpetrators, and might arguably be better interpreted as a single evolving event. The fact that Hobsbawm and Rudé recognised these problems but consigned them to a relatively unimportant footnote was enough to convince Mingay that the work was flawed at source.[16] Happily, the historiography of Swing over the last forty years has not centred exclusively upon the difficulty of counting things, but at least two recurrent questions have been closely related to the problem: firstly, are all expressions of rural dissent between August 1830 and February 1832[17] (or any other parameters) to be counted as 'Swing incidents', and secondly, are we to assume their inter-relationship (that is, do they necessarily cohere to make a social movement)?

One of *Captain Swing*'s great strengths lay in its introduction of a quantitative typology of protest, revising earlier assumptions that Swing was all about threshing machines. Hobsbawm himself had first approached the rising in those more limited terms as far back as 1952, concluding in 'The Machine Breakers' that Swing was 'essentially a major offensive against farm machinery', and Thompson had confirmed it in *The Making of the English Working Class*, where 'the main assault was on the threshing machine'. Rudé revised this view in *The Crowd in History* (1964), which drew fresh attention to local variation and regarded the breaking of threshing machines as simply 'the spark that set the movement off'. A further refinement followed in 1967 when research for *Captain Swing* was almost concluded. Now Rudé was at pains to emphasise other kinds of action, from threatening letters, assaults and robberies to tithe, enclosure and food riots, 'and, in every one of the twenty-five counties affected, there was rick-burning and the firing of farms, barns and country mansions'.[18]

Incendiarism then, has occupied a central position in any subsequent consideration of Swing typology. Back in 1969, Richard Cobb sounded

16 Mingay, Review of 'Captain Swing', 810–14.
17 These dates assume a starting point with the destruction of the first threshing machine at Lower Hardres in Kent and an end point at the close of the Special Commissions.
18 E.J. Hobsbawm, 'The Machine Breakers', *Past & Present* 1 (1952), 58; Thompson, *The Making of the English Working Class*, p. 252; G. Rudé, *The Crowd in History: A Study of Popular Disturbances in France and England, 1730–1848* (London, 1964), p. 150; G. Rudé, 'Rural and Urban disturbances on the eve of the first Reform Bill, 1830–1831', *Past & Present*, 37 (1967), 90.

one of the earliest warnings about conflating incendiarism with Swing, for the covert and anonymous nature of fire-raising meant, 'we cannot even conclude whether they were private persons carrying out vengeance against specified individuals or participants in a mass movement'. Historians should therefore be careful not to read too much into 'what may have been habitual forms of rural pressure and protest'.[19] That incendiarism was an already well established factor in rural social relations is certainly true and Hobsbawm and Rudé were not unaware of it. But for Carl Griffin, perhaps the most prolific of the new generation of Swing scholars, 'the difference between an incendiary attack on a parsimonious farmer during Swing and a similar pre-Swing fire was that the Swing fire was in part inspired by other recent actions and occurred in a context of heightened anxiety'.[20] The point is a fair one. However, if many pre-Swing fires were lit over issues that were not directly connected to 'protest' over deteriorating conditions of employment, we should surely be wary of presuming 'protest' in every fire raised *during* Swing. A.J. Peacock once argued, somewhat speculatively, that 'many' post-Swing fires in East Anglia were 'simply the result of personal pique'. Although he accepted that, since most incendiarists were never caught, the actual number was 'impossible to tell', he nevertheless pronounced, 'the proportion must be very high – perhaps as high as a third or a half'.[21] One doesn't have to endorse parole declarations of this kind to recognise a need for caution however. The brutal hanging of three incendiarists in the Somerset village of Kenn in the summer of 1830 for example, may certainly be seen as an important episode in a loosely defined social war, but its causes were deeply local and associated with the politics of the Informers Act, the prosecution of unlicensed drinking houses and petty agricultural theft, not conditions of employment.[22] Had it occurred a few short months later, it might nevertheless have been erroneously credited to Swing.

19 Cobb, 'A Very English Rising'.
20 C.J. Griffin, 'Swing, Swing Redivivus, or Something after Swing? On the Death Throes of a Protest Movement, December 1830–December 1833, *International Review of Social History*, 54 (2009), 465. Griffin has discussed problems with quantitative approaches to incendiarism in 'Knowable Geographies? The Reporting of Incendiarism in the Eighteenth and early Nineteenth Century English Provincial Press', *Journal of Historical Geography*, 32 (2006).
21 A.J. Peacock, 'Village Radicalism in East Anglia, 1800–1850', in J.P.D. Dunbabin (ed.), *Rural Discontent in Nineteenth Century Britain* (London 1974), p. 30. The trend becomes apparent, wrote Peacock, 'the more one reads the local press'.
22 S. Poole, 'A Lasting and Salutary Warning: Incendiarism, Rural Order and England's last scene of Crime Execution', *Rural History* 19 (2008).

There is another side to this problem. Obvious typological differences between clandestine nocturnal fire-raising on the one hand and open daylight machine-breaking on the other do make the assimilation of incendiarism into Swing difficult without a degree of qualification. Put simply, incendiarism was usually committed by persons at pains to preserve their anonymity; the breaking of threshing machines was not. Did the same people commit both kinds of protest? The objection was grappled with by Hobsbawm and Rudé. 'Arson and the writing of threatening letters were, then, individual acts and, even if related to the general labourers' movement, were rarely part of any organised plan'. Robbery had also to be accommodated with care because it too was 'unorganised' and carried out by 'individuals who had strayed from their original group'.[23] The trouble with all this accommodation, sensed Cobb, was that at the end of it, even Hobsbawm and Rudé seemed uncertain whether to regard Swing as a general rising or as a series of independent episodes. Both multi-form and singular events, overt or covert, were regarded as 'significant' (perhaps because of, rather than despite their anomalous nature) but the connection between them remained unresolved.[24]

The fresh tallies of events produced by the FACHRS project have raised further questions about *Captain Swing's* typological drift. Now that we know what Hobsbawm and Rudé did not know – that incendiary incidents greatly outnumbered incidents of machine-breaking – their assertion that machine-breaking and incendiarism counties were somehow distinct, that incendiarism appeared either as a 'curtain-raiser' for more organised action or else as its 'aftermath', or that 'it rarely appeared where the mass movement was at full strength; and, though a genuine expression of the labourers' grievance, it lay at the fringe rather than at the core of the movement', will require some further reassessment.[25] The FACHRS project tried to distinguish Swing incendiarism from other forms of arson by separating fires on farms from fires on other premises. However, this method produced 1,346 Swing fires and only three non-Swing fires, a not entirely convincing outcome.[26] By these criteria, for instance, Rutland became a Swing county for the first time, but only because a single incidence of incendiarism was discovered at Empingham. Its connection to Swing was assumed from its date rather than its cause, about which little is known, but which, presumably,

23 Hobsbawm and Rudé, *Captain Swing*, p. 205.
24 Cobb, 'A Very English Rising'.
25 Hobsbawm and Rudé, *Captain Swing*, p. 203.
26 M. Holland, 'The Captain Swing Project' in Holland (ed.), *Swing Unmasked*, p. 7.

prevents its being connected with the 'malicious destruction of ten sheep' on a farm in the same parish two years earlier![27]

The uninterrupted presence of incendiarism in the rural south throughout the first half of the nineteenth century raises some important questions about the parameters we place around Swing as an 'event'. For the Hammonds, the savagery of the Special Commissions crushed all resistance and brought Swing to a close early in 1831. In Hobsbawm and Rudé's reading however, Swing had an 'aftermath', measured roughly from the conclusion of the Commissions in January 1831, and characterised by an end to open protest and an upsurge in covert incendiary terrorism. Carl Griffin has recently argued a more adaptive case, in which Swing did not die so cleanly in 1831 but maintained a 'spectral presence' in which 'the resort to open protest was significantly higher than has hitherto been acknowledged'.[28] The demarcation of Swing as an event with temporal and typological boundaries has had the effect of disconnecting it from such open forms of resistance as trades unionism, and little association has been made between Swing and the case of the 'Tolpuddle martyrs' just three years later. Rudé re-emphasised the disconnection in 1980, insisting that Swing's 'old-style form' had nothing in common with unionism and that Tolpuddle was instigated by Owenite Grand National Consolidated Trade Union missionaries from Birmingham.[29] In work focussed on the Swing heartlands of the south east, Wells has strongly argued a contrary case. Urban unionists may have been involved, but fundamentally, 'Unionist mentalities were central to Swing. The demand for work, on improved wages, was repeatedly made …' and any accompanying reassertions of moral economy were simply pragmatic.[30] Nor were unionist continuities confined to the south east. In May 1831, fifty labourers from four different farms around West Lavington, Wiltshire, struck work when magistrates failed to prevent further wage cuts, and there was a similar incident at Ramsbury. As wages continued to plummet in 1832, discontented crowds were monitored uneasily over several nights at Market Lavington, and as the new Poor Law took effect in 1834, fifty labourers blockaded a vestry meeting at Christian Malford. Some Wiltshire JPs now feared that further strikes,

---

27 Holland, 'Captain Swing', p. 283 (table); *Newcastle Courant*, 26 January 1828.
28 Griffin, 'Swing, Swing Redivivus', 468–69, 495–97.
29 G. Rudé, *Ideology and Popular Protest* (London, 1980), pp. 155–56.
30 R. Wells, 'Tolpuddle in the Context of English Agrarian Labour History, 1780–1850', in J. Rule (ed.), *British Trade Unionism 1750–1850: the Formative Years* (London, 1988), pp. 118–19.

accompanied (rather than replaced by) incendiarism, were 'inevitable'.[31] If historians have been wary of linking these protests with trade unionism, Wiltshire' magistrates showed no such qualms. Indeed, E.G. Williams of Marlborough congratulated Melbourne on the firm line taken with the Tolpuddle labourers for, had they not been convicted, the county would surely have been:

> overrun with trades unions, which the agricultural labourers would more readily have joined in hopes of being the means of raising their wages, now so very lamentably low, lower I believe than in 1830. On Saturday last, a brother magistrate asked me if I did not think there would be riots again, he thought the labourers would join the trade unions. I cannot say that they will but I am quite sure the very proper example that has been made of the Dorchester men will act as a salutary check if not a privation.[32]

A second important and recurrent feature of the historiography is the problem of spread and diffusion, and the extent to which escalation might signify a social movement. As suggested earlier, few historians have disputed Hobsbawm and Rudé's conclusion that the counties most affected by Swing fall beneath an imaginary line between Hampshire and the Wash. It is not to the question of static mapping that we turn to here then, but to the pattern of progress. Hobsbawm and Rudé subjected their geographical data to a large range of tests for both association and causation, from parish population density and proportionate land ownership to localised attempts at improvement, and settled, perhaps unsurprisingly, upon broadly *agrarian* factors (and harvest failures in 1829 and 1830 in particular) as determinants. This interpretation was challenged by Charles Tilly who noted an association between the geography of Swing and the displacement of southern rural woollen workers by competition from cotton in the urban north. Hobsbawm and Rudé revisited their data when preparing the Penguin paperback edition in 1972, found insufficient evidence for Tilly's claim, and Tilly himself appears to have abandoned it.[33] More cogently however, historians have

---

31 *Bath Journal*, 6 June 1831; The National Archive, London [hereafter TNA], HO 52/20, T. Scott and W. Hughes to Lord Melbourne, 29 February 1832; HO 52/25, Rev. E.G. Williams to Lord Melbourne, 22 April 1834; Wiltshire Record Office, A1 145 (1834), Quarter Session depositions, information of Henry Hodges, William Baker and Thomas Doyle; examination of Charles Vines and Jane Bath, 8 November 1834.
32 TNA, HO 52/25 Rev. E.G. Williams to Lord Melbourne, 22 April 1834.
33 C. Tilly, review of 'Captain Swing', *Journal of Social History* 4 (1970), 165–66. For Tilly's later work on Swing, see for instance, *Popular Contention in Great Britain, 1758–1834* (Cambridge, Mass., 1995), pp. 315–21.

puzzled over the timing, speed and direction of Swing's geography. Cobb noted that Hobsbawm and Rudé's Swing crowds avoided main roads, pursuing instead an 'erratic course … through semi-secret footpaths or tracks cutting through the greenery, nearly always giving the towns a wide berth, along lines of communication known only to the local man, to the poacher and smuggler, to the ploughman as he plods his weary way back to his airless cottage'.[34] The first important challenge to this approach came in 1979 from Andrew Charlesworth whose spatial analysis of Swing's progress was designed to 'put another nail in the coffin of the Old Faithful model in which social protests are seen as spontaneous, galvanic eruptions, contagiously spreading across the landscape'. The model he produced prompted reconsideration of assumptions about Swing's strictly economic character and renewed interest in the role of political radicals. Essentially, Charlesworth argued that Swing in the Home Counties may have begun in isolated communities but it spread rapidly and methodically only upon reaching main routes to and from London and that it can then be shown to have spread along them. It was this that facilitated the involvement of more sophisticated radicals and prompted more effective organisation and strategic demands: 'The collective protests should thus be considered not as forerunners of the inevitable storm but more as fortuitous events whose significance had to be interpreted by a politically conscious minority'.[35]

Charlesworth's assertion of a shared political consciousness reminds us of the difficulties of interpreting Swing as a social movement with recognisable objectives and something approaching an ideology. Hobsbawm and Rudé refer, somewhat loosely, to the collective events of 1830 as a 'movement' throughout the book, and as Peter Jones has pointed out, the attribution has been 'a given for just about every historian who has treated them seriously over the last forty years'.[36] If for Wells, the unionist demands at the core of Swing were an indication of class consciousness, it had not been Hobsbawm and Rudé's conclusion, for whom Swing remained ideologically backward looking. They reaffirmed the labourer's mental world as ring-fenced by tradition and custom, and offering few 'signs of a new political or social ideology' despite the presence of a few 'village radicals' and nonconformists. E.P.

---

34 Cobb, 'A Very English Rising'.
35 A. Charlesworth, *Social Protest in a Rural Society: The Spatial Diffusion of the Captain Swing Disturbances of 1830–1831* (Historical Geography Research Series, 1, Liverpool 1979), preface and p. 42.
36 P. Jones, 'Finding Captain Swing: Protest, Parish Relations and the State of the Public Mind in 1830', *International Review of Social History* 54 (2009), 429–31.

Thompson and E.L. Jones thought them overly cautious, arguing that insufficient attention had been paid to known rural centres of radicalism, particularly in Hampshire. When revising their text in 1972, Hobsbawm and Rudé acknowledged local exceptions but concluded, 'we do not believe that we overlooked it as a general factor'.[37] Yet Charlesworth believed that the very thing that made Swing significantly different from earlier protests was its 'special conjuncture of circumstances ... the growing number of radicals in the countryside by that date, the outbreak of agitation for parliamentary reform and its culmination in the reform crisis of early November and the effects of such agitation and crises on both the rural middle and working classes'.[38] Indeed, Roger Wells has gone so far as to argue not only that the 'popular, political element to Swing has been seriously underrated by most historians, including Hobsbawm and Rudé', but that the movement, which 'assumed quasi-insurrectionary proportions', was 'the final factor in generating the massive accretion of support for parliamentary reform in the countryside', and later inspired the radical *Champion* newspaper to announce, 'Swing originated Chartism in Kent'.[39] We must be careful, of course, not to presume radical political consciousness among Swing crowds from the evident interest shown in them by urban democrats. This was an area never fully explored by Hobsbawm and Rudé, but David Worrall has now looked in some detail at the use made of Swing by Richard Carlile and his republican circle at the London Rotunda. In February 1831, Carlile, who had already been arrested once for a published lecture 'To the Insurgent Agricultural Labourers', produced a play, *Swing, or Who Are the Incendiaries?*, a clear enough piece of insurrectionary propaganda, in which 'an injured people finally triumphs'. This was the essence of Swing's appeal to urban radicals; it was the perfect vehicle for inspirational theatre, noted Carlile, because 'hitherto, all dramatic efforts to exhibit a resistance to tyranny have represented that resistance as unsuccessful'.[40]

37 Hobsbawm and Rudé, *Captain Swing* (Harmondsworth, 1972), p. xiii.
38 A. Charlesworth, 'The Geography of Protests by Agricultural Labourers, 1790–1850' in A. Charlesworth (ed.), *An Atlas of Rural Protest in Britain, 1548–1900* (Beckenham, 1983), p. 153.
39 R. Wells, 'Rural Rebels in Southern England in the 1830s', in C. Emsley and J. Walvin (eds), *Artisans, Peasants and Proletarians, 1760–1860* (London, 1985), pp.131, 133, 138, 155. See also R. Wells and J. Rule, (eds), *Crime, Protest and Popular Politics in Southern England, 1740–1850* (London, 1997), in which Captain Swing's 'critical misinterpretations' are laid out once again, pp. 9–12.
40 David Worrall, *Theatric Revolution: Drama, Censorship and Romantic Period Subcultures, 1773–1832* (Oxford, 2006), pp. 340–60.

Debates about labouring ideology in the countryside have, unsurprisingly, hinged to a degree upon the actual or anticipated death of rural paternalism and its effect upon the progress of political economy and proletarianisation. For Charlesworth and Wells, ideological distinctions between urban and rural workers in the 1830s have been over-played. On the contrary, radicalism and the class consciousness that gave it expression were carried freely between town and country by men who lived exclusively in neither. Wells' case is supported by the growth of radical meetings in rural and semi-rural areas close to London which drew a mixed crowd of urban and agricultural workers, and where the vigorous pursuit of the New Poor Law after 1834 delivered a *coup de grace* to tradition.[41]

Local studies in rural districts further from the capital however have revealed a different picture. Adrian Randall and Edwina Newman have taken issue over the presumed death of paternalism in Wiltshire, for example, through a closely argued essay on Swing and its aftermath in a single county. 'Where paternalism had survived into the 1830s', they concluded, 'the New Poor Law was much less effective in destroying the values of customary society than some historians have allowed'.[42] Peter Jones has stressed the importance of locally specific work like this without necessarily expecting coherence. On the contrary, Swing is best understood as a series of inter-related events defined by 'an intense localism and an active rejection of anything resembling a guiding principle or set of demands'.[43] His own Berkshire case studies reveal mainly peaceful processions of labourers marching from parish to parish and negotiating terms with JPs and gentlemen as they go. Such activity does little to support their identification as a proletarian movement. In fact, their behaviour is reminiscent of plebeian 'moral economists' and mirrored, for example, by the crowd that toured Stogursey, Nether Stowey, South Petherton, Bridgwater and Otterhampton in the south west in 1801, in pursuit of JPs' signatures to a petition for lower market prices at a time when every community was 'in the same situation and it appears that they are all connected through the different counties'.[44] It would take a brave historian to refer to this as a proletarian 'movement'.

---

41 Wells rehearses the political interpretation most fully in 'Mr William Cobbett, Captain Swing and King William IV', *Agricultural History Review* 45 (1997), 34–48.
42 A. Randall and E. Newman, 'Protest, Proletarians and Paternalists: Social Conflict in Rural Wiltshire, 1830–1850', *Rural History* 6 (1995), 218.
43 Jones, 'Finding Captain Swing', 429–31.
44 Somerset Record Office, Acland Papers, D. Davis to J. Acland, 1 April 1801, DD/AH/59/12/14; *The Times*, 2 April 1801.

In fact, the argument presented in *Captain Swing* was not simply a denial of a rural 'working class'. Rather, it is argued that Swing cohered as a social movement in helping to shape a broader ruralist coalition against the ravages of political economy. In this sense it developed 'the air of a general manifesto of county against town, of past against future, carried by the labourers but signed also by the farmers and even gentry'. Ian Dyck's groundbreaking work on William Cobbett was important in further developing such a view. Dyck broke with traditional representations of Cobbett by locating the great agitator not as an uneasy Tory ruralist, but as a regular rural radical, and something close to a guiding spirit (if not political leader) for Swing. At the very least, Cobbett had predicted the rising and warned both farmers and landowners of its inevitability if the economic condition of the labourer was not improved. For Cobbett, he argued, life on the land 'produced economic co-operation and a sort of natural democracy among all countrymen regardless of their proximity to the means of production'.[45] As a countryside alliance of sorts then, Swing's progenitors might include the previous century's risings against turnpike roads. Open attacks by undisguised crowds on turnpike gates to the south of Bristol in 1749 for instance included not only axe-wielding labourers from a wide range of adjacent parishes, but mounted farmers armed with whips and carrying flags. Urban opposition to the 'country people', mustered by Bristol Corporation, was left to mariners with cutlasses who marched out to engage the Somerset men in a bloody encounter at Totterdown. Anonymous letters delivered to the mayor threatened incendiarism in the city and professed, 'Great at present is ye unesayness between the town and the contery which may as well be in a harmony of peece'.[46] But, in Dyck's view, this alliance of interests had been in grave danger of collapse throughout the 1820s, and in the inexorable breakdown of rural deference after about 1827, Cobbett had observed, 'the development of class consciousness in the countryside, but it was a species of class consciousness that farm workers did not necessarily share with their proletarian fellows in the towns. There was simply too much long-standing mistrust between villagers and townspeople to allow for a

45 Hobsbawm and Rudé, *Captain Swing*, pp. 13–19; I. Dyck, *William Cobbett and Rural Popular Culture* (Cambridge 1992), p. 47.
46 Bristol Record Office, Town Clerks' Letter Box, 1749, Quarter Session depositions and informations, especially bundles 6 and 7, Voluntary examinations of John Old and others, 27 July 1749 and of Aaron Cross and others, 2 August 1749. See also *Bath Journal*, 31 July 1749. For a recent reassessment of the 'country people' in popular protest prior to Swing, see A. Randall, *Riotous Assemblies: Popular Protest in Hanoverian England* (Oxford, 2006) pp.153–78.

town-country axis to be forged on the basis of collective economic identity'.[47]

An important development in recent years has been a growing agreement among historians that complex issues about 'consciousness' need to pay greater attention to regional variation. In fact, *Captain Swing* had highlighted the need for a more systematic approach to regional differences from the start. Its authors were critical, for example, of the Hammonds' over-reliance upon modes of suppression found in those counties that tried rioters by Special Commission, overlooking the differences that characterised responses in counties such as Norfolk.[48] This claim has not been challenged but the response has nevertheless been fragmentary. Hawkins drew attention forty years ago to the thinness of *Captain Swing*'s account of the relationship between local polities of repression and the initiatives of central government, while Cobb thought it insufficiently rigorous in its overall approach to regional difference. Despite their best efforts, he noted, we still had little more than the names, ages, parishes and occupations of participants; oral memory and tradition remained a largely untapped resource; and we had yet to tap such subaltern sources as the contextual commentaries of wealthy water-taking ladies at Tunbridge-Wells. Arguing that detailed local studies were now essential if we were finally to crack open the labourer's mental universe, Cobb issued his oft-quoted directive, 'And now to the study of Lower Hardres', the Kentish parish which 'in a sense launched the whole labourers' collective movement', in Hobsbawm and Rudé's estimation.[49] Re-reading Cobb's appraisal some four decades after its publication only emphasises the role played by *Captain Swing* as a catalyst for the working out of future agendas for rural history from below. In the second edition, Hobsbawm and Rudé readily endorsed further local study, but warned, 'we doubt whether there are more than a very few, not necessarily typical, villages whose micro-history at this period can be written without enormous preliminary labours of local research'.[50] The challenge has, of course, been subsequently taken up, particularly in the south east, and we may see its results, in quite different ways, in Roger Wells's work on the troublesome Sussex village of Burwash, in which a single parish's

---

47 I. Dyck, 'Rural war and the missing revolution in early nineteenth century England', in M.T. Davis (ed.), *Radicalism and Revolution in Britain, 1775–1848: Essays in Honour of Malcolm. I. Thomis* (Basingstoke, Macmillan, 2000), pp. 180–88.
48 Hobsbawm and Rudé, *Captain Swing*, p. 13.
49 R. Hawkins, Review, *Historical Journal* 12 (1969), 716–17; Hobsbawm and Rudé, *Captain Swing*, pp. 205–7; Cobb, 'A Very English Rising'.
50 Hobsbawm and Rudé, *Captain Swing* (Harmondsworth, 1972), pp. xiii, xv.

nineteenth century social relations are closely examined through the incidence of property crime, or in Barry Reay's micro-study of the Herne Hill rising of 1838, and his later more expansive exploration of the same Kentish parishes.[51] The broader approach to micro-history that we have seen in Reay's work is perhaps what Charlesworth was calling for in 1991 when he took rural labour historians to task for 'documenting major episodes of social protest' at the expense of the wider 'productive, social and cultural relationships' that gave rise to them. Selecting the right parishes may not be straightforward however. Lower Hardres, he pointed out, was a poor choice because the atypical nature of the community would only lend strength to the old view of Swing as a discretely agrarian problem. Centres of rural radicalism might be more promising, and then only with the adoption of a systematically comparative methodology. What local studies need is synthesis.[52] Peter Jones has also urged caution. The fitting together of disparate local case studies into a broader structural and explanatory framework has become history from below's orthodox methodology, but in the process, the rough edges of local exceptionalism tend to become smoothed, threatening in turn to simplify further the appearance of Swing's coherence.[53]

Forty years ago, Hobsbawm and Rudé expressed the hope that the apparent conclusiveness of *Captain Swing* would not discourage subsequent historians. In this they clearly need not have worried for not only were they right to note, 'there remains plenty for them to do'; but, as we have seen, many of their own methods and findings have since been scrutinised and questioned. There are many roads still to travel. We still know next to nothing about women and Swing, a little (but not enough) about the disruptive and antagonistic effect of influxes of cheap Irish labour in Swing parishes, and nothing like enough about the social history of the threshing machine, a mechanical intrusion which not only diminished the demand for winter labour, but caused a significant number of deaths and serious injuries to those who used or played near it. The

---

51 R. Wells, 'Crime and Protest in a Country Parish: Burwash, 1790–1850' in Rule and Wells, (eds), *Crime, Protest and Popular Politics*; B. Reay, *The Last Rising of the Agricultural Labourers: Rural life and protest in nineteenth century England* (Oxford, 1990); B. Reay, *Microhistories: Demography, Society and Culture in Rural England, 1800–1930* (Cambridge, 1996).

52 Charlesworth, *Social Protest*, preface; Charlesworth, 'An Agenda for Historical Studies', 234–35. Charlesworth has also urged greater concentration on the role of the authorities, something that practitioners of history from below have tended to neglect despite the obvious fact that 'the ruling elite were clearly key players in social disorder and its control', ibid., 235.

53 For Jones, this is the problem with 'moral economy' as well as with Captain Swing: 'Finding Captain Swing', 429–31.

enthusiasm of historians for researching local specificities is undiminished, and some excellent examples of it will be found here in the essays of Rose Wallis, Judy Hill and Maggie Escott, but broader contextual work considering Swing's relationship with other movements in other places has progressed more slowly. The comparative allusions to Captain Rock in Peter Jones's essay in this collection, together with Alun Howkins's examination of Swing-inspired folksong, may signal a cultural turn in Swing studies broadly complementary to recent work on General Ludd by Kevin Binfield and Katrina Navickas.[54] At first glance, Swing had little in common with Captain Rock, whose armed exploits in rural southern Ireland in the 1820s were more insurrectionary in character and occasioned considerable loss of life, but the predominance of threatening letters, incendiarism and mythical leadership in both outbreaks invites further comparison nevertheless. Moreover, Captain Rock's Irish forebears included Captain Slasher, a purveyor of threatening letters and burnings during moral economy disturbances in the same part of Ireland in 1800 (and, in England, a much older character who clashes with St George in mumming plays).[55] As Adrian Randall shows here however, direct comparison between 'movements' (in this case Luddism and Swing) is as likely to reveal discrepancy as contrast, despite the superficial appearance of common mythical leadership. Many of the problems noted above are addressed directly and in detail in the essays making up this volume. For instance, Dan Myers and Jamie Przybysz revisit debates on the spread, diffusion and the making of movements by applying new quantitative methodologies, Carl Griffin fully addresses the nature and impact of Swing incendiarism as an event type in its own right, and Rose Wallis moves the discussion of local studies forward by directly contrasting the divergent experience of south western and East Anglian counties within the particular framework of the special commissions. New theoretical models are also enriching the field, as Iain Robertson's contribution shows, with its suggestion that 'moral ecology and a sensitivity to the constitutive role of space and local nature/culture relations' might provide a more holistic account of rural protest than we are accustomed to reading. In bringing together many of the most

54 Kevin Binfield (ed.), *Writings of the Luddites* (Baltimore, 2004); Katrina Navickas, 'The Search for General Ludd: the Mythology of Luddism', *Social History* 30 (2005) 281–95.
55 The most recent study of the Irish dimension is James S. Donnelly Jr., *Captain Rock: The Irish Agrarian Rebellion of 1821–1824* (Madison, Wi, 2009), but for Slasher see also Roger Wells, 'The Irish Famine of 1799–1801: Market Culture, Moral Economies and Social Protest' in Adrian Randall and Andrew Charlesworth (eds), *Markets, Market Culture and Popular Protest in Eighteenth century Britain and Ireland* (Liverpool, 1996), pp. 183–85.

important Swing scholars working today, this special edition of *Southern History* amply demonstrates the breadth and depth of approaches to the rising some forty years after the appearance of Hobsbawm and Rudé's seminal book. And, significantly, whether early career researchers or established historians, each of us acknowledges a profound and continuing debt to Hobsbawm and Rudé's masterly study. *Captain Swing* is perhaps unlikely either to be intellectually supplanted or commercially outsold by any future monograph on the events of that troubled autumn and winter, and the length of time it has taken for any new volume to appear is perhaps the most fitting testament to their scholarship. As Roger Wells pointed out after Gordon Mingay's critique in *The Unquiet Countryside* (1989), 'Captain Swing is the only academic history book ever to have achieved a slot in the weekly list of top-selling works of non-fiction'.[56] We hope that this volume will at least be judged a worthy complement to it and a useful signpost for future endeavour.

---

56 Roger Wells, review of Mingay in *English Historical Review*, 108 (1993), 488.

'The Mystery of the Fires': 'Captain Swing' as Incendiarist[1]

Carl J. Griffin

The most suggestive – and most analysed – part of Hobsbawm and Rudé's *Captain Swing* is not a chapter but an appendix: namely, appendix III. Their tabulation of Swing protests not only eloquently attests to the nature, diffusion and intensity of protest but also offers a more certain definition of what defined a Swing incident than the rather impressionistic regional treatments of the 'movement' offered in chapters five to eight. Seventeen protest types are delineated, from incendiarism (number one) to 'sedition' (number seventeen). Using this schema, Hobsbawm and Rudé suggest that the first protests were the sending of threatening letters at Mildenhall and Brandon (both Suffolk) and Chipping Camden (Gloucestershire) in February, March and April 1830 respectively. These events were followed by the destruction on 10 April of the mills used to employ the poor by the Orpington overseer and a political demonstration at Rye on 28 May. But these incidents are not discussed in the main text of *Captain Swing*. The first incident Hobsbawm and Rudé analyse occurred at Orpington (again) on 1 June when farmer Mosyer's ricks were subjected to an incendiary fire.[2]

Mosyer's fire marked the start of the first of Hobsbawm and Rudé's five phases of Kentish protest in 1830, the 'Sevenoaks fires'. As Kent was the county acknowledged to be the birthplace of Swing, the fifteen incendiary fires that occurred near Sevenoaks therefore represent Hobsbawm and Rudé's *de facto* start of Swing. Yet, their text suggests a certain ambivalence as to the role incendiarism played in the events of 1830. It was a protest form, they claimed, that had 'been practiced' before, 'even in this part of England', but it was not the 'characteristic form of unrest' of either the period before Swing or Swing itself. Only after 1830

---

1   The quotation is taken from: Centre for Kentish Studies [hereafter CKS], Maidstone, U840 C250 10/3 Sir Robert Peel to Lord Camden, 22 October 1830.
2   E. Hobsbawm and G. Rudé, *Captain Swing* (London, 1969), p. 312.

did incendiarism become 'the characteristic form of rural unrest'.[3] Whilst to many contemporary observers incendiary attacks on farmers' property were 'the most notable and memorable of "Swing" activities', to Hobsbawm and Rudé 'an element of mystery' surrounded incendiarism in Swing. 'Was it', they asked, 'an integral part, or was it a largely intrusive or alien element?' In attempting to answer these questions they concluded that arson played a different role from place to place, only in East Kent was it closely associated with machine-breaking. 'It lay at the fringe rather than at the core of the movement'.[4]

Hobsbawm and Rudé are not alone in being uncertain as to what role incendiarism played in Swing. John and Barbara Hammond were similarly equivocal. In analysing the Sevenoaks fires they posited that 'it was impossible to say' how 'far' the fires were 'connected with later events'.[5] The relationship between incendiarism (and other 'covert' protest forms) and the various forms of, to use Hobsbawm's phrase, 'collective bargaining by riot',[6] was also central to the so-called Wells-Charlesworth debate. In essence, the debate centred on whether 'overt' or 'covert' protest forms were the most important expression of plebeian discontent in the late eighteenth and early nineteenth century English countryside.[7] Subsequent systematic research has highlighted the elasticity of these concepts when applied to the archive. John Archer has shown that incendiary fires could act as the focus for open, collective protest, plebeian communities joyously gathering by the light of the flames and refusing to assist extinguishing them.[8] Roger Wells has also shown that in the food crises of 1740, 1766, 1795 and (especially) 1800, incendiarism was used alongside food rioting to 'enforce' the 'moral economy'. Notwithstanding this dovetailing of protest forms, incendiarism remained, Wells asserted, 'largely the tactic of

3   Ibid., pp. 12, 98.
4   Ibid., pp. 200, 203.
5   B. Hammond and J. Hammond, *The Village Labourer 1760–1832* (London, 1911/1978), p. 179.
6   E. Hobsbawm, *Labouring Men* (London, 1968), pp. 5–22.
7   The two papers which started the debate were: R. Wells, 'The Development of the English Rural Proletariat and Social Protest, 1700–1850', *Journal of Peasant Studies* 6 (1979), 115–39; A. Charlesworth, 'The Development of the English Rural Proletariat and Social Protest, 1700–1850: A Comment', *Journal of Peasant Studies* 8 (1980), 101–11. These papers, and several responses also first published in the *Journal of Peasant Studies*, were later collected, with new contributions by Mick Reed and Roger Wells as: M. Reed and R. Wells (eds), *Class, Conflict and Protest in the English Countryside, 1700–1880* (London, 1990).
8   J. Archer, *By a Flash and a Scare: Incendiarism, Animal Maiming, and Poaching in East Anglia 1815–1870* (Oxford, 1990), pp. 160–61.

the individual', a response to 'deprivation', a way in which the poor could set 'things right'.[9]

As Steve Poole has recently noted, the debate foundered on unsatisfactory definitions of overt and covert. '[A]rson *might* be used against unpopular tithe collectors, rampaging landlords or the advocates of enclosure, and it *might* then enjoy a positive association with strikes, marches and riots and permit analysis of the relative timings of their use'.[10] In short, there could be much that was furtive about collective protest, and much that was collective, even open, about incendiarism. Our understanding of the relationship between incendiarism and protest 'movements' is thus wracked with uncertainty. Indeed, Peter Jones in his survey of moral economy values in Swing has stated, 'the question of the relationship between arson and overt protest during Swing is complex, and requires a lengthy and ... nuanced treatment'.[11] Was it, as a protest practice, integral to Swing? Or was incendiarism merely incidental to the machine-breaking episodes, the wages demonstrations, and the levying of monies? This essay addresses these questions. The focus is the southern counties of Berkshire, Dorset, Hampshire, Kent, Surrey, Sussex and Somerset, though most of the material drawn upon relates to the four south-eastern counties. The essay is structured as follows. Firstly, it examines the use of incendiarism, as protest practice and as threat, by Swing groups, before, secondly, examining Hobsbawm and Rudé's contention that incendiarism was used as a 'softening up' tactic. Before concluding, the final section explores both the attitudes and responses of both Swing activists and the authorities to incendiarism. Before these analyses, it is necessary to consider what defined a Swing incident.

I Swing's repertoire of resistance

Swing's many historians are unanimous in agreeing that what united all the movement's manifestations was an attempt to improve the rural worker's standard of living. Swing might take multifarious forms – tithe demonstrations, incendiarism, anti-enclosure riots and so on – but these were all united by the universal desire to improve the field workers' lot. That the destruction of threshing machines later assumed the mantle of

---

9 R. Wells, 'Social Protest, Class, Conflict and Consciousness, in the English Countryside', in Reed and Wells (eds), *Class, Conflict and Protest*, pp. 158, 164, 170, 173.

10 S. Poole, '"A lasting and salutary warning": Incendiarism, Rural Order and England's Last Scene of Crime Execution', *Rural History* 19 (2008), 164.

11 P. Jones, 'Swing, Speenhamland and Rural Social Relations: the 'Moral Economy' of the English Crowd in the Nineteenth Century', *Social History* 32 (2007), 271, note 1.

Swing's 'iconic' form is therefore immaterial. In much of Dorset, north west Kent, Somerset, east Sussex, and Surrey, threshing machine-breaking was not even resorted to. Instead, in such locales protests – for protests there were in all these counties – took different forms.

So, could incendiarism be a Swing incident? Elsewhere I have suggested, using social movement theory, that to be a Swing protest, as opposed to an isolated incident separate from any wider movement, the act had to occur in relation to other protest acts. Such a perspective tallies with the understanding deployed by Hobsbawm and Rudé.[12] In part, the number of incendiary fires reported to have occurred in 1830 compared to previous years is therefore telling. Notwithstanding evidential concerns surrounding the reporting of fires,[13] for Hampshire, Kent, Surrey, and Sussex, I have identified 40, 100, 37 and 58 fires respectively for 1830. Of which 38 in Hampshire, 88 (Kent), 35 (Surrey) and 55 (Sussex) occurred in the final five months of the year. This compares to one, two, five and zero fires in 1828, and seven, nine, zero and seven fires respectively in 1829.[14] There can be little doubt then that the level of incendiarism is not only a useful proxy for social tensions but also that it mirrors the resort to forms of collective protest. Or rather, perhaps, that there is a positive correlation between the rise in incendiarism and in less equivocal forms of protest.

To be a movement episode the incident has to be the protest of (an) activist(s) who not only has/have the same broad goal(s) but also recognise that they share the same objectives.[15] Therefore an act of machine-breaking in one parish might inspire a wages gathering in a neighbouring parish, which in turn might inspire an individual elsewhere to fire an overseer's stacks. Thus the difference between any given attack during the heightened atmosphere of late 1830 and, say, two years previously is that the author of the 1830 fire may at least in part be inspired by other activists. The example of a spate of incendiary fires in Bridport is telling. At least 13 incendiary fires occurred in the west Dorset town between the winter of 1829–1830 and early November 1830.[16] By

12 C. Griffin, 'Swing, Swing Redivivus, or Something After Swing? On the Death Throes of a Protest Movement, December 1830 – December 1833', *International Review of Social History* 54 (2009), 464–65; Hobsbawm and Rudé, *Captain Swing*, esp. 195–220.
13 For these problems see C. Griffin, 'Knowable geographies? The reporting of incendiarism in the eighteenth- and early nineteenth-century English provincial press', *Journal of Historical Geography* 32 (2006), 38–56.
14 For a more detailed analysis – and an explanation of method – of these fires see C. Griffin, *The Rural War: Captain Swing and the Politics of Rural Protest* (forthcoming).
15 Griffin, 'Swing, Swing Redivivus, or Something After Swing?', *passim*.
16 *Sherborne Journal*, 4 March 1830, 13 May 1830; *Dorset County Chronicle*, 20 May, 3 and 10 June 1830; *Devizes and Wiltshire Gazette*, 20 May 1830; *Southampton Mercury*, 20 August 1830; *Western Flying Post*, 15 November 1830.

the time of the seventh fire on 16 May, the *Dorset County Chronicle* noted that the 'large rewards' offered by the Fire Office had proved ineffectual in stopping what was now a 'demonic rage for incendiarism, which prevails amongst some miscreants in this town'.[17] One case of incendiarism could, potentially then, encourage others to vent their frustrations.

Some commentators clearly believed this to be true. Incendiarism, fanned by the flames of Swing's open protests, spread like a contagion. When farmer Westmore's barns and stacks were fired at Gosport on the night of 11 November in an act that predated the spread of collective protests in Hampshire by a week, one reporter noted that 'incendiarism is spreading'.[18] It was this fear of contagion that was particularly potent in the public mind in those locales beyond Swing's initial protest centres, not least because of the frequent reports in the southern provincial press of the fires and machine-breaking in Kent. As the *Southampton Mercury* put it in early October, Kent was 'in a very agitated state by an organized system of stack-burning and machine breaking'.[19] Through such reports incendiarism became associated in the public mind with rebellion, with open revolt. Thus when on 5 November the barn of farmer Butt of Thurlbear, near Taunton, was fired, connections were quickly made to the Kent protests. According to the *Western Flying Post*:

> The conflagrations in Kent had produced such an excitement on the public mind, that a report very currently prevailed of the Somersetshire men being about to follow the example, by destroying a threshing machine, which Mr. Butt, the occupier of the farm, had in his possession.

The paper continued, 'We are happy to contradict this report'. The fire was 'an accident caused by a man having imprudently left a pipe near some combustible matter which spread to the teasals'. The *Dorset County Chronicle* and *Sherborne Journal* – the *Post*'s fiercely competitive Sherborne-based rival – denied this series of events. The fire had been deliberately set. 'Great alarm is felt lest the example of Kent should be followed here'. Presumably also with the recent events at nearby Kenn in mind, the hope was that the fire was the product of a 'deluded individual' rather than that of 'a combination'.[20] When an early Wiltshire Swing fire broke out on the Knook farm of Mr. White on 15 November, the *Devizes and Wiltshire Gazette* made this connection explicit. '[P]eople' needed to

17 *Dorset County Chronicle*, 20 May 1830.
18 *Devizes and Wiltshire Gazette*, 18 November 1830.
19 *Southampton Mercury*, 9 October 1830.
20 *Dorset County Chronicle*, 11 November 1830; *Sherborne Journal*, 11 November 1830; *Western Flying Post*, 15 November 1830.

be reminded that at the last Somerset Assizes three men were executed and two men transported for incendiarism. The paper also reminded its readers that John Rowley, one of the executed men, had implored of those gathered at the gallows 'I hope others will take warning by us'.[21]

II Incendiarism as 'overt' tactic

Much of the uncertainty surrounding the connection between incendiarism and the open, collective protests of late 1830 relate not to whether it was possible for incendiarism to be part of Swing's repertoire of resistance but rather what the link was, if any, between covert fire-setting and the 'mobbings'. Some rulers of rural England, as will be shown in the final section, believed there was no connection, either in terms of personnel or in terms of motive. Sir Edward Knatchbull, Tory knight of the shire, east Kent landowner and chairman of the East Kent Quarter Sessions, was of this mind. When sentencing the machine-breakers of Elham at the first Swing trial he asserted that 'it was a species of consolation, that the great number, and a great number there were, Heaven knew, who had engaged in the breaking of machines, felt the same abhorrence as [himself] of the burnings'.[22] Yet of these men – and others in his domain – this was palpably untrue. The primary motive of the Elham gang was to stop the use of threshing machines. This had been twice effected through incendiarism, once at Elham in 1817 and once in neighbouring Lyminge in 1829. The first fire is particularly instructive. 'For some time previous to the fire ... [the] country people in the neighbourhood had shown a great dislike to the use of the threshing machine which had been lately introduced to the parish'. Farmer Fowler had signalled his intention of hiring the machine to thresh some oats and on the morning of 11 October 1817 his oat barn was set on fire and destroyed. Open threats combined with covert terror in setting an important local precedent.[23]

This precedent was also followed directly during the early stages of Swing. After the arrest of several machine-breakers on 27 September and the voluntary surrender on 2 October of a further 50 Elham machine-breakers, the tactics of the gang necessarily had to change.[24] On

21 *Devizes and Wiltshire Gazette*, 18 November 1830.
22 *Cobbett's Political Register*, 30 November 1830.
23 *The Times*, 18 March 1819; *Kentish Gazette*, 29 May; *Kent & Essex Mercury*, 9 June 1829.
24 CKS, U951 C177/18 and 13 Rev. Price, Lyminge, to Knatchbull, 27 September, and, List of persons entered into recognizances (n.d but 2 October); CKS, U951 C14/9, Mary Tylden to Knatchbull, 1 November 1830.

5 October Revd Price's Lyminge farm buildings were set on fire, Price being targeted due to his magisterial involvement in the arrests.[25] On the following day, the very first 'Swing' letters were received by post by two individuals near Dover. Both threatened incendiary attacks. Two days later farmer Pepper of Hougham and Dover also received a 'Swing' letter warning that her threshing machine was to be destroyed and as such she should remove it to an adjoining field immediately. She complied, and that evening the machine was duly broken and set on fire. A reporter for the *Times* was under no illusions as to who the incendiarists were. Now that nearly all the threshing machines had been destroyed or put out of use, the 'labourers have begun to fire [the] barns and stacks of those who retain their machines'.[26] Here the culture of fire-setting, pseudonymous threats, and open, collective protest were intertwined and inseparable in the gang's strategy. Moreover, one of Knatchbull's correspondents in November 1830 – reporting that three fires had occurred the previous night – claimed that the protestors 'assemble by [the] light of the fires', creating the likelihood of 'insurrection by example'.[27]

The next two Swing centres also deployed incendiarism (and incendiary threats) with machine-breaking and attempts to increase wages. On the night before the trial of the Elham machine-breakers Borden overseer Knight had his farm set on fire. A few days later a piece of chilling graffiti was scrawled on a nearby wall: 'Down with machines. Death to informers'.[28] More telling and more important than the graffiti was the fact that the next evening a group of 50 men, many with blackened faces, marched from nearby Newington to Hartlip where they destroyed a threshing machine. Their actions were the result of a concerted plan. Some of the party had been drinking with the local assistant overseer and two farmers at 'one of these abominable nuisances, a new Beershop' in an attempt to divert them until the machine had been destroyed.[29]

25   CKS, U951 C177/31 Deposition of John Wakefield, bailiff, n.d. (probably 6 October); The National Archives, London [hereafter TNA], HO 52/8, ff. 276–77, 281–82 Knatchbull, Mersham, to Peel, 6 October 1830 (twice). For a full treatment of the events surrounding Price's fire, see C. Griffin, 'Policy on the Hoof: Sir Robert Peel, Sir Edward Knatchbull and the Trial of the Elham Machine Breakers, 1830', *Rural History* 15 (2004), 1–22.
26   *Kentish Gazette*, 8 and 15 October 1830; *The Times*, 9 and 10 October 1830.
27   CKS, U951 C14/9 Mary Tylden to Knatchbull, 1 November 1830.
28   *Maidstone Journal*, 26 October 1830; TNA, HO 52/8, ff. 300–1 Rev. Poore, Murston - Peel, 23 October 1830; *The Times*, 30 October 1830; *Maidstone Gazette*, 9 November 1830.
29   TNA, HO 52/8, ff. 300–1 Rev. Poore, Murston, to Peel, 23 October 1830; CKS, U951 C177/35 Poore to Knatchbull, 24 October 1830.

At Ash-next-Sandwich overseer Becker had his stacks set on fire on the same night as Revd Price's fire, rockets supposedly being fired in a line between Ash and Lyminge as some form of signal. This fire predated machine-breaking at Ash by twenty days, in the meantime the parish surveyor also had his stacks set on fire. The following night he was again visited, this time by a 'gang of men' who broke open the stable door and turned 14–15 horses into the road. The men were disturbed though by two persons who had been placed on watch, *The Times* reported, conjecturing that they were attempting to set fire to the farm buildings.[30] On the 25th, upon the machine-breakers being admonished for going about the parish in armed gangs, they sarcastically responded that 'they could not sleep quietly in their beds for fear of the fires' and as such 'were going to break all the threshing machines … then there would be no more fires'. In conversation, two of the machine-breakers also admitted that they had been machine-breaking the previous day at Sandwich *and* had also been at a fire on a farmer's premises in the same town who had refused to 'lay down his machine'. Subsequently one of the machine-breakers was also charged with firing Becker's stacks.[31]

These early Swing fires were not simply coincident with machine-breaking, they were integral to the achieving of the machine-breakers' goals. So too was incendiarism a vital component of campaigns for higher wages and more generous poor relief payments. The two poles of Swing protests in the Weald were typical. At Brede on the night of the expulsion of assistant overseer Abell, a farmhouse was destroyed by an incendiary fire in the parish. At the beginning of November in nearby Battle, the parish poor struck work, demanding that all men should be paid at least 12/- a week. A few days later, overseer Emary and assistant overseer Laincer received letters – the latter signed 'Swing' – threatening that if the labourers' demands were not made good their premises would be fired. The threats were carried out on the night of 3 November when Emary's farm was set on fire. On the following day Laincer quit Battle, farmer Quaife had one of his barns set on fire at 4pm, six hours later farmer Farncomb's stacks were set alight at nearby Icklesham, and at 11pm a mass gathering at the George Inn prompted the authorities to send an express to Hastings for military assistance. Nothing transpired, but threats were openly made that the town would be burnt down that night.

30 TNA, HO 52/8, fff. 216–18 Camden, Canterbury, 22 October, 359–60 Rev. Gleig, Ash, 25 October, to Peel; *The Times*, 23 and 27 October 1830; *Kentish Gazette*, 26 October 1830; *Kent Herald*, 28 October 1830.
31 *The Times*, 27 October 1830; *Kentish Gazette*, 29 October 1830; CKS, U951 C177/36 George Gipps, to Knatchbull, 24 October; TNA, HO 52/8, ff. 359–60 Revd Gleig, Ash, to Peel, 25 October 1830.

Although this did not occur, farmer Watts' farm was set on fire.[32] In both places incendiarism was integral to sustaining *pressure*; the lone protestor's tool of revenge.

In parts of Hampshire the connection between incendiarism and 'mobbing' was even more explicit. On 22 November a group of machine-breakers who had been active that day in the parishes of the Test Valley to the north of Romsey, on returning to East Tytherley that night proceeded to 'take down' the tollhouses on the Broughton and Romsey Turnpike at East Dean and Tytherley. This can only have been partially successful for the following night they were again visited. This time the families were 'dragged out' and the buildings set on fire.[33] Similarly, a group initially emboldened at Leckford to demand an increase of wages proceeded to Stockbridge to levy money. At the house of vicar Hutton their demand for a reduction in tithes and two sovereigns was refused. Instead, the group chanced their luck with Revd Cutler, resolving to demand 25 sovereigns from the clergyman: one for every year he had been 'connected with the parish' and four as 'remuneration for their day's work'. As he resided at some distance from the town, the group compelled the post agent to send an express to the clergyman. If he refused, the agent was warned, Cutler would have his stacks and property set on fire. As the *Hampshire Chronicle* relayed, 'their menaces were too successful'.[34]

Occasionally threats were carried out instantaneously. In the early hours of Sunday 21 November a group, reportedly 200 strong, assembled at Shoddesden in the parish of Kimpton. After levying money and victuals of farmer Barnes his threshing machine was destroyed and his barn fired. A cottage on his farm, occupied by an 'old woman' who was given 20 minutes to get dressed and collect her effects, was also fired. This tactic of combining assembly with incendiarism (and threats of incendiarism) was also deployed later that day by another 'mob' at Fyfield where threats were made to burn Mr. Bishop and other individuals'

32 TNA, HO 52/10, ff. 359–60, 361–62, 363–64, 364–66, Barton, Battle, 4 and 5 November and Ticknall, Battle, Thomas Quaife, Battle both 5 November, to Peel; *The Times*, 8 November 1830.
33 *Dorset County Chronicle*, 25 November 1830; *Berkshire Chronicle*, 27 November 1830; *Hampshire Advertiser*, 27 November 1830; *Southampton Mercury*, 27 November 1830; *Portsmouth, Portsea and Gosport Herald*, 28 November 1830; *Hampshire Telegraph*, 29 November 1830; *The Times*, 29 December 1830; TNA, HO 52/7, ff. 65–67, 93–94 Mr. W. Hay, Romsey to Mr Lockhart, nr Abingdon, 23 November, and, Isaac Goldsmith, Dulwich Hill House, Camberwell to Phillips, 24 November 1830.).
34 *Hampshire Chronicle*, 29 November 1830; *The Times*, 31 December 1830; TNA, HO 130/1 Calendar of the Winchester Special Commission case numbers 216 and 217 (Leckford).

property, and at Weyhill where it was declared they intended to burn the booths of the famous sheep fair.[35]

Elsewhere in Hampshire, as at Battle, open, collective protests during the day were often followed by incendiary fires at night. On 19 November alone, fires at Barton Stacey and St. Mary Bourne followed demonstrations in the day, and in the case of a Whitchurch fire only two days after a wages protest in that parish. On the 20th an assemblage at Andover was followed by the near demolition of Tasker's Iron Foundry at Upper Clatford. Only when darkness descended did the men quit Tasker's and return to Andover. During the night some men 'loitered' in the streets of Andover, whilst the corn barn of South Park Farm in Andover was set on fire causing some £2,000 of damage. The very number of such occasions suggests the improbability that these were coincidences.[36] An examination of the Barton Stacey fire shows they were not. On the evening of the 19th a small group of men visited the Newton Stacey farm of William Courtney. Claiming that there were 1,600 other men behind them and that the farmer should 'look over at the hills at Barton Stacey for a light' – a blatant threat of incendiarism – they managed to levy fifteen shillings as well as bread, cheese and beer from Courtney. Less than two and a half hours later the Barton Stacey farm of Sir Henry Wright Wilson Bt. was ablaze.[37]

This tactic was even deployed in the penultimate machine-breaking episode in Kent in 1830. On catching farmer Hannam of Alland Grange and his specially assembled force of 30 special constables off-guard, the men quickly started destroying one threshing machine. A mêlée ensued and blows were exchanged, Hannam threatening to shoot the men if they persisted. This threat was met by another threat: if Hannam fired they would fire his stacks. Fearlessly, the gang continued their destruction. A second machine, the wheels of a chaff cutter, a bean mill, malt mill, and a wheat mill were all dispatched. They then demanded the keys to a barn, again threatening to set fire to the premises if resisted. Instead, they broke

35 TNA, HO 52/7, ff. 46–47 Sir L. Curteis Cart, Ramridge, nr Andover to Peel, 21 November 1830; *Hampshire Advertiser*, 27 November 1830; TNA, HO 130/1 Calendar of the Winchester Special Commission case numbers 98 and 154 (Kimpton).

36 TNA, HO 52/7, ff. 42–43 Andover Bench, 20 November to Peel; *Hampshire Advertiser*, 20 and 27 November 1830; *Portsmouth, Portsea and Gosport Herald*, 21 November 1830; *Hampshire Chronicle*, 22 and 29 November 1830; *The Times*, 25 November, 23 and 24 December 1830; TNA, HO 130/1 Calendar of the Winchester Special Commission case numbers 263–265 (Barton Stacey).

37 *Hampshire Advertiser*, 20 November 1830; *Hampshire Chronicle*, 22 November 1830; *The Times*, 23 November, 23 and 31 December 1830; Hampshire County Record Office, Winchester, 92M95/F2/9/1 Memorandum regarding prisoners whose cases have not been fully settled, December 1830.

the down the barn doors to find another two threshing machines. These were soon in pieces, the men victoriously giving three cheers before departing across the fields.[38]

Even farmers used the threat of fire. On 20 November at Nether Wallop in west Hampshire the 'agricultural population' rose and successfully demanded from the farmers an increase in their wages from eight to ten shillings a week. In turn the farmers went to demand an immediate 30 per cent reduction in their tithes, threatening tithe holder James Blunt that his house would be set on fire if they were refused.[39]

Another tactic, initially deployed in East Kent but more frequently deployed in Swing's fringe, was the openly setting on fire of threshing machines.[40] On 1 December on the Somerset-Dorset border 'a body of rioters' assembled at Henstridge and set fire to Mr. Grey's threshing machine. They then physically destroyed Mr. Davis' machine at Yenston, before proceeding to Tomer where a further two threshing machines were set on fire.[41] Similarly, a group of threshing machine and hay-making machine-breakers active at Baverstone, Newnton and Chavenage on the Wiltshire-Gloucestershire border also set one threshing machine on fire near Tetbury.[42]

III Incendiarism as a 'softening-up' tactic?

As Hobsbawm and Rudé noted, incendiarism heralded the start of open, collective protests in all counties west of East Sussex. Writing about Wiltshire, they claim that 'there had been the usual preparatory "softening-up" by threatening letters and incendiary fires'.[43] But to what extent did these fires actually directly relate to other forms of movement activity? Were they simply coincident precursors? What evidence do we

38 TNA, HO 52/8, ff. 33–34, 97–99 John Boys, clerk to Margate Bench to Maule, 23 November; R. Cobb Esq, Solicitor, Margate to Melbourne, enclosing deposition of William Liley, waggoner, both 28 November. TNA, TS 11/943 Prosecution Briefs for the King vs. George Moore, James Dunk, James Pointer and George Hollands, Kent Winter Assizes 1830; Evidence of George Hannam Esq, John Forster, James Pointer, and George Hollands.
39 TNA HO 52/7, ff.46–47 Sir L. Curteis Cart, Ramridge, nr Andover to Peel, 21 November; *Southampton Mercury*, 27 November 1830; *Hampshire Chronicle*, 29 November 1830.
40 The first recorded example of this tactic during the autumn and winter of 1830 occurred at Hougham near Dover. Widow Pepper after receiving one of the first 'Swing' letters removed, as instructed, her threshing machine to an adjoining field where it was subsequently broken and then set on fire. *Kentish Gazette*, 15 October 1830.
41 *Western Flying Post*, 6 December 1830.
42 *Keene's Bath Journal*, 6 December 1830.
43 Hobsbawm and Rudé, *Captain Swing*, p. 122.

have of incendiarism being used to 'soften-up' farmers and the rulers of rural England? The first incendiary fire in West Sussex after the spread of protests into neighbouring East Sussex occurred at Coldwaltham on the night of 12 November. The next day the first 'rising' to occur in West Sussex happened at Kirdford, some 40 miles distant from Mayfield, the previous most westerly parish to rise. But this is crude geography, for there was no discernible connection between the events at Coldwaltham and twenty mile distant Kirdford.[44] In Hampshire a flurry of incendiary letters were received at Gosport around the 11 November – at least one of which was signed 'Swing' – 'asking' the farmers to remove their threshing machines. The threats were carried out on the aforementioned farmer Westmore on the 11th. The subject and pseudonym of the letters were obviously a direct reference to the events in Kent, the Hampshire press hoping that the fire was not 'a prelude to the outrages which have for some time disgraced several neighbouring counties'.[45] These fears were well-founded but there was no connection between this localised conflagration and the sustained start of protests around Havant on 18 November. Nor was there any obvious connection between a fire at Longparish on 13 November and the start of open protests in that area on 18 November.[46] That no clear connection existed suggests that the incendiarists, notwithstanding that they might have been inspired by events to the east, or were potentially attempting to provoke others into collective action, were not part of any coordinated action to 'soften up' farmers as a prelude to the 'real' protests.

Nor was there any concurrence between 'early' incendiarism and open protests in Berkshire. As Gash originally demonstrated, and Hobsbawm and Rudé later confirmed, most of the early fires in that county occurred in the heavily forested and wooded eastern areas which largely remained free from collective protests that winter.[47] Evaluating evidence from neighbouring Wiltshire is less straightforward. Hobsbawm and Rudé note that 'Swing' letters were received at Codford St. Peter and Horton on or about 15 November, whilst fires occurred at Knook on the 15th, Collingbourne and Ludgershall on the 18th, Oare on the 19th and

44 TNA, Ho 52/8, ff. 621–22 Earl of Egremont, Petworth to Peel, 13 November 1830; West Sussex County Record Office QR/Q 51 Indictment of John Champion and Thomas Champion, labourers, West Sussex Epiphany Sessions 1831.
45 *Southampton Mercury*, 13 November 1830; *Hampshire Chronicle*, 15 November 1830; *The Times*, 16 November 1830; *Devizes and Wiltshire Gazette*, 18 November 1830; *London Gazette*, 23 November 1830.
46 *Hampshire Chronicle*, 22 November 1830.
47 N. Gash, *The Rural Unrest in England in 1830 with Special Reference to Berkshire* unpublished BLitt thesis, University of Oxford (1934), pp. 56–58; Hobsbawm and Rudé, *Captain Swing*, p. 134 and appendix 3.

Stanton St. Bernard on the 20th. Threshing machine-breaking started on the 21st at All Cannings and Hippenscombe.[48] Mapping these early Wiltshire protests demonstrates an extraordinary overlap between covert protests – excluding the fires to the south of Wilton – and machine-breaking. The machine-breaking on the Wiltshire-Hampshire border might have in part been inspired by the aforementioned events around Andover on the previous two days but the fires predated these Hampshire protests. The exact link here will be forever obscure, but the timing and geography are – if nothing else – highly suggestive of a connection.

In the counties of Berkshire, Hampshire and Wiltshire, where Swing as a movement flared with extraordinary intensity but was very short-lived, there was little opportunity beyond the opening skirmishes to 'soften up' farmers in any preconcerted way. Instead, Swing was established both as 'contagion' – at Havant and Petersfield in Hampshire, at Hippenscombe in Wiltshire – and as indigent but coincident poles of protest – Thatcham in Berkshire, Whitchurch and the Dever Valley in Hampshire, and All Cannings in Wiltshire. Once these initial protests occurred, protests diffused in a matter of days to cover most of their respective counties. There was, in short, not enough time to develop complex *plans* that deployed multiple protest forms.

Most fires that occurred were either attempts to consolidate the message (or even gains) from other forms of protest, as at Barton Stacey and Andover, or were the work of opportunist individuals. Indeed, many of the 'protest' forms deployed by Swing's multifarious activists disavowed the attainment of public and symbolic goals and instead, influenced and emboldened by the urgency and confidence of the surrounding overt actions, sought to right personal wrongs. When on 9 November 1830 Elizabeth Studdam, a young single-woman, fired a hay stack in the grounds of the poor house at Birchington in the Isle of Thanet, this was in revenge for *her* treatment at the hands of the parish poor law officials.[49] The atmosphere engendered by Swing not only emboldened some individuals to give a more public life to specific grudges but also to make more generic public statements. Brothers Henry and William Packman were found guilty of firing the farm of William Wraight at Hernhill on 20 November but their initial plan was to fire a faggot stack of Mr. Paven. Upon leaving the public house that Saturday night, the would-be incendiarists changed their minds. They would now fire Wraight's

48 Ibid., pp. 122–23 and appendix 3.
49 TNA, TS 11/943 Prosecution Brief prepared by the Treasury Solicitor in the case of the King vs. Elizabeth Studdam for arson, Kent Winter Assizes 1830.

premises 'as it would not be so much trouble'.⁵⁰ Yet notwithstanding these very personal motivations, their actions, and those of many other fire raisers, may nevertheless have been toasted in public houses and beershops throughout southern England.

IV Incendiarism in the Public Mind

Knatchbull's belief that the Elham machine-breakers viewed incendiarism with the same 'horror' that the rulers of rural England did might have betrayed a profound misreading of his local charges, but how true was it of other Swing activists? Such an understanding is hard to directly assess. The resort to open incendiary threats suggests a willingness – at least on behalf of some Swing groups – to embrace fire raising. Further evidence is derived from support for incendiarism from Swing activists in mobile groups. Robert Price, a 48 year-old politically-active Maidstone shoe maker who led a group active in the area south of the Kent county town, was one such individual. In a parley with Mrs. Stacey of Stockbury, Price launched into a tirade about the state of the poor, to which Stacey suggested they wait for the new Parliament to see what the King did, the expectation being that he was going to 'take off five millions in taxes'. Price exploded: 'King, we have no King … Five millions of heads will be taken off before that is done'. The 'burnings' were therefore:

> [N]ecessary to bring people to their senses, it is your dandy Houses and your dandy habits and your sinecure places that have brought the Country to this state … you are all too high and must come down from the Head. If you go to Church you only go to look at the … fashions … Now we have righted this Parish we are going thro' every other Village and Parish to do the same thing.⁵¹

Further evidence is provided by the refusal of plebeian parishioners to help extinguish incendiary fires. A Sevenoaks correspondent to the *Rochester Gazette* reported in relation to the wave of fires in the vicinity:

> The expressions of the mob are dreadful: they said 'Damn it, let it burn, I only wish it was a house: We can warm ourselves now: We only want some potatoes, there is a nice fire to cook them by!'

50 TNA, TS 11/943 Prosecution brief prepared by the Treasury Solicitor in the case of the King vs. Henry and William Packham for Arson, Kent Winter Assizes 1830.
51 CKS, Q/SBw/124/7,8 and 9 Defence of Robert Price, Depositions of Daniel Green, farmer, and Charlotte Stacey, wife of Courtney Stacey, all 19 November; CKS, U951 C14/6 Poore, Murston, to Knatchbull, 29 October 1830.

At a fire on Mrs. Minet's farm in early September the pipes of the attendant fire engines were so badly cut that they were rendered useless, pails having to be passed along a half-mile human chain.[52] 'The most disgusting feature', wrote one Kentish correspondent, 'is to see the sangfroid with which the lower orders speak of their 'Bonfires' and still more the exultation evinced by the Mob present at them'.[53]

Elsewhere in Kent other labouring communities made similarly defiant displays at farmyard fires. Lord Darnley's farm at Cobham was fired on 24 October. Some 200 labourers gathered but, in the words of the *Maidstone Journal*, showed 'total apathy'. A fire on Lord Sondes' Selling farm attracted the assistance of the dredgers from nearby Faversham but not the local labourers who 'just looked on'. A week later a similar fate befell farmer Catt's farm in neighbouring Chartham. When Mr. Dawson's Stockbury farm was set ablaze on 24 October a large number of labourers flocked to the scene but very few helped. Those who simply watched the flames not only 'scoffed' at those who did help but also later proceeded through the village carrying a black flag. As Archer has shown in his study of East Anglian arson, the actual conflagration at incendiary fires offered a focus for displays of open dissent.[54]

Such hard heartedness was not always – or even usually – the case. Many fires during late 1830 attracted large numbers of local labourers and artisans who were potentially prepared to risk their own safety to save the property of the farmer. The example of a fire on the Fareham farmer Merrett's premises on 17 November is instructive. The 'inhabitants' of Fareham were soon on the spot of the fire and helped confine the flames to a hay stack. Within days not only had a massive £500 reward for information leading to a successful prosecution been offered, but further subscriptions were raised to 'distribute' money to those who helped put out the fire and to pay £100 to any 'labourer' over the next twelve months who detected an incendiary. Such payments were an attempt to buy loyalty, to perform community solidarity in the face of the coming storm from Kent and Sussex.[55]

52 TNA, HO 52/8, ff. 259–60, 313 and Managing Director of the County Fire Office, Regent Street, 31 August, and, Mr. Manning, New Bank Buildings, 3 September, to Peel; *Rochester Gazette*, 14 and 21 September 1830.
53 TNA, HO 52/8, ff. 203–5 B. Sandford, Farningham and Dartford to John Irving M.P., 8 October 1830.
54 TNA, HO 52/8, ff.361–62, 365–66 Post Office Deputy Sharp, Faversham, to Sir Francis Freeling, General Post Office, 26 October, and Rev. Poore, Murston to Peel, 25 October; *Kent Herald*, 28 October 1830; *The Times*, 30 October 1830; *Maidstone Journal*, 26 October and 9 November; Revd Poore, Murston to Peel, 25 October 1830; *Kentish Gazette*, 5 November 1830.
55 *Hampshire Advertiser*, 20 November 1830; *Portsmouth, Portsea and Gosport Herald*, 21 November 1830.

Notwithstanding the offer of a huge reward – invariably a move that was more symbolic than effective – the strategy adopted at Fareham also intimated that 'strangers' rather than local labourers were the authors of the fires. This relationship between loyal local labourers and strange shadowy fire setters was also tested at Whitelackington in Somerset. On the evening of Sunday 12 December the dairy house of Messrs T. and W. Stephens was set on fire. It contained, one assumes not coincidentally, a threshing machine. The local labourers 'made great exertions' in extinguishing the fire. They were not the supposed culprits. Instead, 'an unknown person' had been seen on the premises an hour or so before the fire was suspected.[56]

Sightings of strangers – with the emphasis often on the *strange* – were extraordinarily common before fires in late 1830. Farmer Quaife at Battle reported to the Home Office that 'incendiaries', 'gentlemen in appearance', were travelling about the county in gigs. One such alleged incendiary was seen at Quaife's farm at noon in the day of the fire, but his 'respectable appearance' had prevented any initial suspicion. Quaife's father also went to the trouble of writing to Home Secretary Sir Robert Peel to inform him of his profound belief that the fires at Battle were not the product of local labourers but were instead caused by a 'very different class'.[57] In the area between Dartford and Reigate the strangers supposedly 'traversing' the parishes were reported to be 'above the description of common labourers'.[58] Similarly when a threshing machine on the Silton Estate at Bourton was set on fire of the night of 3 December it was reported in the Dorset press that the culprits were thought to be 'two men on horseback' who had been there during the day asking questions about the rate of wages.[59] Even the duke of Wellington was not immune from strange fire setters. When his Strathfieldsaye farm was targeted in December two strangers were reported to have been seen in the vicinity at dusk. The correspondent of the *Hampshire Advertiser* even went as far as to the claim that they were 'political incendiaries' whose work was to 'harass the Government'.[60]

These 'strangers', invariably deemed to be incendiaries, were represented as working in small cells as part of some broader shadowy organisation. In early December at Axminster a large number of special

56 *Sherborne Journal*, 16 December 1830.
57 TNA, HO 52/10, ff. 359–60, 364–66 Thomas Quaife, Marley Farm, Battle to Peel, 5 November, James Quaife, Hackney Coach Office, Essex to Peel, 8 November 1830.
58 TNA, HO 52/8, ff. 318–19 Rev. Sir C. Farnaley, Wickham Rectory, Bromley to Melbourne, 29 November 1830.
59 *Western Flying Post*, 6 December 1830.
60 *Hampshire Advertiser*, 18 December 1830.

constables were sworn in to 'scour the neighbouring countryside by day to look out for the incendiaries' it being believed that 'several' were 'lurking about the neighbourhood'. Elsewhere in Somerset, a 'sharp lookout' was kept at Taunton for all strangers and 'revolutionary incendiaries'. Around Lewes in early November it was thought that 'incendiarists' were travelling about the countryside in groups of three or four dressed in smock frocks to evade detection.[61] Even Home Secretary Peel was convinced that there was some sinister plan afoot. Treasury Solicitor Maule's dispatch to help the Kentish judiciary was primarily precipitated by Peel's belief that the fires had not been caused by 'the resident population of the county' but had 'been devised by other hands, and executed by other hands', thus making them 'a national, not a local matter'.[62]

All such pronouncements attest to the genuine fear amongst rural communities of fire. As a Canterbury resident later recalled:

> Scarcely a night passed without the citizens of Canterbury being startled by messengers riding into the place at full speed to summon the assistance of the fire-engines ... I have gone up the Mount of Dane John, for several nights in succession, and have seen three and four, sometimes five, farms blazing away at one time.[63]

Even those sympathetic to the plight of the machine-breakers – 'their crying wants would never have reached the unfeeling hearts of [the farmers] otherwise' – were quick to claim to the Home Office that incendiarists were:

> [In the] purses & influence of radical scoundrels who think they can produce revolution by the anarchy and confusion which they expect to arise from ... [the] destruction of the common means of subsistence.[64]

The two grand old radicals that were inculcated in the movement, William Cobbett and Henry Hunt, were at pains to disassociate themselves from the fires. 'There was very little danger', Cobbett

---

61 *Brighton Gazette*, 11 November 1830; *Dorset County Chronicle*, 2 December 1830; *Western Flying Post*, 6 December 1830.
62 TNA, HO 41/8, pp. 24–25 Under Secretary Phillips, Home Office to Maule, Maidstone, 31 October; TNA, HO 40/27, ff. 54–55 Maule, Maidstone, to Phillips, 1 November 1830. For a detailed examination of Maule's deployment see R. Wells, 'Mr. William Cobbett, Captain Swing, and King William IV', *Agricultural History Review* 45 (1997), 37–38.
63 R. Stanley (ed.), *Passage from The Autobiography of a 'Man of Kent'* (Paris, 1866), p. 53.
64 TNA, HO 52/7, ff. 14–15 John Pearce, Chilton Lodge, Hungerford to Melbourne, 5 December 1830.

proclaimed, 'in the machine-breaking, and the sturdy begging, or rioting and robbing ... but as to the fires it was quite another matter'. Hunt, addressing an audience at Taunton, stated that the only 'panacea for the distress of the country' was parliamentary reform. Incendiarism, which he 'deprecated in the strongest terms' as not 'manly, peaceable and Englishman like in manner', was 'not the way to right their grievances'.[65]

V Conclusions

Was Captain Swing an incendiarist? The answer is simple. Yes, whenever he – and occasionally she – needed to be. Many individuals drawn up by the euphoria of Swing, or pressed against their will into the movement, no doubt abhorred the actions of incendiaries. As many commentators were quick to point out, the political economy of rick firing was absurd. It would act, albeit nominally, to force up food prices and would reduce the farmers' capital and hence their ability to employ labour. Yet to many Swing activists the landlords and farmers were their tormentors, the reason their families' bellies were empty. There might then be little economic 'logic' in firing the means and results of production but there was a certain logic in intimidating farmers in the hope of increasing wages. And occasionally it worked, as the actions of the Foulmere (Cambridgeshire) vestry as reported to the 'Rural Queries of the Poor Law Commission' attested.[66] Besides, protest does not always have to have a particular end in mind, its aims can be diffuse, its purpose psychological.

Swing's aim – a universal attempt to improve the fieldworkers' lot – could partly be achieved through an appeal to magistrates', landowners', farmers' and clergymen's sense of humanity. But fifteen years of patient appeals had got labourers (and rural artisans, mechanics and operatives) nowhere. As Jones has recently reiterated, it is extraordinary then that Swing was so often reliant on deferential forms.[67] Yet for every mannered request for higher wages there was an equally confident performance, again often backed by customary ritual, which did not shy from deliberately engendering fear. Incendiarism and threats of incendiarism represented one such strategy. If it is impossible to judge what proportion of fires that occurred in the autumn and winter of 1830 were deliberately set to effect broader social goals and what proportion were set to settle an individual score, it is telling that the level of incendiarism was far in

65 William Cobbett, *Two-Penny Trash*, issue 8, February 1831; *Dorset County Chronicle*, 9 December 1830.
66 *Report from His Majesty's Commissioners for Inquiring into the Administration and Practical Operation of the Poor Laws, 1834*, British Parliamentary Papers, Appendix B1, 10, 3.
67 Jones, 'Swing, Speenhamland and Rural Social Relations', *passim*.

excess of anything hitherto witnessed in southern England. As Kevin Bawn has shown for Dorset, even if one excludes 'Swing' fires, 1830 was a record year for fire setting.[68]

Beyond asking whether 'Captain Swing' was an incendiarist and whether he supported incendiarism we can also answer, with a reasonable degree of confidence, whether arson was integral to Swing as a movement. In the public mind the answer is undoubtedly yes. Of the eight 'instant histories' I have identified as written in the final weeks of 1830 and the early months of 1831, only one focuses on machine-breaking whereas five explicitly address incendiarism.[69] In a practical and political sense too incendiarism was integral to the movement. It was deployed (and threatened) in tandem with other protest forms to achieve specific objectives. Nowhere was this connection made more explicit than at Barton Stacey in the Dever Valley. The parish hosted multiple 'risings' between 18 and 20 November, that of the 19th, as noted above, followed by a fire on the farm of Sir Henry Wright Wilson. Two nights later the cart house and stable, the only buildings to escape the previous conflagration, were set on fire and destroyed. Thomas Berriman and Henry Hunt were found guilty of the first fire and executed at Winchester in March 1832. Fourteen months earlier Thomas' father had been transported by the Hampshire Special Commission for his involvement in the Dever Valley mobilisations.[70]

The example of the Berrimans serves to remind us that incendiarism was not something understood and practiced only by revolutionaries or the 'mad' (the judgement often returned by juries against alleged incendiaries). Rather, fire setting was as much a part of labouring culture as hunger, cramped housing and inadequate wages. By 1830 there were

68 K. Bawn, 'Social Protest, Popular Disturbances and Public Order in Dorset, 1790–1838' unpublished PhD thesis, University of Reading (1984), appendix II.
69 C.Z. Barnett, "Swing!" A Farce, in One Act (London, 1830); R. Taylor, Swing: or, Who are the Incendiaries? A Tragedy [in Five Acts, in Prose and in Verse] (London, 1831); 'Francis Swing' (pseud.), The History of Swing, the Noted Kent Rick Burner. Written by Himself (London, 1830); G.W. (Gibbon Wakefield: pseud.), A Short Account of the Life and Death of Swing, the Rick-Burner; Written by One Well Acquainted With Him (London, 1831); Francis Swing, The Genuine Life of Mr. Francis Swing (London, 1831); Anon. ('Swing'), A Letter from Swing to the People of England (Lichfield, 1830); E. Wakefield, Swing Unmasked; or, the Causes of Rural Incendiarism (London, 1831); J. Parker, Machine-breaking and the Changes Occasioned by it in the Village of Turvey Down. A Tale of the Times (Oxford, 1831).
70 Hampshire Advertiser, 20 November 1830; Hampshire Chronicle, 22 November 1830; Portsmouth, Portsea and Gosport Herald, 28 November 1830; TNA, HO 130/1 Calendar of the Winchester Special Commission case number 271 (East Stratton). For Thomas Berriman's prosecution, see The Times, 5 March 1832; Hampshire Chronicle, 19 March 1832.

few southern parishes that had not either hosted an incendiary fire or were next to a parish that had. The rural poor understood the power and the meaning of incendiarism. Archer's analysis of the ages of East Anglian incendiarists suggests that it was a young man's practice, the fire setters typically being in their early 20s. But elsewhere I have shown that plant maimers – those individuals who maliciously cut flora as a form of protest – had a remarkably similar demographic. Indeed, Hobsbawm and Rudé's analysis of those Swing activists tried shows that they were also overwhelmingly in their 20s and early 30s.[71] There was, therefore, nothing different about incendiarists. They were the same people as the machine-breakers, the money leviers and the vestry lobbyers. Protest was a young man's game.

Rural workers had a wide variety of protest tools at their disposal and often deployed multiple weapons at once. As Archer has suggested they were 'selective in their choice of tactics', combining 'open' and clandestine forms at will.[72] Quite how all protest tactics were learnt is perhaps forever lost to the archive but some points of brief speculation are worth considering. Bushaway, Pettit and, most recently, Jones have all noted the marked similarity between rural 'processing' and 'quête' customs and Swing's door-to-door demanding of monies and parading the parish to call for higher wages.[73] Machine-breaking was rather more novel, an adaptation – both literally and in a social Darwinian sense – of other collective forms for the age of the machine. All such forms were relatively infrequently deployed in most of the south after the last major wave of food rioting in 1800–1801. As noted, incendiarism and other 'covert' protest forms were rather more commonly deployed. Not only was fire setting an important weapon of the weak it was also an integral part of plebeian rural culture. To set a fire was an important life skill. Through cooking and providing heat it was perhaps the most important everyday practice of the rural poor. It was an essential skill for survival. And in Swing it was so deployed. The many fires that lit up the night skies of southern England were attempts to forge a new agrarian equipoise, to find a new way of surviving.

71 Archer, *By a Flash and a Scare*, pp. 165–97; Hobsbawm and Rudé, *Captain Swing*, p.257; C. Griffin, '"Cut Down by Some Cowardly Miscreants": Plant Maiming, or the Malicious Cutting of Plants as an Act of Protest in Eighteenth- and Nineteenth Century Rural England', *Rural History* 19 (2008), 29–54.
72 J. Archer, 'The Wells-Charlesworth Debate: A Personal Comment on Arson in Norfolk and Suffolk 1830–1870', *Journal of Peasant Studies* 9 (1982), 281.
73 B. Bushaway, *By Rite: Custom, Ceremony and Community in England 1700–1880*, (London, 1983); T. Pettitt, '"Here Comes I, Jack Straw": English Folk Drama and Social Revolt', *Folklore* 95 (1984), 11–12; Jones, 'Swing, Speenhamland and Rural Social Relations', 285.

'The Luddism of the Poor':
Captain Swing, Machine Breaking and Popular Protest

Adrian Randall

On the morning of Tuesday 23 November 1830, Mr Robert Pile, a prosperous farmer of 600 acres in Alton Barnes, a village in north Wiltshire, saddled his horse and rode the seven miles north to Marlborough to attend the fair. It was not a propitious time to stray from home. The day before, riots had broken out in Enford, a village only seven miles to the south of his farm. Surrounded by a large crowd of labourers, a meeting of the vestry, convened to discuss wages, had recommended two shillings a day and 'a gallon loaf and six pence, as it had said in the paper'. The labourers agreed to return to work but first 'they would break all the machines'. Jonathan Smallbones' workshop making the ironwork for threshing machines was attacked and all his stock destroyed. Then, moving southwards down the Avon valley, they systematically smashed threshing machines in all the farms around. Other disturbances had broken out around Burbage, nine miles to the east, while, even closer, a mob had broken a threshing machine belonging to William Ferris at Wilcot. But Pile clearly weighed the risk and decided to travel: he had some sheep for sale and he also had heard that the labourers 'intended to meet from the different villages at Marlborough' that day. If so, he could keep an eye on them.

At Marlborough, Pile's day took an unexpected turn. He was a private in the Everley troop of the Wiltshire Yeomanry, but, mid-morning, the Marlborough troop was mustered to tackle a band of rioters who had destroyed threshing machines at Rockley, a few miles north of the town. Pile joined them and assisted in 'apprehending some rioters at Rockley Temple'. But, arriving back in Marlborough, he heard news that, rather than meeting up, numerous mobs had been gathering in the villages between Devizes and Pewsey. His farm lay in the epicentre. He galloped home to find the lane outside filled with labourers, some carrying sledge hammers, iron bars or bludgeons. Inside his yard others were throwing bits of mangled metal from the barn. These were pieces of his threshing machine which, fearing reprisals, Pile had already dismantled. Pile was furious. He demanded that the labourers leave and, drawing his pistol, he fired it over their heads. Some ran off, others retreated into the barn or the rickyard. Pile dismounted and followed them, encountering the men breaking his threshing machine. 'I asked whether I had done them any harm'. 'No, you have done us no harm', came the reply, 'we have nothing to say against you, Mr Pile: but we thought we might as well break your threshing machine as we have broken those of others'.[1]

Similar attacks were taking place all across north Wiltshire. That day at Wanborough, nine miles north of Marlborough, a mob of labourers had assembled early at the farm of John Langford and broken his threshing machine. They left quietly but later they, or another mob, returned, smashed the parts which remained unbroken and then marched up to Langford's house. They demanded food and drink. Langford gave them 5 shillings. They then proceeded through the village, stopping at various houses and demanding money. By the time they reached the farmhouse of James Spicer, they were carrying a tricolour flag. They demanded two sovereigns. Spicer had already dismantled his machine. Nonetheless he gave them two sovereigns. Two other farmers in the village, John Wells and Thomas Baker, then had their machines broken. Labourers to the east of Marlborough were doing the same. In South Savernack a mob arrived at the farm of Robert Lyne. Lyne's threshing machine had already been smashed and he showed them the pieces. Lyne asked Maurice Pope, the apparent leader of the mob, if he were satisfied with this evidence. Pope replied that they 'must have a sovereign'. They had 'had it everywhere else and must have it here also'. Lyne replied that he would not give them money but 'that if they were civil I would give them beer'. The leaders were adamant: they must have the sovereign. Lyne duly handed it over.[2]

The destruction of threshing machines was one of the characteristic modes of the Swing riots of 1830. Indeed, according to Hobsbawm and Rudé in their pioneering study, *Captain Swing*, it was *the* characteristic mode: 'The distinctive hallmark of "Swing" – even more than arson or

[1] *Devizes and Wiltshire Gazette*, 25 November 1830, 6 January 1831; *Salisbury and Winchester Journal*, 29 November, 1830, 10 January 1831; The National Archives, London [hereafter TNA] WO13/4044, Muster rolls, Wiltshire Yeomanry, 1830–1; Wiltshire and Swindon History Centre, Chippenham [hereafter WSHS], 1553/12, Woodman to Cobb, 25 November 1830; *The Times*, 7 and 10 January 1831.

[2] *Devizes and Wiltshire Gazette*, 2 December 1830, 6 January 1831; *The Times*, 6 and 7 January 1831; *Salisbury and Winchester Journal*, 10 January 1831.

the threatening letter that gave the riots their name – was the breaking of machinery'. Swing, they opined, was 'the greatest machine-breaking episode in English history – and by far the most successful'. Their compilation of Swing 'events' revealed that machine breaking actions, some 390 in all, easily outnumbered arson attacks (316), 'robbery' (219) and 'wage riots' (162) with Swing letters (99), the very artefacts which gave the riots their apparent coherence, following 'riots/assaults' (100) in only sixth place. It was this 'Luddism of the poor' which gave Swing its identity, from the very first attack on a threshing machine in Lower Hardres in Kent on 28 August 1830, which 'came as a bolt from the blue', to the last, the smashing of a threshing machine at Bromsbarrow in Gloucestershire on 11 January 1831. Between these dates, 'Continuous machine breaking went on'.[3] Indeed, Swing outdid its more famous antecedent: 'Of all the machine breaking movements of the 19th century, that of the helpless and unorganised farm labourers proved to be the most effective. The real name of King Ludd was Swing'.[4]

What are we to make of this ascription? Was Captain Swing the true inheritor of General Ludd? Were the Swing riots Luddism redux? The first thing we might note is that the statistical basis for this paramount placing of machine breaking has been undermined by subsequent research which has demonstrated that Hobsbawm and Rudé seriously underestimated the scale of Swing disorder, in particular that of arson. A recent study by the Family and Community Historical Research Society (FACHRS), combining the efforts of local historians across the country, has now identified a total of 3283 'Swing' incidents, as against *Captain Swing*'s 1475. Of these, arson easily tops the list with some 1292 incidents. Machine breaking, with 539 recorded incidents, comes a distant second, though with double the number recorded for threatening letters and incidents of robbery.[5] So machine breaking, though important, was not the predominant mode of Swing activity. Moreover, Hobsbawm and Rudé's own evidence demonstrated that machine breaking was not ubiquitous. Their appendices showed that only 20 out of 38 counties experiencing Swing activities saw threshing machines destroyed while, of the 390 attacks on threshing machines they identified, some 217 of these

---

3   E.J. Hobsbawm and G. Rudé, *Captain Swing* (London, 1969), pp. 17, 98, 169, 197, 303–5 Appendix 1 Distribution of Disturbances by Counties.
4   Hobsbawm and Rudé, *Captain Swing*, p. 298.
5   M. Holland (ed.), *Swing Unmasked: The Agricultural Riots of 1830 to 1832 and their Wider Implications* (Milton Keynes, 2005), p. 5. The table also lists 272 Swing letters, 252 incidents of robbery and 284 'wage riots'. Family and Community Historical Research Society (FACHRS) also publish a CDRom listing Swing events (http://www.fachrs.com).

events occurred in only three counties, Berkshire, Hampshire and Wiltshire. And, even here, it was only in Wiltshire and Berkshire that machine breaking accounted for a clearly predominant share of protests.[6] The FACHRS study likewise shows that extensive machine breaking, if more widespread than *Captain Swing* supposed, was concentrated in relatively few counties.[7]

Why, one might wonder, did Hobsbawm and Rudé choose to associate Swing so closely with Luddism? One attraction might well have been the apparent novelty. Where riot and even wage disputes, if not commonplace, had precedents in the English countryside before the late summer of 1830, machine breaking had, until 1830, been regarded as something confined to industrial districts. Arson, if widespread, resulted from 'individual acts ... rarely part of any organised plan' and was confined to a narrow parochial stage. It was only the threatened displacement of labourers by machinery which motivated collective resistance on an unprecedented scale and generated 'the labourers' movement'. Even if the 'Swing movement was entirely traditional', the destruction of threshing machines, and other machinery, at least indicated that Hodge was acquiring some new weapons from his urban cousins.[8]

But is the characterisation appropriate? Was Captain Swing a late developing Luddite? The very notion, of course, presupposes that Luddites were themselves a coherent and focussed body with clear and transcendent aims. We know that this is not the case. The circumstances which led to the outbreaks of concerted attacks by the framework knitters on the wide frames in Nottinghamshire in 1811 were not the same as those which provoked the croppers of Yorkshire to attack shearing frames or the cotton workers of Lancashire to assault the cotton mills in early 1812. In each, different industrial contexts and histories shaped behaviour and modes of operation, even if the common context of a rapidly collapsing economy, and the fearful imaginings of a paranoid government, provided an over-arching commonality.[9] But did Swing share characteristics with any of the three Luddite disturbances?

6   Hobsbawm and Rudé, *Captain Swing*, pp. 304–5. Kent, the original 'Swing' county, came in only fourth in machines destroyed. Their figures showed that machine breaking constituted 24 per cent of protests in Kent, 22 per cent in Hampshire, 33 per cent in Norfolk, 45 per cent in Berkshire, and 47 per cent in Wiltshire.
7   The FACHRS evidence is not aggregated into types of incident by county but the data in the accompanying CDRom reinforces the pattern demonstrated by *Captain Swing*.
8   Hobsbawm and Rudé, *Captain Swing*, pp. 205, 294.
9   The most recent studies of Luddism are: K. Binfield, *The Writings of the Luddites* (Baltimore, 2004); K. Navickas, 'The Search for "General Ludd": the Mythology of Luddism', *Social History* 30 (2005), 281–95; A.J. Randall, *Riotous Assemblies: Popular Protest in Hanoverian England* (Oxford, 2006).

Hobsbawm and Rudé termed Swing 'the Luddism of the poor' but Luddism in 1811–12 was not a consequence of poverty. Indeed, the croppers of Yorkshire would have vigorously refuted any such ascription: they were an honourable craft, well paid and, even in the face of total displacement by shearing frame and gig mill, a powerful combination. As a letter in the *Leeds Mercury* noted in 1803, 'the cropper strictly speaking is not a servant. He does not feel or call himself as such, but a cloth worker'. Such was the influence of their trade union that Fitzwilliam described them as 'the tyrants of the country'.[10] Many of the cotton weavers who gathered in very large numbers to assail mills such as those at Stockport, Edgeley and Middleton, would have certainly regarded themselves as poor. But they would have reacted very strongly to the suggestion that they were as 'poor' as the agricultural labourers: realistically they were a debased trade but they clung tenaciously to the ethos of a craft, whatever the reality. The same was true of the framework knitters. They were, they claimed, an honourable craft, if fallen on hard times. Neither cropper nor cotton weaver pleaded poverty as excuse for their machine breaking activities in 1812. The framework knitters were more comfortable claiming 'poverty' when working on public opinion: Edward Ludd accused Charles Lacy of having 'reduced to poverty and misery seven hundred of our beloved brethren ... by making fraudulent cotton point nett of one thread stuff'. But in their dealings with the hosiers they sought to re-establish the reciprocity of master and independent master worker: 'we have nothing in view but a reciprocal Advantage in the Trade, both for ourselves and you'.[11] Moreover, all three groups employed machine breaking in 1811–12, as they had done many times before, as a deliberate, calculated and hitherto proven weapon to safeguard their employment and status. This was not true of the agricultural labourers. The 'Luddism' of Swing, Hobsbawm and Rudé assumed, was the reaction of desperation, stemming directly from increasing poverty.[12]

If we examine the modes of action employed, we can again see that the Swing rioters' attacks on threshing machinery generally bore only limited resemblance to those of the Luddites. The Yorkshire croppers, like the Wiltshire shearmen before them,[13] attacked cloth dressing machinery at

10 *Leeds Mercury*, 15 January 1803; TNA, HO 42/66, Fitzwilliam to Pelham, 27 September 1802.
11 TNA, HO 42/119, 'Declaration: Extraordinary', November 1811; *Nottingham Review*, 29 November 1811.
12 Randall, *Riotous Assemblies*, pp. 295–97.
13 A. Randall, 'The Shearmen and the Wiltshire Outrages of 1802: Trade Unionism and Industrial Violence', *Social History*, 7 (1982), 283–304.

night when the cover of darkness might best hide their identities. They well understood that, if seen, they would be most likely recognised. These attacks in the main involved relatively small bands of men, at least until their success against the smaller cropping shops brought the croppers into inevitable collision with the new large and heavily fortified factories recently erected by men such as Horsfall and Cartwright. For example, Samuel Swallow deposed that 'a number of people came to this house and began to demolish tools' between one and two in the morning in early March 1812, while the shearing mill owned by William Thompson at Rawden was attacked at night by about forty men who tied up the watchman and then smashed the shearing frames. Reports, as that about the men who attacked Mr Smith's workshop near Holmfirth, spoke regularly of blackened faces.[14] In the east Midlands in 1811, the early protests against the wide frames were open, as in the case of the large crowd at Arnold which smashed fifty frames in March 1811. But thereafter most attacks on the frames of obnoxious hosiers were clandestine affairs: 'The operations were conducted with so much secrecy and dispatch that the business was accomplished long before any force could be collected to resist them'. As in Yorkshire, most were carried out by small bands of men. 'The persons engaged in these depredations proceed in small companies, disguised so that their persons are not known'.[15] The impact of these night time predations was heightened by their suddenness, their secrecy and the difficulty of obtaining any evidence retrospectively as to who were involved. Wiltshire Swing rioters, like those elsewhere, did not eschew night attacks – between two and three on the morning of 23 November, William Robbins of Chirton was awoken by two men who told him they had come to smash his threshing machine. Robbins said he would resist them so one of the men left and shortly returned with a mob which duly broke the machine. This mob was part of the larger one which later in the day attacked Pile's farm. And, shortly after midnight the same day, some forty or fifty labourers arrived at William Smith's farm at Cricklade and smashed his machine, using his foreman's lanthorn to light their efforts.[16] Nonetheless, here as elsewhere in November 1830, most Swing machine-breaking episodes took place in daylight.

14 TNA, HO 42/121, examination of Samuel Swallow, 6 March 1812; *Nottingham Journal*, 4 and 28 April 1812.
15 *Nottingham Journal*, 16 March, 23 March, 30 November 1811.
16 *Devizes and Wiltshire Gazette*, 6 and 13 January 1831; *The Times*, 6 and 10 January 1831; *Salisbury and Winchester Journal*, 10 January 1831.

Only the Lancashire Luddites employed mass daylight attack as their principal form of action. This had been the way the earlier protests against the spinning jenny and the flying shuttle looms in the 1770s had occurred and the mode was to be employed once more, to powerful effect, in what was in fact the greatest outbreak of Lancashire Luddism, the 1826 attacks on new power loom factories.[17] Here too, daylight attacks increased the risk of identification and subsequent prosecution but the sheer numbers of the Lancashire Luddite crowds (the crowd which attacked mills in Edgley was said to number over 3,000)[18] provided significant protection against recognition. Besides, the cotton towns were growing so rapidly that the ability of property owners to identify 'local' people was very limited. In the case of Swing, however, the chance of recognition was very much higher, given that most attackers came from the near locality and, more importantly, from small communities. The 1831 census listed total population of 138 for Alton Barnes, 961 for Enford, 1448 for Burbage and 677 for Wilcot. If we aggregate all the populations of the villages within five miles of Alton Barnes we have a combined population of just over 8,500. This was very much a 'face-to-face society' where faces were known. Charles Davis, the 'captain' of the mob at Alton Barnes, had been born in Wilsford and lived in Marden, both only three miles from Pile's farm.[19] At Heytesbury, the local justice, Col. A'Court, confronted a large mob which was intent upon smashing Ambrose Patient's threshing engine. He later noted: 'William Smith was there. I was much shocked at seeing him. He is a labourer of my own. I saw him with the bill hook'.[20] Not only did few Swing rioters make any attempt at disguise: several went to lengths to identify themselves as leaders. John Reeves, a leading figure in the mob at Wanborough on the 23 November, wore a reddened handkerchief round his hat which he told John Langford had been dipped in blood. Charles Gerrard, one of the leading figures in the mob at Tisbury, wore a distinctive coloured sash. He was warned by John Benett: 'Young man, that sash will hang you'.[21]

---

17 A.J. Randall, *Before the Luddites: Custom, Community and Machinery in the English Woollen Industry, 1776–1809* (Cambridge, 1991), pp. 72–85, 98–100; D. Walsh, 'The Lancashire 'rising' of 1826', *Albion*, 26 (1994).
18 *The Times*, 17 April 1812; *Nottingham Journal*, 21 April 1812.
19 J. Chambers, *Wiltshire Machine Breakers: The Rioters* (Letchworth, 1993), pp. 66–67. This book lists a rich array of evidence carefully compiled on each convict from the Wiltshire Special Assizes in January 1831.
20 *The Times*, 5 January 1831.
21 *The Times*, 6 January 1831; *Devizes and Wiltshire Gazette*, 6 January 1831; *Salisbury and Winchester Journal*, 29 November 1830; *The Times*, 3 January, 1831. Benett was not quite right, Gerrard got seven years' transportation.

Thomas Goddard, the 'Ramsbury Ranter', bore a tricoloured flag and rode his horse. And Maurice Pope, the Bedwyn blacksmith who led the rioters at Savernack and Wooton Rivers on the 24th, was a famous boxer, 'the celebrated Wiltshire pugilist' and well-known in the London ring. It was not likely he would remain unrecognised. Indeed, Robert Lyne easily identified him.[22]

Luddites in 1811–12 made little attempt to parley with those whose property they were targeting, other than through threatening letters, since they knew from earlier experience that discussion was worthless.[23] They recognised, in Yorkshire and Lancashire in particular, that theirs was a battle between the power of industrial capital and the raw labour power of mass menace. In contrast, Swing rioters frequently engaged in protracted discourse with those whose property they intended to destroy. The men who destroyed Pile's threshing machines had already broken John Clift's machines. They were very open about their intentions, with Charles Davis, James Lane and Laban Stone prominently to the fore. They next visited the rector, Reverend Hare, who refused their request for money. He followed them and had a 'long conversation' with Davis and two others at Pile's farm before the irate Pile arrived. Davis had again been quite open about their intentions, asking for money 'but not in a threatening manner'.[24]

This is not to say that there was nothing in common between Luddism and Swing. The evidence from the trials and other sources suggests that Luddite gangs in all three regions were composed principally of men mainly in their twenties and thirties. Some 69 per cent of those tried in the Wiltshire Special Assizes were in this same age group.[25] Older men, such as the Jacobin John Baines, were tried at the Luddite Special Assizes in 1813 but they were accused of 'twisting in' men into a wider conspiracy and were not engaged in machine breaking. The evidence from the Wiltshire Special Assizes, however, shows that nearly one in twelve of those taken up for disorder were in their forties and fifties, a very different pattern. Indeed, one man, George Hawkins, arrested and tried for taking

---

22 *Devizes and Wiltshire Gazette*, 25 November 1831; *Salisbury and Winchester Journal*, 10 January 1831; *The Times*, 7 February 1831. Goddard was a prosperous tanner, said to be worth over £1,000.
23 Occasionally there was some interchange. The men who smashed Samuel Swallow's shearing machines asked for arms and then, 'after wishing goodnight, they left'. TNA, HO 42/121, examination of Samuel Swallow, 6 March 1812.
24 *The Times*, 7 and 10 January 1831; *Salisbury and Winchester Journal*, 10 January 1831.
25 M.I. Thomis, *The Luddites: Machine-Breaking in Regency England* (Newton Abbot, 1970), p. 112; Gloucestershire County Record Office, D1571/X64, County of Wilts, Calendar of Prisoners, 1831.

part in the riot at Rockley on 23 November, was aged 60.[26] This was a ripe age for rioting.

Historians have noted that, while in the main Luddite ranks were composed of those threatened by technological displacement, they also included men – and, in the case of Lancashire, women – who were not directly affected by the new technology, betokening a wider community support for the aims of the machine breakers. The same was true of Swing. Hobsbawm and Rudé noted the importance of 'the role played within it by the town and village craftsmen' among the rioters. Indeed, they saw the role of such groups as pivotal, citing the view of Mr Justice Park at the Wiltshire trials: such men 'have been the foremost in the destruction of the threshing machinery and the violent and often felonious acts which the mob, in the pursuit of that purpose, have so often committed'.[27] A'Court stated that Patient's threshing machine 'was broken in a minute, evidently by persons who understood the trade – I should think by blacksmiths and carpenters'.[28] Blacksmiths, of course, possessed the necessary tools to dismantle and smash the cast iron machines. Some, such as Maurice Pope, took part voluntarily, others, such as Edmund White of Tisbury, as pressed men.[29] Small farmers were also suspected of supporting the attacks on machinery, in just the same way that some petty capitalists – small hosiers, master dressers and master weavers – were suspected of support for the Luddites: 'the small farmers if they do not aid are evidently glad to see the labourers at work [breaking machines] fancying it will tend to their benefits, lowering tythes etc', Col. Mair noted from Wiltshire.[30] Finally, the response of central government likewise was very similar in both sets of disorders. While local authorities in both periods oscillated between an insistence upon maintaining local management and desperate requests for troops, central government in both periods saw the events unfolding in the regions as dangerous threats to public order and increasingly intervened, both directly through the

---

26 T.J. Howell, *Complete Collection of State Trials and Proceedings for High Treason and Other Crimes* (London, 1823), 31, pp. 1074–92. Hawkins was one of the men taken up on the day by Pile and the Marlborough yeomanry troop. One of his colleagues, William Baily, was 53. Along with many others, he pleaded guilty. Baskerville, the magistrate they had attacked, put in a plea for mercy and all were bound over for two years under a heavy recognizance of £50 each. *Salisbury and Winchester Journal*, 10 January 1831; *The Times*, 10 January 1831.
27 Hobsbawm and Rudé, *Captain Swing*, p. 245.
28 *The Times*, 5 January 1831.
29 Ibid., 3 and 6 January 1831; WSHC, 413/23, Confession of Edmund White.
30 TNA, HO 52/11, Mair to Melbourne, 26 November 1830. The role of farmers in the riots in Wiltshire is discussed in E. Billinge, 'Rural crime and protest in Wiltshire 1830–1875', unpublished PhD thesis, University of Kent (1984), pp. 175–78.

army and indirectly through pressure upon the Lords Lieutenant and then through Special Commissions.

Yet if government was alarmed by Swing, Luddism had frightened them far more. While no one died at the hands of the Luddites until William Horsfall was murdered near Marsden on 27 April 1812, there was a palpable sense of violence in the air. Firearms were regularly carried by Luddite bands in all three regions.[31] Conversely, for all their threatening language and occasional personal confrontations, Swing rioters remained, according to Thompson, 'curiously indecisive and unbloodthirsty'.[32] Brotherton wrote from Wiltshire, 'I cannot find any trace of firearms among them. The weapons they have are but the fragments of the machines they have broken'.[33] And Denman noted from the Commission that 'there has been such an absence of cruelty as to create general surprise'.[34] Wiltshire Swing rioters in the main carried only sledge hammers (often purloined, as by Peter Withers from the forge of John Chumm in Ogbourne on the morning of the 24th prior to the attack at Rockley),[35] iron bars and bludgeons. That is not to claim that they were pacific or that they could not turn nasty. But when violence broke out in Wiltshire, it often was in response to aggressive behaviour by a farmer or magistrate. For example, at Alton Barnes the mob did not become violent until the choleric Pile arrived. According to Hare, even when Pile swore at the men in his yard and fired over their heads, the mob remained respectful towards him and, as noted, emphasised their lack of personal animus. That did not last once Pile, now armed with a loaded double barrelled gun brought to him by Rev. Hare and still carrying his pistol, advanced on the machine breakers. Faced with this weaponry, the men in the barn chose to escape but a fracas ensued and the gun went off, apparently injuring some rioters. Only at this point did the mob turn ugly, beating him and smashing his gun.[36] The pattern was replicated elsewhere.[37]

In all three Luddite regions there was much talk of military-style leadership: 'twisting in' was certainly practised in both Yorkshire and

---

31 Randall, *Riotous Assemblies*, p. 295.
32 E.P. Thompson, *The Making of the English Working Class* (London, 1968), p.250.
33 TNA, HO 52/11, Brotherton to Melbourne, 28 November 1830.
34 TNA, HO 40/27, Denman to Melbourne, 5 January 1831.
35 *The Times*, 10 January 1831; *Devizes and Wiltshire Gazette*, 13 January 1831.
36 *Devizes and Wiltshire Gazette*, 25 November, 9 December 1830, 6 January 1831; *The Times*, 7 January 1831; *Salisbury and Winchester Journal*, 10 January 1831.
37 Even at Tisbury events began peacefully enough until Benett's forceful intervention. See A.J. Randall and E. Newman, 'Protest, Proletarians and Paternalists: Social Conflict in Rural Wiltshire, 1830–1850', *Rural History* 6 (1995), 210–11.

Lancashire while military-like organisation infused all Luddite attacks. Thus in Nottinghamshire and Yorkshire there were reports of men 'on a regular systematic plan and with the most minute attention to the commands of the leader'. The group which attacked Balderstone's shop at Crosland Moor 'marched off in military order'.[38] Such organisation severely frightened many property owners. Thomas Garside, a mill owner from Stockport saw Luddism as 'the most desperate and best organised conspiracy that the world has ever witnessed'.[39] General Maitland in Yorkshire faced 'an evil combination of destruction'[40] while the *Nottingham Journal* believed the county faced 'little short of rebellion'.[41] But the authorities could detect little sign of any directing agency in Swing, in spite of serious searching. Brotherton noted from Wiltshire: 'The insurrectionary movement seems to be directed by no plan or system, but merely actuated by the spontaneous feeling of the peasantry and quite at random'.[42] Luddite bands marched to and from attacks. Swing mobs travelled often considerable distances but few manifested any sort of formation nor was their bearing very military. They were at best a troop of irregulars under their Captain – they lacked a General like Ludd.

If the Swing riots in Wiltshire, the county which witnessed the most machine breaking, compare poorly with the Luddite disturbances, they demonstrated clearer parallels with other earlier disorders. They certainly bore more than a passing resemblance to the riots which greeted the introduction of preparatory machinery into the textile industries in the later eighteenth century. These too had seen large mobilised crowds, a determined destruction of technology and an apparent lack of prior organisation.[43] Indeed, in Wiltshire, and in other counties, Swing saw a limited reprise. The rioters who had assembled at Enford on the 23rd eventually reached Figheldean where they demolished all the machinery in a defunct woollen mill. At Quidhampton, the working woollen mill owned by William Nash was attacked by a mob of three or four hundred. They smashed the windows, broke in and destroyed many spinning machines, parts of which were thrown in the mill pond.[44] And at Wilton an even larger mob attacked John Brasher's Crow Lane woollen mill and

38   *Leeds Mercury*, 29 February 1812; *Nottingham Journal*, 1 March 1812.
39   TNA, HO 42/122, Garside to Ryder, 21 April 1812.
40   Sheffield Archives, Sheffield, Wentworth Woodhouse MSS., F45/112., Maitland to Fitzwilliam, 26 April 1812.
41   *Nottingham Journal*, 1 February 1812.
42   TNA, HO 52/11, Brotherton to Melbourne, 28 November 1830.
43   Randall, *Before the Luddites*, pp.100–7.
44   *Devizes and Wiltshire Gazette*, 25 November, 2 December 1830; *The Times*, 5 and 7 January 1831; *Salisbury and Winchester Journal*, 10 January 1831.

smashed five carding engines. Asked why, their leader, John Jennings, allegedly replied, 'in order to make more work for the poor people'.[45] Such attacks echoed the bitterness demonstrated against the early spinning jennies and scribbling engines which had destroyed the major bi-occupation for many agricultural labourers' wives and daughters forty years before.

A better parallel can be drawn with the food riots which up to 1801 had periodically swept through the region. The sudden appearance of food-rioting mobs, demonstrating surprising unity, determination and sense of legitimacy had frequently shocked the authorities.[46] Like Swing, food riots arose apparently without warning or earlier preparation, but rapidly swept up large crowds from market place, workplace and public houses. Like Swing rioters, they made a point of pressing the willing and unwilling alike to take part in their collective actions, a fact demonstrated by the numbers at trial before the Special Commissions in both 1766 and 1831 pleading that they had been coerced into joining. Food rioters were frequently summoned by horns or drums, to the terror of the respectable classes. They also frequently bore flags, often bolting cloths seized from corn mills. Wiltshire Swing rioters certainly carried flags but rarely seem to have horns or drums. Thomas Langford, perhaps ironically, told the flag-bearing mob which arrived at his farm at Wroughton on 23 November that he was surprised that did not have a drum.[47] But Swing crowds frequently carried broken threshing machine parts, both as trophies and as evidence of intent. And, like food rioters, Swing mobs moved from place to place quite openly and apparently without fear of recognition. That lack of deference was seen even at the trials. The *Times* correspondent noted the 'bold and confident air' of the prisoners.[48]

Food rioters evinced a strong sense of legitimacy which rested upon reference to the old legislation which regulated food markets. Indeed, in Gloucestershire and Wiltshire they often referred to themselves as 'regulators'.[49] Swing rioters did not have legal precedents to turn to but a strong sense of moral purpose characterised their behaviour. Threshing machines were clearly viewed as devices to 'steal' their rightful labour as

45 *Salisbury and Winchester Journal*, 29 November 1830, 10 January 1831; *The Times*, 5 January 1831. Neither of leaders at Figheldean and Wilton were agricultural labourers. Thomas Piggot at the former was a chimney sweep, John Jennings at Wilton a whitesmith.
46 On food riots, see E.P. Thompson, 'The Moral Economy of the English Crowd in the Eighteenth Century', *Past & Present* 50 (1971).
47 *The Times*, 6 January 1831.
48 Ibid., 8 January 1831.
49 A. Charlesworth and A.J. Randall, 'Morals, Markets and the English Crowd in 1766', *Past & Present* 114 (1987), 209–11.

their discourse with farmers often showed. The demand for payment for breaking threshing machines can be read in this way and stands in marked contrast to the actions of both Luddites and earlier machine breakers. Luddites sometimes demanded money – they certainly demanded firearms – but there was no explicit correlation of payment with their actions, no recorded incidence of a Luddite demanding a sovereign, or any other sum, as compensation for his trouble in smashing the hated machine. The labourers in 1830 appear to have wanted more than just the end of the threshing machines. They wanted acknowledgement that introduction of the threshing machines had been a breach of a long-standing social contract. The farmers' recourse to taking down threshing machines in advance of trouble, though in the main a tactical device to assuage a difficult situation, could well have been read by the labourers as acceptance of 'guilt'. And it is notable how few threshing machines seem to have been reinstated in 1831 when market power, coupled by state coercion, would certainly have allowed it. In Wiltshire in 1833 there were still 'not many – in fact scarcely one to every hundred that used to exist'.[50]

This sense that machine breaking might be justifiable was even to be seen at the Special Commission. Thomas Lawrence was convicted of extorting money from Spicer though, along with others, he was acquitted of the charge of breaking Langford's threshing machine since the evidence showed that it had been destroyed by the earlier mob. Lawrence, 'very active in the mob', and having 'the appearance of a gypsy', was sentenced to death. On the other hand, Charles Bowerton was found guilty of breaking John Wells' threshing machine at Wanborough in the same series of events. A local married labourer with one child, he had been earning only seven shillings a week. Though he had been 'very active in the destruction of the machine', he was given a good character. Baron Vaughan, sentencing him, noted that the machine breaking was his 'only offence and was not accompanied with robbery, and as you had very low wages, which probably might have been the reason why you were so easily led into this crime'. Bowerton, clearly not looking like a gypsy, was given three months hard labour in the house of correction.[51]

One motif of Swing was incendiarism, something rarely associated with food riots but not unknown in earlier anti-machinery disturbances.[52] Hobsbawm and Rudé remained uncertain of the role of arson in Swing.

50 P.P. 1833, 612, 5, *Select Committee appointed to inquire into the state of agriculture*, p. 64.
51 *The Times*, 10 January 1831.
52 For example, Wiltshire shearmen, battling against the introduction of finishing machinery in 1802, used arson as a means to put pressure upon their employers. Randall, 'The Shearmen and the Wiltshire Outrages of 1802', 293–4.

Was it the work of disgruntled individuals or in some way part of a wider coordinated response? Wiltshire, which they characterised as one of the '*machine-breaking* counties' as distinct from the '*incendiary* counties',[53] had fewer blazes than in south-east England but witnessed examples of both clandestine and openly celebrated incendiary attacks. For example, on the night of 21 November a fire which destroyed a hay rick at Amesbury was suspected to be the work of two 'strange' men in snuff-coloured clothes seen heading for the turnpike. But three nights before at Oare, near Pewsey, a major fire at the farm of Mr Fowler, which destroyed all his wheat, barley, beans and oats, took a different form. While the respectable inhabitants fought the blaze, the labourers of the place gathered and 'appeared to take pleasure from the situation', refusing to help.[54] Nevertheless, many Swing participants, often without obvious pressure, denounced arson, even though it plainly assisted their cause in frightening farmers. Wanborough farmers were particularly alarmed by threats to their ricks –one had recently suffered an arson attack - and on the 22 November they all went to Swindon to be sworn in as special constables. When the next day rioters arrived at his farm, Spicer demanded of them: 'Are you firemen? If you are I would sooner die on the spot than give you anything.' They vigorously refuted the suggestion. They were 'only machine breakers'. They must, however, have a sovereign for every threshing machine that they broke.[55] John Benett too had parlayed with the labourers before the infamous 'battle of Pyt House'. He warned them that the government had just issued a proclamation which offered a reward of £50 for anyone impeaching a machine breaker and £500 for an arsonist. 'We don't burn. We have nothing to do with the fires', they indignantly replied.[56] Charles Davis told Rev. Hare 'that they would not burn any property, that they would discover the incendiaries if they could, and deliver them up to justice; and that hanging was too good for them'.[57]

Food rioters claimed that they did not tolerate thieving, sometimes with justification, but it certainly occurred.[58] They also had frequent recourse to sturdy begging and worse. Swing rioters likewise pressed passers by for 'alms'. The Ramsbury rioters stopped coaches at Froxfield and solicited money from the passengers, though no violence was offered.[59] And, as in all disorders, there were some who took the

53 Hobsbawm and Rudé, *Captain Swing*, pp. 200, 203.
54 *Devizes and Wiltshire Gazette*, 25 November 1830; 13 January 1831.
55 Ibid.
56 *Salisbury and Winchester Journal*, 29 November 1830; *The Times* 3 January 1831.
57 *Devizes and Wiltshire Gazette*, 6 December 1831; *The Times*, 7 January 1831.
58 Randall, *Riotous Assemblies*, p. 120.
59 *Devizes and Wiltshire Gazette*, 25 November 1830.

opportunity to steal. Shadrack Blake was a leading figure in the attack at Mr. Fulbrook's farm in Hippenscombe. Fulbrook had repulsed an earlier attempt but late in the evening 'a mob of around 300 people returned ... broke the doors and windows ... and about 20 people got into the house'. Fulbrook provided a lanthorn to enable the men to see to break his threshing machine but, when the mob left, a tea caddy, two tea ladles and a linen table cloth had gone with them. Next day Blake was part of a large mob which visited the farm of William Barnes at Shalbourne. Barnes had already dismantled his machine but the mob smashed the parts to pieces. Blake was spotted trousering a brass spindle box. Barnes handed over the requisite sovereign but had some consolation when three days later a special constable searched Blake's lodgings and found the tea caddy.[60] Disorder encouraged men to push the boundaries of legality. At Hannington in the early evening of 24 November, a crowd of 40 or 50 men arrived at the house of Mr Shewry, demanding 'Drink, drink!' They went on to the house occupied by a magistrate's widow, Mrs Montgomery, shouting up at her window that they had visited all the houses in the village and at each they had been given beer or money. They were thrown some money and left. At last, about ten o'clock, they arrived at the house of Thomas Jefferies with the same cry. He was warned 'there was no law for that night'. But one man also told him that 'he hoped the farmers would have their rents lowered and we would have our wages raised'.[61]

Food rioters judged their actions with half an eye on the justices since they hoped for magisterial support in what they saw as the re-imposition of morally-responsible marketing practices. Swing labourers likewise were far from shy about engaging the justices. Some at least believed that the justices endorsed their actions, a claim frequently expressed by food rioters. Reverend Hare, who witnessed the events at Pile's farm, noted in his evidence at the Commission:

> I feel it my duty to say, that, in consequence of the long conversation I had with Davis and two other men, I believe that they were acting under the misapprehension of some advice that they had heard that morning from a magistrate, and that they fancied that they were not breaking the law ... They said that they only wished that every man should live by his labour.[62]

As in food riots, some justices in 1830 were clearly more interventionist than others. Take the case of Sir Richard Poore, one of

60 *Salisbury and Winchester Journal*, 10 January 1831; WSHC, 2320/1, Diary of Richard Massey, Shalbourne, 25 November 1830; *The Times*, 8 January 1831.
61 *Devizes and Wiltshire Gazette*, 13 January 1831; *The Times*, 10 January 1831.
62 *Devizes and Wiltshire Gazette*, 6 December 1831; *The Times*, 7 January 1831.

the leading gentlemen in the Devizes division. Poore had been away from his home at Rushall on 22 November when the Enford labourers had come calling. His gardener informed the mob of his absence and told them that Lady Poore was ill in bed. They waited quietly while he reported their concerns to her and then brought back a £5 note, most of which was then spent at the Poore Arms in nearby Charlton. The next morning Poore went out to find the mobs who were now breaking machines all around. At Manningford Abbots he came upon a large crowd and rode in among them, warning them against destroying property, assuring them 'that if it was in his power to redress their grievances, he would use his utmost endeavour to do so; that he would mediate between them and the farmers, or landlords, or magistrates and that he was satisfied that their wages ought to be raised.' They received him well and Poore, assuming that the labourers were now going to disperse, gave them a sovereign and rode home. The labourers, however, continued the work of machine breaking and at midday joined with others at the Rose and Crown at Woodborough. Thereafter they marched as one body under the leadership of Charles Davis until they arrived at Pile's farm. Clearly it was Poore's advice to which Davis and the others talking to Hare were alluding.[63]

Poore was not alone in following the old paternal intervention model. While he and his fellow justices in the Devizes division published a notice on 23 September which condemned disorder, six days later they published a second which urged the farmers to raise wages 'so that every able bodied labourer shall received for his full labour wages at the rate of ten shillings weekly'. At Christian Malford, Paul Methuen and his fellow justices parlayed with a large mob which likewise demanded 10s but also urged that the tithe owners and landlords should reduce their charges in proportion to assist the farmers. 'The magistrates promised the men that they should have the wages they desired; upon hearing which they gave three cheers and dispersed'.[64] In taking such actions, the justices echoed the practices of their predecessors who, when food riots raged, publicly ordered tenants to sell grain at 'fair' prices and denounced forestallers. However, the instrumental power of the justices was not what it had been, a fact exposed by food riots in 1801.[65] The occupiers of land in the Devizes Division immediately responded to the magistrates' promptings

63 *Devizes and Wiltshire Gazette*, 25 November 1830. Poore, undismayed, went to Pewsey the next day but found no labourers to meet him, 'so well were they satisfied that the worthy Baronet would mediate fairly between them and their employers'. *Salisbury and Winchester Journal*, 29 November 1830.
64 *Devizes and Wiltshire Gazette*, 2 December 1830.
65 Randall, *Riotous Assemblies*, pp. 238–39.

with their own notice which 'humbly' requested 'that the Proprietors and Tithe owners will openly and candidly declare what REDUCTION they intend to MAKE to their Tenants, without which they cannot possibly accede to their wishes'. Watson Taylor at Erlestoke was able to persuade all his tenants to comply, but elsewhere the recommendation led the labourers to believe that 10s was now the compulsory wage. When farmers refused to pay, disorders and strikes followed, as at Marston. Poore and Estcourt were forced to beat a hasty retreat at the Petty Sessions, emphasising that:

> the magistrates had no intention of interfering between the farmer and labourer; they had no power, indeed; and if they had, it would be far from their inclination; they barely *recommended* 10s a week wages; conceiving that was a fair remuneration.

It was an embarrassing climb down. The farmer who was prosecuting the strikers agreed 'to see his brother and endeavour, if possible, to effect some arrangement' on rent reduction, but the case demonstrated the shifting power balance, a balance shifted further by the New Poor Law.[66]

Food rioters tended to treat all justices with some deference. Swing rioters were less inhibited, a remarkable fact given their often close economic relationship. At Heytesbury, Col. A'Court managed to disperse a crowd late on the evening of 24 November with paternal rhetoric but early the next morning the mob gathered again and refused to listen – 'the more he spoke the more they hooted'. They proceeded to Ambrose Patient's farm where, notwithstanding the justice's presence, they smashed Patient's machines and then proceeded to do the same at another farm.[67] Not all justices bothered to proffer mediation. The rioters who massed at Ogbourne St Andrew early on the 22nd encountered Justice Baskerville on their way to Canning's farm at Rockley. Baskerville ordered them to return to their homes. He got short shrift: 'they didn't care a d—n for the magistrates for though there were only 40 or 50 of them, there were 1,300 or 1,400 waiting to join them'. Baskerville told them he would not allow the breaking of machines, flourished his pistol and he and Oliver Codrington, an unsworn special constable, both on horseback, lashed out with their whips. A fracas quickly ensued, which ended when a hammer, thrown by Peter Withers, hit Codrington, knocking him senseless from his horse. The justice withdrew, pending reinforcements, and the mob proceeded to destroy the threshing

---

66 *Devizes and Wiltshire Gazette*, 2 and 9 December 1830; Randall and Newman, 'Protest, Proletarians and Paternalists', 211–12, 214, 217–18.
67 *Salisbury and Winchester Journal*, 29 November 1830, 10 January 1831; *The Times*, 5 January 1831.

machines. It was this same mob, Withers included, who were arrested by Pile and the yeomanry troop later that morning.[68]

Clearly the willingness of the rioters to listen to the justices depended upon the standing and trust such men had in the eyes of labouring society and, even when dealing with proven paternalists like Poore, rioters still continued with their own interventions. But this is again in marked distinction to the actions of the Luddites. All bar the framework knitters had long despaired of active and benevolent intervention by the bench in industrial confrontations. And even the framework knitters in 1811 recognised that the justices in the hosiery districts had little instrumental power to help them.[69] Swing labourers in Wiltshire evidently still retained glimmering hopes that the justices might be willing to carry out their paternal duty.

If Swing had more in common with food riots than with the Luddite disturbances, does this have implications for our view the events of 1830? I would suggest that it does, since it raises questions about the way in which successive historians have followed Hobsbawm and Rudé in conceptualising Swing as a 'movement' and its events as parts of a whole. Historians of food riots recognise the common context of rising prices, food shortages and growing tensions in the market place. They identify a common set of responses which were informed by a shared belief in a moral economic model. They do not, however, speak of a food rioting 'movement', even though rioters had a common aim in restoring the 'just price', used similar means to effect that end, utilised similar symbols to identify themselves and the riots themselves were spread by neighbouring precedents, by reports in the newspapers, and by the active intervention of roving crowds of 'regulators', all of which also characterised Swing. Hobsbawm and Rudé indeed described Swing as the 'defence of customary rights', presciently anticipating Edward Thompson's concept of 'moral economy'. However, they constantly referred to Swing as a movement, even though they found Swing wanting in all aspects of modernity.[70] *Captain Swing*, of course, was written in an era when political scientists and historians were much taken with contemporary

68 *Devizes and Wiltshire Gazette*, 25 November 1830; *The Times* 10 January 1831; *Salisbury and Winchester Journal*, 10 January 1831.
69 D. Gray and V.W. Walker, (eds), *Records of the Borough of Nottingham* (Thos. Forman, 1952), 8, 1800–1835, p. 157.
70 The 'weapons with which the labourers fought were archaic'; neither machine breaking nor arson 'needed much in the way of social inventiveness'; and the labourers demonstrated few 'signs of a new political or social ideology. On the contrary, there is evidence that the labourers still accepted the ancient symbols of ancient ideals of stable hierarchy.' Hobsbawm and Rudé, *Captain Swing*, pp. 16, 17, 18.

peasant 'movements',[71] yet subsequent historians have persisted with the model. One of the exceptions has been Roger Wells who, in a wide ranging essay, explicitly and convincingly identified Swing, as here, as having a clear lineage back into the moral economic world of the eighteenth century.[72]

Moving away from the 'movement' model allows historians to focus upon the local contexts of Swing disorders and to examine the ways in which they mediated, exacerbated or even prevented Swing outbreaks.[73] Food riots did not break out in every market or parish, even though sharp upward spikes in food prices quickly translated to all markets in a district. Sometimes this reflected the active interventions of the landlords or justices or poor law authorities, sometimes the strength of dominant power structures, sometimes the lack of protest precedents, sometimes the weakness of plebeian will. The Pewsey Vale, as we have noted, witnessed unprecedented popular activism in late November 1830, yet the adjacent districts to the west of Devizes saw no disorder and little conflict. This was not because of an unwillingness to challenge power, as the frequent clashes in and around Potterne in the years following Swing demonstrated. Indeed, a decade later the 'Potterne lambs' had become notorious for their hostility to the new police.[74] Was Swing 'absent' here because of labour weakness or, paradoxically, because of its perceived strength?

A refocus upon the local context also allows us to re-address the question, posed by Andrew Charlesworth, as to how and why the riots spread. Study of the events in the Pewsey Vale indicates that the labourers followed a seemingly systematic approach, with multiple mobs

71 See, for example, B. Moore, *Social Origins of Dictatorship and Democracy: Lord and peasant in the Making of the Modern World* (London, 1967); H.A. Landsberger, (ed.), *Latin American Peasant Movements* (Ithaca, NY, 1969); H.A. Landsberger, (ed.), *Rural Protest, Peasant movements and Social Change* (London, 1974); E.R. Wolf, *Peasants* (Eaglewood Cliffs, 1966); E.R. Wolf, *Peasant Wars in the Twentieth Century* (New York, 1970).
72 R. Wells, 'The Moral Economy of the English countryside' in A.J. Randall and A. Charlesworth (eds), *Moral Economy and Popular Protest: Crowds, Conflict and Authority* (London, 2000), pp. 209–72. Wells, like the Hammonds, refers to Swing as a 'revolt'. See also Wells, 'William Cobbett, Captain Swing, and King William IV', *Agricultural History Review* 45 (1997), 34–48.
73 An insistence upon understanding the 'local' characterises the work of two important young historians, Carl Griffin and Peter Jones. See C. Griffin, '"There was No Law to Punish that Offence" Re-Assessing 'Captain Swing': Rural Luddism and Rebellion in East Kent, 1830–31', *Southern History*, 22 (2000); P. Jones, 'Finding Captain Swing: Protest, Parish Relations and the State of the Public Mind in 1830', *International Review of Social History* 54 (2009).
74 Randall and Newman, 'Protest, Proletarians and Ppaternalists', 217, 219–21.

quartering first their immediate district and then the districts round about. Where did this model of action come from? Charlesworth argued that the highways carried the contagion of Swing. The story from north Wiltshire suggests we might do better to switch attention from the arterial routes back to the lanes and cart tracks of rural England. Charlesworth also argued that it was the press reports which provided the spur.[75] The labourers at Enford on the 23 November certainly wanted what they believed others had obtained, 'as it had said in the paper', but did they draw their methods from such reports? As with food riots, we are left to wonder where their leadership came from, since there was no clear 'trade' hierarchy to build upon as in the case of industrial workers. Charisma, moral stature and serendipity clearly played a part. Charles Davis was more than a labourer: his occupation was later listed as 'Ploughs, reaps, milks, mows and spadesman'. Maurice Pope and Thomas Goddard had nothing to do with agriculture. Pope, prize fighter and blacksmith, was clearly a celebrity in Bedwyn. Goddard, a tanner 'in a comfortable way of business', had ridden to Aldbourne with the intention of taking a mediating role. He arrived at Church's farm following the smashing of a threshing machine and at the point when the customary sovereign was being levied, whereupon the mob 'called out for Mr Goddard to receive the money for them'.[76] Historians of Swing, blessed with the quality and depth of both local and national newspaper reportage of the Special Commissions, together with the detailed criminal records, are better placed than students of any previous mass disorders to tease out the answers to these questions.

A focus upon the local also allows sharper comparison with other and earlier outbreaks of popular protest. In so doing we recognise another real contextual difference between Swing and the Luddite disorders. Framework knitters, handloom weavers and croppers might, and regularly did, clash with their employers, but they knew that there were other employers who might offer them work. Hosiers, cotton manufacturers and master dressers likewise rarely owned cottage properties and had only limited control over the local poor law. The agricultural labourers of Wiltshire and of southern England collided with their employers at very much greater peril. There were rarely many farmers offering employment on a significant scale and those who did dominated the vestry and often had numbers of tied cottages. This is what makes Swing, and above all the openness of many Swing actions, so remarkable. Only the rural disorders

---

75 A. Charlesworth, *Social Protest in a Rural Society: the spatial diffusion of the Swing disturbances, 1830–31* (Norwich, 1979), pp. 25–27, 37–39, 44–45.
76 Chambers, *Wiltshire Machine Breakers: The Rioters*, pp. 66–67, 86–87, 172–74.

occasioned by the Militia Acts in 1757 and again in 1796 saw such direct and such vigorous clashes *within* rural society. These disorders similarly saw the world turned upside down.[77] They, like the Swing riots in north Wiltshire, can only be understood as an outbreak of collective outrage at the evident abandonment of every precept of moral responsibility of the rich to the poor which the introduction of the threshing machines symbolised.

Hobsbawm and Rudé saw Swing as the precursor to the more formalised trade unionism of the 'Revolt of the Field' later in the century.[78] I would suggest that Swing was more of an end than a beginning. Riots can be read as a dialogue, acted out through a mixture of discourse, symbolic action and disorder. The dialogues of Swing, much more locally specific than those of the Luddites, marked the curtain call of the moral economy.

---

77 Randall, *Riotous Assemblies*, pp. 166–72, 175, 177, 318.
78 'The point is that up to 1830 ... the labourers' agitation was essentially the sort of movement which could and ought to have been trade unionist'. Hobsbawm and Rudé, *Captain Swing*, p. 292.

The Diffusion of Contentious Gatherings in the Captain Swing Uprising*

Daniel J. Myers and Jamie L. Przybysz

I Introduction

The end of the 18th, and beginning of the 19th, century produced marked changes in the agricultural economy of southern and eastern England. Several poor growing seasons combined with an accelerating introduction of agricultural machinery transformed the relations between agricultural owners and labour. Landless farm labourers experienced a reduction in pay and at least believed that they were being replaced by the threshing machine, conditioning an acute crisis of unemployment and poverty. The chances of subsisting as a casual workforce made many long for earlier farming arrangements that were more dependent on person power.

As the autumn of 1830 approached, the situation in East Kent had become so desperate that parish magistrates urged farmers to discontinue the use of threshing machines – many complied but others did not and became targets for the growing resentment among the labourers. On Saturday night, 28 August 1830, the hired machine of Cooper Inge was destroyed, the first of many. By the third week of October, over one hundred threshing machines had been destroyed in East Kent.

As ruined machines accumulated, the tactical strategy was apparent – not just because the implement blamed for the economic problems was destroyed, but also because of selective targeting: farmers who pledged not to use the machines were less likely to be targeted by the mob despite

---

*   This research was partially supported by grant SBR 96-01409 from the National Science Foundation, USA. We thank Mike Welch, David Hachen, Robert Fishman, the members of the University of Notre Dame Working Group on Politics and Social Movements, and the participants of the 2009 conference, *Captain Swing Reconsidered*, for comments on earlier drafts.

widespread destruction. The selectivity helped the public at large and even some local authorities to view the destruction sympathetically. Soon after, threatening letters began to arrive at the residences of intended victims. The letters, signed by the legendary anonymous character 'Captain Swing', provided a moniker for the wave of collective action that would continue to spread across England between August and December of 1830.[1]

Did this wave of action constitute a social movement? It is easy to imagine how these events might have accelerated, given the lack of social condemnation or repression by authorities. And, indeed, in addition to machine breaking, the repertoires of protestors expanded to include marches, wage meetings, riots and arson. At first glance, then, it seems intuitively clear that these events must have been related and, therefore, in some sense, constituent pieces of a social movement. One incident, and the rhetoric that surrounded it (such as the letters attributed to the good Captain), seem likely to have fuelled others.

Despite these appearances, prior analyses of the Swing uprising do not agree even on the question of whether and how the events might have been related to each other (the diffusion question), much less whether they were part of something that might have some coherence as a movement. Some scholars viewed the events as largely isolated incidents, while others even believed that elements of intentional coordination connected one event to another. The difference is important not just to describe and trace the development of the wave, but also because it has implications for the burgeoning development of a rebellious political consciousness among the landless agricultural labourers of this time and place – a consciousness that has been denied by some observers of the period.

Here, we re-examine the Swing wave to determine if, in fact, there is substantial evidence for event-to-event influence – in other words, to determine if diffusion influence was a substantial contributor to the Captain Swing uprising. If the diffusion patterns reveal influence among events, then we have a foundational piece necessary to understand how a collective political movement, however loosely aware of itself as coordinated collective action, may have developed in the countryside of agricultural Britain.

---

1 This brief account is derived from those provided by J. Stevenson, *Popular Disturbances In England, 1700–1832* (New York, 1992); A. Charlesworth, *Social Protest in a Rural Society: The Spatial Diffusion of the Captain Swing disturbances of 1830–1831* (Historical Geography Research Series, 1, Liverpool 1979); E. Hobsbawm and G. Rudé, *Captain Swing: A Social History of the Great English Agricultural Uprising of 1830* (New York, 1975); G. Rudé, *The Crowd in History, 1730–1848* (New York, 1964); C. Tilly, *Popular Contention in Great Britain: 1758–1834* (Cambridge, Mass., 1995).

II Background
Social Diffusion Processes and Collective Action

Social scientists have long recognised that incidents of social behaviour are rarely independent.[2] Scholars of collective action have not been oblivious to these interdependencies, and there has been a patchy, yet substantial scholarship devoted to the spread of collective action events across time and space.[3] These scholars and others have increasingly recognised the need to understand the connections among events and the people that produce them, in order to understand the trajectory of protest waves. Despite increasing calls for attention to the dynamic elements of protest, rebellion, and all kinds of collective contention,[4] it is fair to say that progress in understanding diffusion processes has been stalled by three problems. The first is the unfortunate history of the idea of 'contagion' in early crowd theories. For example, Gustave Le Bon writing in 1895 and Sigmund Freud in 1921, posited notions of mob contagion under which individuals in crowds could be 'infected', by an unconscious, primitive craze.[5] Such notions of crowd behaviour have been thoroughly debunked,[6] yet analysts have remained reluctant to examine diffusion notions for fear of resurrecting these misleading ideas. Modern variants of social diffusion recognise it as a rational form of inter-actor influence. Potential actors observe and evaluate the outcomes of others' behaviours, and then make a decision for themselves about whether or not to adopt the behaviour.[7]

The second impediment to progress in understanding social diffusion, and the diffusion of collective action in particular, has been a lack of analytic apparatus necessary to test diffusion hypotheses. In particular, competitive tests of formal mathematical models against other long-standing hypotheses about waves of social behaviour were difficult to

---

2   For a thorough retrospective summary, see E.M. Rogers, *Diffusion of Innovations* (New York 1995).
3   A thorough history of the development of crowd and collective behaviour research may be found in C. McPhail, *The Myth of the Madding Crowd* (New York 1991); R.H. Turner and L.M. Killian, *Collective Behavior* (Englewood Cliffs, NJ, 1972). V. Mahajan and R.A. Peterson, *Models for Innovation Diffusion* (Beverly Hills, Ca., 1985) provides an introduction to diffusion theory and how it links to collective behaviour.
4   D. McAdam, S. Tarrow, and C. Tilly, *Dynamics of Contention* (Cambridge, 2001).
5   G. Le Bon, *The Crowd: A Study of the Popular Mind.* (London, 1952 [original 1895]); S. Freud, *Group Psychology and Analysis of Ego* (London, 1921).
6   McPhail, *The Myth of the Madding Crowd.*
7   A. Oberschall, 'Loosely Structured Collective Conflict', *Research In Social Movements, Conflict and Change* 3 (1980), 45–68; A. Oberschall, 'The 1960 Sit-ins: Protest Diffusion and Movement Take-off', *Research In Social Movements, Conflict and Change* 11 (1989), 31–53.

construct.[8] This problem was solved in a series of studies by Strang, Tuma, and Greve in the 1990s in which they demonstrated how event history techniques could be effectively used to examine diffusion hypotheses.[9] Of particular importance was the new models' ability to (1) include time-varying predictors, and thus a wide variety of diffusion hypotheses, and (2) simultaneously to test diffusion hypotheses against other kinds of static and dynamic variables. This contribution has opened up a whole new way to study and understand the dynamic and continually changing mutual influence of social actors.

The third obstacle to progress in understanding the diffusion of collective action resulted from a discontinuity between collective protest events and the kinds of phenomena usually examined under the 'diffusion of innovation' programme so often associated with Everett Rogers. The classical programme, for example, concerned itself with the spread of innovations that, once adopted, were assumed to remain adopted in perpetuity. Thus, an actor can only experience the event of interest (adoption) once, following which they are no longer at risk of another event – the move from non-adopter to adopter is irreversible and unrepeatable. While this assumption is very useful for simplifying mathematical models of diffusion, it does not hold for many social phenomena that may spread via diffusion. Non-routine collective action episodes, which are repeatable and often unfold as waves of activity, are one of these. Myers has shown how event history diffusion models can be applied to collective political events without invoking these debilitating assumptions.[10]

This set of advances in diffusion modelling calls for a re-examination of prior studies and conjecture about the diffusion of collective action. With these new tools, we can better examine collective action waves to identify and understand their dynamic elements. And so, we return to the Captain Swing uprising – particularly important to this line of work because the diffusion of the collective activity in the wave has long been suspected by scholars, but never adequately assessed.

8 Mahajan and Peterson, *Models for Innovation Diffusion*.
9 D. Strang, 'Adding Social Structure to Diffusion Models: An Event History Framework', *Sociological Methods and Research* 19 (1991), 324–53; D. Strang and N.B. Tuma, 'Spatial and Temporal Heterogeneity in Diffusion', *American Journal of Sociology* 99 (1993), 614–39; H.R, Greve, D. Strang, and N.B. Tuma, 'Specification and Estimation of Heterogeneous Diffusion Processes', *Sociological Methodology* 25 (1995), 377–420.
10 D.J. Myers, 'Violent Protest and Heterogeneous Diffusion Processes: The Spread of U.S. Racial Rioting from 1964 to 1971', *Mobilization* 15 (forthcoming).

Captain Swing and Diffusion

Past scholarship on diffusion in the Captain Swing uprisings is contradictory. While some studies denied that inter-actor influence operated, others gave a strong impression that diffusion played a role in the progression of events. Nevertheless, even these latter studies stopped short of making strong claims because the authors simply did not have convincing evidence. For example, one of Rudé's studies of Swing mapped diffusion by plotting the protests in each series and then interpolating the path between these locations. Because he found that the sequence of events appeared to cross major transportation routes, rather than flow along them, Rudé concluded that the events were mainly independent local phenomena having little to do with national lines of communication.[11]

Hobsbawm and Rudé's classic study also attempted to detect a pattern connecting the Captain Swing events. Their meticulous analysis of archival sources details locations of events, and the types and targets of action. In their account of the uprising's spread, they often imply that there was an underlying 'movement' connecting the agricultural labourers. In the end, however, they downplay (as did the contemporaneous authorities) the notion that there was a greater-than-local collective consciousness that somehow connected the events. To Hobsbawm and Rudé, agricultural workers simply did not have an apparatus of social thinking that extended beyond their own atomised existences. They did recognise the possibility of diffusion processes operating, but focused the bulk of their attention on the presence of local economic conditions – 'triggers' – that determined 'the timing and nature of local outbreak' and were ultimately limited to 'the region in which cereal farming was combined with low wages'.[12] Although they recognised that 'an immense movement of this kind generates its own momentum, and there is no reason to be surprised because it overflowed its 'natural' geographical boundaries …', they did not possess the analytical tools necessary to connect events convincingly, and thus they defaulted to the characterisation of the movement as spontaneous, unplanned, and unsystematic.[13]

John Bohstedt contested this notion, however. Responding to Marxist scholars who denied these workers any sense of revolutionary or class consciousness, he observed that English workers in the nineteenth century:

11 Rudé, *The Crowd in History*.
12 Page numbers herein refer to the 1975 New York edition, Hobsbawm and Rudé, *Captain Swing*, p. 215.
13 Ibid., pp. 173, 220.

... could and did become conscious of themselves as a class within a class system of power and property that exploited them, without either becoming practically revolutionary or accepting the existing system and its 'bourgeois' values as legitimate. Rather, in many instances they held to a radical critique of the system as an ideal, while working pragmatically for less than ideal improvements ...[14]

Given that labourers had to concern themselves with basic everyday survival, it should be expected that the particular modes of behaviour they pursued would be closely aligned with more local, immediate aims and therefore would vary somewhat from place to place even in the presence of a common or collective consciousness linking the diverse events. Thus, localism does not necessarily preclude diffusion. If a collective consciousness was developing through recognition of structurally congruent positions, then agricultural workers in one location would have good reason to take cues from the actions of protestors in other locations – who were protesting the same kinds of conditions, often successfully and under the relatively tolerant, and sometimes even approving, eye of the public and authorities. If such social and political dynamics were operating, we should be able to detect substantial diffusion effects in the Captain Swing wave, even in the absence of a specifically class-based consciousness.

Scholars studying Swing[15] have also suspected that the spatial and temporal patterning of events might have been driven by the spatial distribution of radicals in England, rather than by an actual diffusion process. Thus, protest activity would first appear in areas with a high concentration of radicals and later appear elsewhere. If radicalism was concentrated geographically, the resulting pattern of events might be misinterpreted as diffusion. Contrary to expectations however, Hobsbawm and Rudé found widely recognised centres of Radicalism within unaffected counties.[16]

Subsequently, Andrew Charlesworth applied a geographer's eye to the Swing events. Reflecting the ascendance of resource mobilisation and political opportunity structures, he began by insisting that the economic grievances formulation was too simplistic to explain the pattern of events. He was dissatisfied with Hobsbawm and Rudé's treatment of political radicalism, feeling that they had set aside prior evidence about the role of radical consciousness, despite recognising the short-comings of their own

14 J. Bohstedt, *Riots and Community Politics in England and Wales 1790–1810* (Cambridge, Mass., 1983), p. 300.
15 Charlesworth, *Social Protest in a Rural Society*, p. 37.
16 Hobsbawm and Rudé, *Captain Swing*.

approach.[17] The notion developed in Charlesworth's research then, was that political consciousness spread with events and cultural critiques along cross-region modes of communication. Charlesworth's evidence was derived from plotting Swing events on maps and interpolating paths among the events. One insight garnered from the analysis was that although there may have been a national diffusion pattern, it also seemed likely that there were more localised diffusion patterns where events spread from multiple nuclei of radicals. Nevertheless, the analytical techniques did not, in the end, produce convincing evidence about the diffusion question and Charlesworth concluded that the pattern of spread was just as likely to have resulted from the geographic distribution of radicals in England.[18]

More recently, Tilly also found evidence of patterned action among the events. Although Swing was only a small part of Tilly's study of changes in collective action repertoires in Great Britain between 1758 and 1834, his research locates Swing in broader historical context and reveals a longer-term development of the collective consciousness that partially fuelled, and was further invigorated by, the Swing uprising. Tilly discerned connections between several of the events of the period and concluded that they were not spontaneous outbursts.[19] There is no doubt that the events were geographically clustered – events were concentrated along main roads in London's market region. They also reflected local conditions – larger, open parishes with significant numbers of non-agricultural workers and localities with a history of parish wage-fixing were disproportionately involved. In addition, however, areas were more likely to be involved where collective demands for higher wage rates were made by labourers using a 'rights' legitimating frame – reflecting the strong possibility of a broader collective political ideology. It was not, however, Tilly's purpose to examine the diffusion question or to account for the cross-regional spread of action. Therefore, although his findings point toward questions about Swing diffusion, local characteristics again end up dominating the account of Swing.

The purpose of our study, then, is to determine if the spread of contentious gatherings during the Captain Swing protests can be more fully understood using inter-actor diffusion models. To achieve this objective, we examine three subsidiary questions: First, does the overall event wave cluster events in a manner that is consistent with inter-actor diffusion models? Second, does the inter-actor influence of a past event

17 M. Dutt, 'The Agricultural Labourers Revolt of 1830 in Kent, Surrey and Sussex', unpublished PhD thesis, University of London, (1966).
18 Charlesworth, *Social Protest in a Rural Society*, p. 37.
19 Tilly, *Popular Contention in Great Britain*.

change (either increase or decrease) over time? Third, are contentious events more influential over shorter distances? The models we use permit us to examine these questions while simultaneously reconsidering past explanations for the sequence of Swing events. We find that both diffusion processes *and* the effects of economic conditions are important to our understanding of these collective action dynamics.

III Analysing Event Data for Diffusion Patterns
Classic Diffusion Wave Patterns

A cursory examination of any collective violence wave often reveals a pattern similar to many social diffusion waves: the general form of the cumulative event count is sigmoid and the rate of occurrence is wave-like – starting low, peaking, and then dying out.[20] Classic diffusion processes exhibit this kind of pattern because adoption acts are a function of those who have previously adopted (spreaders) and those who have yet to adopt (targets). In the early parts of the wave, there are relatively few spreaders – who collectively have limited influence. As the number of adoptions grow, so does the number of spreaders and their growing combined influence increases the adoption rate. Later, the process slows because although the spreaders have gained considerable momentum, the pool of targets is becoming depleted – and those who remain are likely to be the most resistant to adoption.[21]

An initial question for any diffusion wave, then, is whether or not the pattern of adoption exhibits this pattern of adoption rates. Strang and Tuma demonstrated how event history models could be used to assess this question in a reanalysis of Coleman, Katz and Menzel's study of the diffusion of tetracycline.[22] In its simplest form, the heterogeneous diffusion model they propose introduces a simple covariate, the total number of adoptions that have occurred by a particular point in time. If the adoption pattern is consistent with a classical diffusion process, the effect of this variable should be curvilinear – exhibiting a positive effect in the first part of the wave as the adoption rate increases and a negative effect in the latter parts where the process is dying out.[23] Should this pattern be observed, it does not unequivocally demonstrate that diffusion

---

20 B.L. Pitcher, R.L. Hamblin, and J.L.L. Miller, 'The Diffusion of Collective Violence', *American Sociological Review* 43 (1978), 23–35; Mahjan and Peterson, *Models for Innovation Diffusion*.
21 Rogers, *Diffusion of Innovations*.
22 J.S. Coleman, E. Katz, and H. Menzel, *Medical Innovation* (Indianapolis, 1966).
23 Myers, 'Violent Protest and Heterogeneous Diffusion Processes'.

is operating, but it lends plausibility to claims that clustering of events changes the chances of other events occurring.

Our primary aim in this paper is not to examine these longer-term diffusion patterns but instead to examine the data for diffusion clusters that are considerably smaller in both temporal and spatial scale. To achieve that goal convincingly, however, it is necessary to control for the longer-term trend. If we did not control for the clustering of events that typically occurs in the middle of an event wave, short-term temporal effects would likely be over-estimated.

Collective Violence, Diffusion, and Event History Models

Despite similarities to classic diffusion processes, the collective action phenomena we examine diverge from classic diffusion phenomena in several significant ways. First, the conventional assumption of continuous and irreversible adoption is invalid: collective action tends to appear for a short period of time, disappear, and then can return again – even in the same location.[24] In part, this means that units of analysis can adopt repeatedly – they do not exit the risk pool once they have acted. Instead, once an event terminates, the unit returns to a state of peace and can later erupt to produce another event.

Second, diffusion processes driving collective action, particularly violent or destructive collective action, are characterised by disrupted adoption waves. Repression attempts, social sanctions, and exhaustion all operate intermittently to tire and subdue participants.[25] The combination of repeated risk and interruption in the cycle mean that influence from prior adoptions is not constant over time – diffusion effects are often time-limited. In other words, a collective event may indeed propel further action, but this effect is likely to die out as the time from the initial event grows. The result is a series of mini-cycles containing acceleration and deceleration in the rates of adoption – a pattern of 'waves within waves'.[26]

24 D. McAdam, 'Tactical Innovation and the Pace of Insurgency', *American Sociological Review* 48 (1983), 735–54.
25 As documented in many studies of protest and rioting such as W.R. Kelly and L. Isaac, 'The Rise and Fall of Urban Racial Violence in the U.S.: 1948–1979', *Research in Social Movements Conflict and Change* 7 (1984), 203–33; R. Koopmans, 'The Dynamics of Protest Waves: West Germany, 1965 to 1989', *American Sociological Review* 58 (1993), 637–58; A. Oberschall, 'The Decline of the 1960s Social Movements', *Research In Social Movements, Conflict and Change* 1 (1978), 257–89; P.E. Oliver, 'Bringing the Crowd Back In: The Nonorganizational Elements of Social Movements', *Research In Social Movements, Conflict and Change* 11 (1989), 1–30.
26 P.E. Oliver and D.J. Myers, 'The Coevolution of Social Movements', *Mobilization* 8 (2003), 1–24.

Third, many classic diffusion models assume homogeneous mixing or full information about the behaviour of all actors in the system. In other words, all actors have the same chances of influencing each other's behaviour. Clearly this is not a viable assumption with respect to collective action. In particular, the separation of social actors in physical space reduces the influence that one actor has on another.

These three deviations produce a much more complicated field than can typically be recognised by diffusion-of-innovation models. In effect, these characteristics of collective action are constantly changing the likelihood of an event occurring to potential actors in other locations, depending on spatial and temporal proximity to prior events. Strang and Tuma's event-history formulation of diffusion allows the researcher to model the impact of characteristics of the adopter (spreader), the adoption event itself, and the proximal links between them. The event history approach to diffusion modelling has been used in a variety of empirical contexts including Davis and Greve's analysis of changes in corporate governance practices, Soule's examination of tactical diffusion of a protest innovation, and Soule and Zylan's study of state-level social policy reform.[27]

The prior work that is most similar to our present analysis is Myers's analysis of U.S. collective violence in the 1960s.[28] Using Spilerman's riot data,[29] Myers experimented with an event-history framework to compare the effects of competition theory and diffusion explanations for riot hazard rates in the wave of U.S. civil disorders in the 1960s. In addition to Spilerman's finding that the non-White population of a city and its regional (southern) location dominated the determination of how much rioting occurred, Myers found that other structural variables were also important contributors to rioting. More relevant to the present paper, he also presented strong evidence that diffusion effects produced outbreaks of collective violence. In a more methodological treatment, Myers refined the event history diffusion approach to address a series of

27 G.F. Davis and H.R. Greve, 'Corporate Elite Networks and Governance Changes in the 1980s', *American Journal of Sociology* 103 (1997), 1–37; S.A. Soule, 'The Student Divestment Movement in the United States and Tactical Diffusion: The Shantytown Protest', *Social Forces* 75 (1997), 855–83; S.A. Soule and Y. Zylan, 'Runaway Train? The Diffusion of State-Level Reform in ADC/AFDC Eligibility Requirements, 1950–1967', *American Journal of Sociology* 103 (1997), 733–62.
28 D.J. Myers, 'Racial Rioting in the 1960s: An Event History Analysis of Local Conditions', *American Sociological Review* 62 (1997), 94–112; D.J. Myers, 'The Diffusion of Collective Violence: Infectiousness, Susceptibility, and Mass Media Networks', *American Journal of Sociology* 106 (2000), 173–208.
29 S. Spilerman, 'The Causes of Racial Disturbances: A Comparison of Alternative Explanations', *American Sociological Review* 35 (1970), 627–49.

difficulties involved in applying these techniques to collective events,[30] many of which are used herein with the Swing events.

IV Diffusion Hypotheses

Baseline Diffusion Pattern

We first examine the wave for consistency with the classic diffusion pattern – which predicts the general shape of the hazard to be curvilinear: a low rate of event occurrence at the start of the cycle, a higher rate in the middle, and a tapering of activity toward the end. To test for this trend, we introduce a polynomial variant of the cumulative count of all events prior to the given point in time. In the analysis, the county-day is the unit of analysis, therefore, for a given county-day, this variable is simply the count of *all* events that have occurred in *all* counties prior to that date.

As discussed above, verifying this trend indicates that a general diffusion pattern is plausible, but it is mainly introduced in the models as a control for clustering in the centre of the wave. It also, however, introduces the most basic notion of homogenous diffusion effects and modifications of that notion are reflected in other diffusion covariates. When simply counting the number of prior events, the analysis assumes both temporal and spatial homogeneity. In other words, all past events are equally contagious no matter where or when they occurred. As we have already discussed, this notion is quite implausible for most social behaviour and in particular for the collective action events we examine. In subsequent hypotheses, we relax this assumption.

Temporal Proximity

The diffusion-related effects of riots and protests do not last forever. Instead, they die out over relatively short periods of time. Certainly, it is hard to imagine a riot that occurred several months ago having much contagious influence. How long the effect lasts, though, is an open question and may differ depending on the type of event and the historical context.[31] We examined several possible influence durations for this data set, ranging up to 60 days. Periods longer than seven days did not appreciably improve the models, therefore we constructed the variables presented herein assuming that the short-term inter-event influence during the Captain Swing rebellion lasted for only seven days – after which the event no longer

---

30 Myers, 'Violent Protest and Heterogeneous Diffusion Processes'.
31 D.J. Myers, 'Media, Communication Technology, and Protest Waves', paper presented at Social Movement Analysis: The Network Perspective, Ross Priory, Scotland, 2000.

had influence on future events. To test this notion in our models, we simply constructed a covariate that, for any particular county-day, counts the number of events that had occurred in all counties over the prior seven days. This model assumes that the contagious influence of an event only lasts for one week (a limited notion of temporal heterogeneity), and that it exerts the same effect on all other potential actors irrespective of distance (still maintaining the notion of spatial homogeneity).

Rather than influence remaining constant for a week and dropping off completely, a more plausible model might suggest that influence from a prior event declines gradually over the course of the week, such that its maximum influence is felt the day after it occurs and very little influence is felt when seven days have passed. To operationalise this notion, we simply reduce the influence from any event by one-seventh of its maximum value for each day that passes. Thus, the proportion of the maximum influence exerted is hypothesised to be 1.0 on the first day following the event, six-sevenths the second day, and so forth. When the eighth day is reached, the influence of the event drops to zero. To calculate the total diffusion influence exerted for a particular county-day, this value is summed over all events that have occurred in the past seven days. Again, this model only considers temporal heterogeneity and still maintains the notion that distance between actors does not matter (spatial homogeneity).

Spatial Proximity

Spatial heterogeneity recognises that the diffusion influence from a close neighbour will be greater than the influence from a relatively distant actor. This effect is expected in part because proximal actors will have more information about nearby events due to interpersonal communication flows and mass media networks,[32] and because nearby actors may have greater structural similarity than those farther away.[33] To test for spatial diffusion effects, one must calculate an influence covariate that declines as a function of distance. The most commonly used function is simply $1/\text{distance}$. However, this function introduces several problems,

---

32 P.E. Oliver and D.J. Myers, 'Networks, Diffusion, and Cycles of Collective Action', in M. Diani and D. McAdam (eds), *Social Movements and Networks: Relational Approaches to Collective Action* (Oxford, 2003); C. Mueller, 'Media Measurement Models of Protest Event Data', *Mobilization: An International Journal* 2 (1997), 165–84; D.J. Myers and B.S. Caniglia, 'All the Rioting That's Fit to Print: Selection Effects in National Newspaper Coverage of Civil Disorders, 1968–1969', *American Sociological Review* 69 (2004), 519–43.
33 Myers, 'The Diffusion of Collective Violence'.

including the potential for divide-by-zero for events occurring to the same unit (county) and an arbitrary change in the function depending on the unit of distance used (kilometres versus miles, for instance). Therefore, in this analysis we used a decay function derived from the relative distribution of the event pairs and county pairs.[34]

It is also possible to consider combinations of influence decay. For example, instead of just weighting the influence of events by either a distance factor or a time factor, it is possible to weight by both. Doing so recognises both that an event's initial influence is lower if it is farther away and that this influence will decline as time from the event increases. A covariate weighted by both decay functions simultaneously recognises both temporal and spatial heterogeneity in diffusion influence.

V Alternative Explanations

Beyond diffusion processes, there are, of course, other conditions in the local environment that may contribute to collective action. First, there is the basic demographic reality that larger populations increase the chances of any kind of event occurring. Therefore, we control for county population in our models. Second, although past evidence is contradictory in terms of the role of local economic conditions in propelling collective action of all kinds,[35] local economic hardship dominates the account of the Swing riots. Particularly as we assess the diffusion patterns, it is important to control for local economic conditions – if poor conditions contribute to collective action, and local conditions are clustered in particular ways, they can produce the appearance of diffusion. To assess the economic argument and to control for grievance clustering, we include county-level wages for agricultural labourers.[36]

Third, despite the fact that the participants in Swing events 'rarely included political activists or unionised workers',[37] there exists a long-standing argument that the geographic distribution of radicals could have produced the appearance of diffusion.[38] This argument would predict that Swing events should cluster around, and radiate from, London. Thus, we control for the distance of each county from London.

---

34 See Myers, 'Violent Protest', for information on how this decay function is calculated.
35 See, for example, S. Spilerman, 'The Causes of Racial Disturbances; 'Structural Characteristics of Cities and the Severity of Racial Disorders', *American Sociological Review* 41 (1976), 771–93.
36 E.H. Hunt, 'Industrialization and Regional Inequality: Wages in Britain, 1760–1914', *Journal of Economic History* 46 (1986), 935–66.
37 C. Tilly, *The Politics of Collective Violence* (Cambridge, 2003), p. 186.
38 Charlesworth, *Social Protest in a Rural Society*, p. 37.

In addition, each county may have a baseline propensity to generate radical action, exhibited in part by the amount of action produced over time. As Bohstedt and Williams put it, geographic areas can develop a 'tradition of rioting' during the course of a collective action wave.[39] Essentially, this means that if rioting had been used at an earlier time and deemed a successful tactic, it is likely that supportive elements needed to carry out subsequent actions, such as modes of organisation, tactical knowledge, and cooperative attitudes, would already be in place. If true, we should also expect to see a reinforcement pattern.

Finally, we control for the day of the week. In most collective action waves, certain days are more likely to produce action than others due to work patterns, worship, marketing and so forth. These weekly clusters of activity can masquerade as short-term diffusion effects if not controlled. Therefore, we enter dummy variables for each day of the week into the analysis. As we will show, most of these factors (population size, economic conditions, distance from London, and tradition of rioting) do predict Swing events, but diffusion elements predict collective contentious actions beyond these basic considerations.

VI Data and Estimation

Several scholarly compilations of Swing events exist that use different assumptions and definitions to produce overlapping data sets. Decisions about (1) how one defines an event, (2) which original sources are consulted, and (3) determining whether or not a candidate event is associated with Swing (including decisions about the relevant geographic and temporal windows) can produce extraordinarily different data. The data used herein are drawn from Horn and Tilly's 1988 data set, *Contentious Gatherings In Britain: 1758–1834*. 'Contentious gatherings' are defined by Horn and Tilly as 'occasions on which ten or more persons outside the government assemble in a publicly-accessible place and visibly, by word or deed, make a claim that would, if realized, affect the interests of some person or group outside their own number'. In sum, Horn and Tilly identified 285 Swing events across England between August and December of 1830, as reported in seven national periodicals.[40]

---

39 J. Bohstedt and D. E. Williams, 'The Diffusion of Riots: The Patterns of 1766, 1795, and 1801 in Devonshire', *Journal of Interdisciplinary History* 19 (1988), 1–24.
40 For more detail, see N. Horn and C. Tilly, 'Contentious Gatherings in Britain, 1758–1834'. Distributed by the Inter-university Consortium for Political and Social Research, #8872, 1988, (Machine Readable Data File and Documentation), p. 7; Tilly, *The Politics of Collective Violence*.

In contrast, others use considerably less restrictive operationalizations than Horn and Tilly and therefore identify many more events. Hobsbawm and Rudé, for example, identified 1,475 incidents they considered to be part of Swing.[41] More recently, the FACHRS Swing research project has "unmasked" a total 3,282 incidents, ranging in character from animal maiming and anonymous letters to machine breaking and wage riots.[42] The decision about which data set to use involves a number of trade offs. Our choice of Horn and Tilly data has several advantages. For one, these events are relatively homogeneous and therefore we are not encumbered with the assumption that an anonymous letter is equivalent to a wage riot. These events also have a clear collective character, have a physical gathering at their core, and are substantially visible – and thus are likely to be socially contagious. And of course, a well-used data set produces comparability with prior studies that have also depended on it. Indeed, one of the most important contributions of this study is applying a new method to shed new light on an old question – and focusing on previously engaged data is particularly useful in that context.

At the same time, we also lose a broader range of events, and even if these are not commensurate with Horn and Tilly's notion of a collective gathering, they are still likely to be related and thus exerting some kinds of social influence on each other. With the present foundational analysis in hand then, researchers are encouraged to delve further into the diffusion dynamics using data such as the FACHRS data. Doing so will allow inquiry into a new set of question about the flow of action within the wave: Is one kind of act (letter writing) more contagious than another (such as, animal maiming)? Does letter writing produces machine breaking, but not the other way around? Or, perhaps some types of activity actually slow subsequent action, while others speed it up? The methodological foundation laid in the present article points the way toward these and many other interesting permutations of diffusion thinking.

We use discrete-time event history analysis focusing on county-days as the unit of analysis. The choice of the county (as opposed to the city or parish level) is driven in large part by the availability of data for this period of time. It is, therefore, more blunt than would be ideal for this analysis. At the same time, however, given that we are primarily concerned with identifying diffusion effects, the broader geographic units are likely to mask diffusion effects, rather than to artificially

41 Hobsbawm and Rudé, *Captain Swing*, Appendix I.
42 M. Holland, *Swing Unmasked: The Agricultural Riots of 1830 to 1832 and Their Wider Implications* (Oxford, 2005).

produce them. Therefore, we may be confident that the procedure is a conservative estimate of diffusion effects.

Given that the individual units of analysis (counties) each contribute multiple observations to the analysis, dependence between observations introduces a downward bias in standard error estimates.[43] We address this problem in two ways. First, we adjust standard errors for clustering on county. In addition, we include a variable reflecting the history of events in the county. This variable, the number of prior events in the county, not only provides a control for unobserved heterogeneity among observations within single counties, but also has substantive meaning as a measure of the tradition of contention in the county.

VII Results of the Analysis

Local Conditions, Trends and Controls

Table 1 presents estimates from four models that examine our hypotheses. The first model examines long-standing explanations related to local conditions. For example, we can easily see that the distance from London did indeed decrease the chances of an event occurring. This confirms earlier observations that events were clustered toward London. It also supports the notion that radicalism, which was concentrated closer to London, may have been a critical contributor to the politics of Swing. The magnitude of the coefficient means that the odds of having an event decrease by about 8 per cent for each 10 additional miles from London.

The measure of local economic conditions does not have the effect predicted by structural notions. Rather than poorer economic conditions predicting unrest, there is a significant *positive* zero-order relationship between agricultural wages and the likelihood of an event (not shown in table). Although such an effect might seem consistent with many studies of unrest that connect protest to *positive* structural conditions, a problem with the data may also explain this effect: Earnings from this period may be underestimated because they often fail to account for payments-in-kind (housing, food, etc.).[44] If payments-in-kind replace monetary wages, then the results could be interpreted to mean that Swing events were more likely in areas where wages dominated agriculture earnings rather than payments-in-kind. This interpretation is consistent with structural/ grievance notions because the replacement of traditional arrangements with more wage pay would accompany the transition to more modern

---

43 P.D. Allison, 'Discrete-Time Methods for the Analysis of Event Histories', *Sociological Methodology* 8 (1982), 434–53.
44 E.H. Hunt, 'Industrialization and Regional Inequality'.

Table 1: Diffusion Effects in Captain Swing

	Model 1	Model 2	Model 3	Model 4
Control Variables				
Distance from London	−.00744**	−.00745**	−.00218	−.00202
	(.0025)	(.0024)	(.0022)	(.0021)
1794–1795	.311	.308	.244	.236
Agricultural Wages[a]	(.22)	(.22)	(.21)	(.21)
County Population[b] (logged)	.658**	.661**	.912***	.918***
	(.24)	(.24)	(.25)	(.25)
Monday	.554	.265	.326	.194
	(.28)	(.32)	(.36)	(.36)
Tuesday	.266	.515	.583	.590
	(.28)	(.28)	(.32)	(.31)
Wednesday	.0602	.540	.598	.610
	(.34)	(.37)	(.41)	(.40)
Thursday	−.0714	.391	.433	.428
	(.24)	(.22)	(.24)	(.23)
Friday	.284	.631*	.678*	.689*
	(.26)	(.30)	(.31)	(.32)
Saturday	.0750	.370	.409	.430
	(.41)	(.39)	(.43)	(.42)
Cumulative CGs at t	.0552***	.0659***	.0865***	.0894***
	(.0090)	(.012)	(.014)	(.015)
(Cumulative CGs)^2 × 10^{-3}	−.201***	−.244***	−.312***	−.324***
	(.026)	(.037)	(.044)	(.047)
Previous CGs in County	.0640***	.0655***	.0508***	.0524***
	(.0099)	(.010)	(.010)	(.010)
Diffusion Due to CGs in the Previous Week				
Total		.0372***	−.0042	.0442***
		(.010)	(.021)	(.012)
Weighted by Time		−.0698***	−.0815***	−.171***
		(.016)	(.020)	(.038)
Weighted by Distance			.0187***	
			(.0059)	
Weighted by Time and Distance				.0335***
				(.0099)
Constant	−11.30	−11.60	−13.23	−13.21
Model χ^2 (df)	414.01	717.56	602.73	609.53
	(12)	(14)	(15)	(15)

[a] Shillings; see Hunt (966) for primary data sources.
[b] See B. R. Mitchell, *British Historical Statistics* (Cambridge, 1988), pp. 30–31, for primary data sources. * $p < .05$, ** $p < .01$, *** $p < .001$ (two-tailed tests). Robust SEs (in parentheses) are adjusted for clustering on county.

forms of farming and the incorporation of machinery into agricultural production. Thus, Swing unrest would be key to the grievances brought about by these agricultural transitions.

It also seems likely that these transitions would be more likely to occur in locations with higher populations, in which the ability to take advantage of economies of scale were more apparent. If true, we would expect more Swing events in areas with higher populations, not just because of increased numbers of potential actors, but also because grievances would be higher in these better developed areas. Indeed, both of these explanations seem supported by the data because there is a positive association between population and unrest, but there is also a collinearity between wages and population that eliminates the zero-order wage effect when both variables are placed in the model (see Model 1 in the Table).

The control for days of the week rarely demonstrates any substantive differences among days, although the variables are maintained throughout the analysis to help control for possibility of unobserved weekly cycles (described above). In the full diffusion models (described below), Fridays tend to produce more events than Sundays, but there are few significant differences among other pairs of days.

Model 1 also presents the findings related to the most simple diffusion effect, Strang and Tuma's notion of the 'diffusion intercept'. The curvilinear (polynomial) variant of the prior event demonstrates compatibility with the pattern expected from a long-term diffusion trend. This trend is robust throughout the models examined in the analysis. Again, we emphasise that this trend does not demonstrate a diffusion process conclusively, but that it *suggests* that inter-actor influence is occurring. More importantly, controlling for this trend in the model provides a more stringent test of short-term diffusion effects because it controls for temporal clustering in the middle of the event wave. Finally, we also introduce the county-level prior event count variable in Model 1. It is apparent that the number of prior contentious gatherings in the county predicts the likelihood of future ones. Thus, a history of radical action seems to reinforce itself, especially within the cycle, perhaps reflecting development of organizational tools necessary for collective action and sharing knowledge of effective repertoires. The pervasive influence of this control variable suggests an important role of planning and organization of contentious gatherings.

Temporal Effects

Model 2 begins the examination of short-term diffusion effects. Model 2 shows the effect of both the simple count of events in the prior one-week period and the effect when we weight the influence of each event (in the prior week) according to its age in days. Both the total count and the count weighted by time are both significant predictors, but in opposite directions. The positive effect of the 'total' coefficient shows that recent events do increase the chances that another event will occur. For each additional event in the prior week, the odds of another event occurring increase by about 4 per cent. However, the time decay effect works opposite from predictions. Instead of the influence *decaying* as the event ages, it instead *increases*. Thus, while imitation effects do occur following an event, it takes time for these imitations to get started.

When examining the U.S. urban unrest of the 1960s, Myers found the opposite effect of time-decay.[45] Two key differences between the sets of events studied may underlie the seemingly contradictory effect. First, the communication technology transmitting information in the Swing era was much slower than the television transmissions thought to underlie the diffusion of 1960s riots.[46] In effect, information had to carried personally by individuals travelling from town to town, thereby delaying imitative response. Second, individual Swing events exhibited more coordination than the urban riots. Planning, organising, and targeting the collective events may have also delayed the response.

Spatial Effects

To examine spatial effects, Model 3 adds the distance decay variant of the diffusion measure. The distance decay variable operates as expected: increased proximity increases influence. It is important to note that this variable completely subsumes the effect of the simple count of events in the prior one week. Thus, the effect of the simple event count is captured in the more complex construction of the diffusion notion that incorporates distance factors.

It is particularly striking that this effect persists even though the distance from London is controlled. In fact, incorporating the distance decay variable also completely subsumes the effect of the distance from London, which has become non-significant. The positive coefficient means that we are detecting differences in spatial influence among events *after* the London-related clustering is controlled. This is powerful evidence that spatial diffusion was, in fact, an important element in producing unrest in the Swing uprising. Model 4 enters a variable that weights influence of each event by both time and distance

---

45 Myers, 'Violent Protest and Heterogeneous Diffusion Processes'.
46 Myers, 'The Diffusion of Collective Violence'.

simultaneously. Although strongly significant in Model 4, this effect is due primarily to the overlap with the simpler distance decay version used in Model 3 (results not shown). Thus, we reject the time and distance combination on the grounds of parsimony and suggest that Model 3 is the best representation of diffusion in these data.

VIII Discussion

Swing as a Movement

The Captain Swing uprising occurred at an important juncture in the history of collective action. As Tilly's *Popular Contention* demonstrates in much more elaborate detail, the period within which Swing occurred ushered in a significant transition in contentious repertoires – a change to types of action that were more dependent on social organisation. This does not mean, of course, that Swing was driven by a unified, national-level organisation that coordinated or planned the timing and location of individual events in the wave. The layout of incidents, however, does suggest that the wave of events were connected to each other in ways that reflected the social fabric of the times. The dependence of the events on each other demonstrates that, as the repertoires of contention were changing, the rationalist model of diffusion was also becoming relevant. This notion of structure and logic conditioning the spread of events is demonstrated in several ways in this study.

First, it is clear that the pattern of events demonstrates that they were far from independent from each other. For each event that occurred, it increased the chances that another event would occur – at least for a week. Thus, actors not involved in the first event attended to the initial event and were connected to it through a communication network that linked prior actors with those who might act in the future. The social structure that produced this communication network therefore influenced the transmission of both radical action and the ideas that supported it.

Second, this communication network, and thus the diffusion effect, was geographically constrained. The results demonstrate that the instigating effect of prior events declined as distance from the prior event increased. This implies that social networks were constructed such that influential others were concentrated nearby and that collective actors gathered information about repertoires of action and their effectiveness mainly from people they knew best and from whom they perceived as sharing structural positions that in turn produced common motivations and constraints for collective protest.

Third, there was an apparent delay in the imitation that followed an event. While this delay in part reflects the relatively slow transmission of information from place to place (compared to modern times), travel time is probably not enough to produce the amount of delay that occurred in the Swing wave.[47] In addition, subsequent events were likely delayed as those who heard about prior events collectively considered the outcomes of these events and coordinated a subsequent event.

Finally, as has been a common observation in the social movement literature, actual experience with collective protest is critically important in determining future action. Consistent with the reinforcement pattern observed in this data, prior activism has been shown to provide actors with the tools (organisational know-how, a network of activists, and efficacy) that make activism more likely and more effective in the future. Once a collective has engaged in, or even observed, protest, it becomes more likely to do so in the future because the costs of organising and coordinating the action have gone down.

Do these patterns mean that the Captain Swing events were a movement? Without reiterating long and unresolved arguments about what constitutes a movement, the answer to this question clearly depends on how 'movement' is defined. Participants in these events were not members of a social movement organisation that coordinated activities, chose strategies, consciously coordinated framing attempts, and many of the other activities we commonly associate with modern social movements. The connections between the events and the rhetoric that accompanied them, however, indicates that some kind of common consciousness had developed among agricultural labourers. At a minimum, the diffusion patterns demonstrate that farm workers recognised that their plight was similar to others and that they could import tactics used elsewhere to address similar circumstances. Whether they viewed their own efforts as having an impact beyond their local environment (in terms of providing a model for others or forming a mutually supportive collective identity) remains an open question.

Warnings, Reminders, and Agendas

As important as the diffusion effect in the Swing wave may be, we should not set aside the other explanations regarding the distribution of radicals and the economic conditions. These factors are as essential to

---

47 For more detail on the amount of time required to travel between Swing event locations, see A. Charlesworth, 'The Geography of Protests by Agricultural Labourers 1790–1850', in A. Charlesworth, (ed.), *An Atlas of Rural Protest in Britain 1548–1900*, (Philadelphia, 1983).

understanding the temporal and spatial distribution of events as diffusion is, and in fact, can work hand-in-hand with diffusion to produce waves of collective action. In particular, our results suggest that more analysis of the role of radicals, the distribution of their ideas via pamphlets and publications, and the travels of specific individuals (as thought leaders) is needed because they may have fuelled geographically concentrated mini-waves of activity. One clear pattern in the Swing data is that the rebellion consisted of a series of 'waves-within-waves' – bursts of activity radiating from multiple temporal and geographic nuclei. One plausible explanation for this pattern is a two step process in which the ideology supporting the action diffused to radicals and those radicals in turn set off smaller concentrated waves of activity. Hedström and colleagues noted these kinds of 'meso-level networks' as key determinants of the spread of collection action,[48] and they may be operating in the Swing wave as well. More exact spatial data would be required to investigate these multiple-level questions.

Just as this analysis opens up questions about the operation of meso-level networks in Swing, it also produces a series of other questions related to diffusion processes. For one, we have only begun to scratch the surface in terms of the characteristics of actors and events that may have shepherded or inhibited the flow of events across the countryside. In this analysis, we examined the spatial locations of actors as characteristics that may have conditioned the diffusion process, but there are many others – especially in terms of local conditions – that may not have directly caused events, but may have changed the way diffusion operated. For example, Strang and Tuma identify 'susceptibility' factors in their diffusion model which are characteristics of a target actor that do not directly increase the chances of adoption, but rather increase the likelihood of imitation once another has adopted. In addition, we have not considered (due to data limitations) how repression may have affected inter-actor influence or the role of other kinds of social networks that do not coincide perfectly with the geographic distribution of actors.

The imperfection of data is an issue in all studies, and historical studies that depend on newspaper data are particularly susceptible to criticism, given the known limitations of this type of data.[49] The data used in the

48 P. Hedström, R. Sandall, and C. Stern, 'Mesolevel Networks and the Diffusion of Social Movements: The Case of the Swedish Social Democratic Party', *American Journal of Sociology* 106 (2000), 145–72.
49 See reviews by Mueller, 'Media Measurement Models of Protest Event Data'; J. Earl, A. Martin, J.D. McCarthy, and S.A. Soule, 'The Use of Newspaper Data in the Study of Collective Action', *Annual Review of Sociology* 30 (2004), 65–80; D.G. Ortiz, D.J. Myers, N.E. Walls, and M.D. Diaz, 'Where Do We Stand with Newspaper Data?', *Mobilization* 10 (2005), 397–419.

present study were gathered from seven English national periodicals and although these data are considered relatively high quality by the scholarly community and have been used in important studies of the period, using them introduces questions about the trustworthiness of findings and subsequent interpretations. There is little doubt that the data does indeed miss events that actually occurred and that these events have a certain character. Given the findings of methodological studies, one can safely assume that smaller Swing events and those located farther from the publication's home (London) are under-represented in the data. How might this affect the results? Studies of the diffusion of collective protest indicate that smaller events tend to flow from larger ones. Given that smaller and more distant events are missing from the data, it is possible that the diffusion effects we have identified are actually understated, given that imitator events are more likely to be missing than the imitated models.

In sum, our study reveals important inter-actor influences – patterns that reveal that Swing was not merely a set of spontaneous local responses to common economic conditions. Neither, of course, were they centrally directed. But they do reflect a process that is, in some sense, 'organised' by the social structure and the social networks that condition action, even if they do not coordinate them. Furthermore, the diffusion processes that occurred in this action wave are consonant with a rationalist understanding of the diffusion of collective action from one place and time to another. Thus, one recommendation that flows from this research is a reorientation in our approach to diffusion influences in collective action waves. Clearly, we should not invoke diffusion or 'contagion' in the way proposed by older crowd theorists, but neither should we avoid the influence of inter-actor influence for fear of being attached to wrong-headed ideas. Instead, we should recognise that diffusion is an important social process rooted in rationalist notions of imitation and combine these two approaches to produce new hypotheses. For example, traditional social movement theoretical notions – such as resource mobilisation and political opportunity structures – imply specific kinds of inter-actor influence and diffusion patterns. Thus, diffusion ideas should no longer be seen as a defeated, debunked variant of Le Bon's notion of contagion, but should be appreciated as an opportunity to extend our most useful theories of social movements and add considerable nuance to our understanding of the dynamic elements of contentious political behaviour.

'Two steps forward; six steps back': the dissipated legacy of Captain Swing

Iain Robertson

'*Captain Swing* remains a seminal publication and any new study of the riots still, perforce, begins with an acknowledgement of the debt owed to the book. After forty years, that remains a real achievement'.[1]

This paper will engage in some depth with the legacy of *Captain Swing*. This is perhaps best captured in the above quotation, taken from a recent survey of the Swing literature by Adrian Randall. The legacy of *Captain Swing* is both inspirational and, in its ubiquity, something of a sheet anchor to further progress in our understanding of manifestations of social conflict in rural England in the first half of the nineteenth century. Take, as exemplar, the following two incidents; in December 1830 a rick was set ablaze at Pardon Hill near the town of Winchcombe in the county of Gloucestershire.[2] On the 11 June 1831 Warren James led a large group of men and women from the Forest of Dean in the breaking of the forest enclosures.[3] Convention dictates that only the latter should be included in any discussion of Swing, and, of course, strictly speaking this is correct. The Warren James riots were different. And yet post Hobsbawm/Rudé histories of 'Swing' have demonstrated that their strict typology can be called into question. This is the problem of protest historians need to categorise. The argument here is that this is as much a liability as it is an asset and that we need to look again at Swing and other protest events to see if we cannot find a way of approaching these critical events more holistically. What we should be looking for, it is argued, are explanatory devices which allow us to view 'in the round' the two incidents noted above: to resist the bifurcating effects of compartmentalisation, in other words. This essay, then, is based on the belief that such has been the

---

1 A. Randall, '*Captain Swing*: a retrospect', *International Review of Social History* 54 (2009), 419–27.
2 E.J. Hobsbawm and G. Rudé, *Captain Swing* (London, 1969), p. 128.
3 *Gloucester Journal*, 11 June 1831.

failure to advance our understanding of manifestations of social conflict (and overt protest in particular) in rural England in the first half of the nineteenth century that it has allowed attention to drift away from this vitally important area to embrace conceptually and narratively different perspectives. From this the view is taken that the somewhat dissipated legacy of *Captain Swing* needs to be recovered (a project that is well underway) and re-worked to address new models. Further, it is suggested that those models that will be the more effective in restoring the legacy of *Captain Swing* are those which permit the development of more holistic perspectives on protest more generally (and that of the first half of the nineteenth century more specifically).

The view taken here is that the legacy of *Captain Swing* is of an over-heavy reliance on the events of the early 1830s to the detriment of our understanding of events of protest more generally. To achieve greater balance may require a different explanatory model. That model may be moral ecology and a sensitivity to the constitutive role of space and local nature/culture relations. To view protest in this way, as deriving from and drawing on local, informal and vernacular expressions of ecological ethics, takes us into the realm of nature/culture interactions and into the contested politics of quotidian experience in ways that are potentially more satisfactory than those hitherto pursued. It needs to be stressed, however, that this paper has neither the substance to, nor the intention of advocating a complete overturning of long-established interpretations or the advancement of moral ecology as the only way forward. The intention here is to demonstrate the need to advance our understanding of early nineteenth century social conflict and to suggest, but nothing more, that moral ecology may well be one such path to progress. Moreover, the case studies undertaken here should be viewed more as demonstrations of the overshadowing legacy of *Captain Swing* rather than as evidence of the existence of moral ecology as motivating device.

Prior to embarking on a discussion of moral ecology, however, the legacy of *Captain Swing* must first be explored. Unquestionably the work of Eric Hobsbawm and George Rudé has been inspirational. Alongside Thompson's moral economy thesis *Captain Swing* set the agenda for the study of social protest, ensured that rural riot would never more be written out of history, and placed protest more generally in a central position in social histories of both early modern and modern England, a position, it was assumed, it would never relinquish. The particular legacy of *Captain Swing* goes much further than that, however. Its enduring centrality comes from the fact that it remains virtually the only national survey of 'Swing' that seeks to advance a sophisticated analysis of these events as well as just enumerate events. This is not, however, to denigrate enumeration. The task of counting 'Swing' and any other protest event is, as Wells has demonstrated,[4] a problematic but vital one, providing the basis from which much interpretation can proceed. What we can derive from the approach adopted by Hobsbawm and Rudé is a concern for the lives and livelihoods of the rural dispossessed alongside the appreciation of the need for fine-grained localised studies that pay close attention to the particularities of place and of the nature of social relations in-place. In recognising the centrality of the local economic, social and cultural milieu, Hobsbawm and Rudé's work has played a significant role in the emergence of a rural history that aspires to rich and often very local contextualisation of change.

So here, then are the two steps forward. It could be Hobsbawm and Rudé but actually it is *Captain Swing* and moral economy. And undoubtedly both provided a powerful legacy that has engendered a number of important insights. But we must also acknowledge that such powerfully defining moments, reflected in an inability not to begin any discussion of protest without an in-depth engagement with one or both, can hold back debate and the advancement of any protest theme.

Prior to Poole's valuable essay in the current volume, the most recent overview of the Swing literature has come from Adrian Randall.[5] Here he reminds us of the lack of distance we appear to have travelled from *Captain Swing* and of the seemingly continuing dominance of the quantitative methodology and the need to categorise protest events. Randall draws attention to the historical geography work of Andrew Charlesworth and his focus on the diffusion of riot. Here we have the first questioning of the Hobsbawm/Rudé thesis and their downplaying of the local context; in particular the role and influence of local radicals. Further questions were raised over what has come to be seen as Hobsbawm/Rudé's over-simple understanding of the complexities of nineteenth century rural society and of the endurance of the pre-modern customary world.[6] Finally, Randall points to the ongoing re-counting of Swing incidents. All aspects it would seem – machine breaking, arson, Swing letters, robbery and wage riots – were seriously under-reported in the original monograph. Here we should note in particular the work of Family and Community History Research Society project which has widened both the geographical and temporal range of the disorders.[7] A

4   R. Wells, 'Counting Riots in Eighteenth-century England', *Bulletin of the Society for the Study of Labour History*, 37 (1978), 68–72.
5   Randall, '*Captain Swing*'.
6   Randall, '*Captain Swing*', 423–24.
7   M. Holland (ed.), *Swing Unmasked: The Agricultural Riots of 1830 to 1832 and their Wider Implications* (Milton Keynes, 2005).

further excellent example of this is Carl Griffin's recent discussion of the oversimplified understanding of arson, and therefore the debate over the supposed transition from overt to covert forms of protest in the 1790s, which arise from an uncritical utilisation of the provincial press.[8] Similar issues arise over the need to classify and develop protest event typologies and come from the inevitably dynamic nature of events of protest. The written record and the need to classify will only ever capture particular 'moments' within otherwise complex and fluid events. Thus, as Randall asserts, virtually every aspect of any event could change character and therefore fit uneasily within any attempt at compartmentalisation.[9] There was a perceived need, therefore, to move beyond the dominant paradigm and its essentially quantitative methodology. It is to be regretted, however, that Randall's review begins to fade out at the point at which some of the most recent writers start to build this new paradigm.

One aspect of this new approach has been a turn towards the linguistic and the eponymous 'Swing'. Here the discussion has centred on the rhetorical construction of the Captain and on what may be said to bring coherence to the 'disparate set of discourses which constituted protest across time and space'.[10] The work of Katrina Navickas on General Ludd has proved valuable here in leading to the suggestion that the eponymous Swing may well be the visible tip of a protest mythology.[11] Creating a figurehead was a product of a psychological need to reflect unity. In Luddism the need appears to come more from within the protestors themselves whilst in Swing the need appears to be more from those in power, the figurehead being a means to focus 'fear and disapproval'.[12]

Navickas' other major contribution to date has been to draw attention to the important constitutive role of space in shaping and giving meaning to protest. Working on protest events in the West Riding of Yorkshire in the first half of the nineteenth century, Navickas explores the crowd's use of moors, fields and routes as both symbol and spectacle.[13] Landscape, she argues, is given meaning by crowd action, it served to act as both passive host of such action, and active, through the shaping of the landscape.

8 C.J. Griffin, 'Knowable Geographies? The Reporting of Incendiarism in the Eighteenth- and early Nineteenth-century English Provincial Press', *Journal of Historical Geography* 32 (2006), 38–56.
9 Randall, '*Captain Swing*', 424–27.
10 P. Jones, 'Finding Captain Swing: Protest, Parish Relations, and the State of the Public Mind in 1830', *International Review of Social History* 54 (2009), 436.
11 K. Navickas, 'The Search for General Ludd: the Mythology of Luddism', *Social History*, 30 (2005), 281–95.
12 Navickas, 'The Search for General Ludd', 284; Jones 'Finding Captain Swing', 442.
13 K. Navickas, 'Moors, Fields, and Popular Protest in South Lancashire and the West Riding of Yorkshire, 1800–1848', *Northern History* 46 (2009), 93–95.

Topography becomes a tool in such actions and a legitimising 'ground' from the long tradition of crowds assembling in particular places. Landscape, in this view, can be understood as a social and cultural construct; a symbol and resource for counter hegemonic meanings. Chartist political rhetoric, actions and identities, for instance, drew heavily on the symbolic power of both moors and fields. In one memorable passage centring on the landscape, Navickas is able to draw parallels between Swing arson attacks and Chartist meetings:

> Malcolm Chase has commented on the sense of threat created by the flames of the torchlight processions, lighting up the famished faces of the participants and echoing the arson of the Swing riots in 1830, a fear though now potentially transposed from the southern arable flatlands to the northern moorland environment. Viewed close up, the processions must have conveyed these associations to the authorities. Viewed from a distance, by contrast, the torchlight processions created a more subliminal scene. Lines of light highlighted the contours of the moors, visually displayed the extent of support, and ensured that the protesters were simultaneously anonymous yet visible to an almost hyper-real extent.[14]

What this all points to is a very welcome new sensitivity to space and a strong move away from compartmentalisation in our approach to the study of protest events. And yet the compartmentalising urge remains strong, and the reader is often left with the conviction that truly innovative work in the study of Swing often fails to get beyond the restrictions imposed on it by the power of the original thesis and momentum has often been difficult to maintain. *Captain Swing* has become such a field of force in its own right; it has come to epitomise what nineteenth-century rural protest actually *was*. We can identify two distinct consequences of this dominance. First, there is very little of the healthy controversy that accompanied, for instance, the publication of Michael Fry's revisionist interpretation of the Highland Clearances.[15] Second, even such a welcome intervention as that by Peter Jones feels the need to begin with the assertion that historians of Hanoverian popular disturbances have generally underplayed (at best) the fact that these were 'essentially local affairs'.[16] This emphasis on the local and particular was, as already noted, something that appeared in the very early critiques of *Captain Swing*. Jones, however, attempts to do something more than just

14 Navickas, 'Moors, Fields, and Popular Protest', 106; M. Chase, *Chartism: A New History*, (Manchester, 2007).
15 M. Fry, *Wild Scots* (London, 2005)
16 Jones, 'Finding Captain Swing', 431

critique. In an exploration of 'Swing' events in Berkshire in November 1830 Jones takes what he terms a 'micro-historical' approach to demonstrate the absence of an agricultural labourers' movement in these episodes, whilst paying close attention to the crucial influence of local socio-economic relations. From this Jones is able to argue for 'Swing' as a 'meta-movement': a series of essentially local events that had wider connections but lacked wider guiding principles or ambitions. This, however, is a view with which Carl Griffin is not hugely sympathetic. Rather, in an important change of emphasis, he sees Swing as a protest *movement*, albeit one which linked 'essentially localised movements'.[17]

This need to pay due respects to our intellectual debt has given rise to something approaching complacency. In wider social history the perspective has shifted whilst specific studies of social protest can lag some way behind. A good example here is the work of John Walter. His early study of the grain riots in Maldon in 1629 typifies, and draws on, the Thompsonian perspective whilst his most recent work on the 'politics of subsistence' is a radical departure. Here he almost immediately dismisses the focus on riot as 'a lazy shorthand for the complexity of crowd actions', preferring instead to 'recover that broader "infrapolitics" of the ruled'.[18] In this, Walter is echoing a trend in the study of protest more generally: away from the study of overt events and towards the work of James C. Scott and what Michael Braddick and Walter term in their introduction to the same volume 'the tactics by which the relatively powerless seek to defend their interests'. The problem, however, with such an approach is one they themselves recognise. To move away from overt protest forms may result in producing histories of power 'without victims'.[19] In stressing the negotiating and vitiating power of 'hidden transcripts' and 'everyday resistance' Braddick and Walter come close to arguing for the mediation of power relationships. In turning the focus away from crowd actions and conflict they come close to denying the reality of power inequalities in social relationships. That they draw back from this position is to their credit but any turn away from the material realities of social conflict is to

17 Jones 'Finding Captain Swing', 433–34; C.J. Griffin, 'Swing, Swing Redivivus or Something after Swing? On the Death Throes of a Movement, December 1830–December 1833', *International Review of Social History* 54 (2009), 465.
18 J. Walter, 'Grain riots and Popular Attitudes to the Law', in J. Brewer and J. Styles (eds), *An Ungovernable People* (London, 1980), pp. 47–84; J. Walter, 'Public Transcripts, Popular Agency and the Politics of Subsistence in Early Modern England' in M. Braddick and J. Walter (eds), *Negotiating Power in Early Modern England* (Cambridge, 2001), p. 123
19 M. Braddick and J. Walter, 'Introduction' in Braddick and Walter (eds), *Negotiating Power*, pp. 7, 41.

be regretted. Whatever analytical model is applied, it is difficult to deny that to study popular protest is to study the victims of unequal power relations. Complacency and the monolithic presence of *Captain Swing* can give rise to the impression that rural disorder in the nineteenth century is all about 'Swing'. But it isn't, of course, and a short case study of disorder in and around the town of Winchcombe (Gloucestershire) by way of illustration is appropriate at this juncture.[20] If we consult only *Captain Swing* then we get a picture of an isolated incident on the periphery of the main 'Swing' locales. Social relations and conflict in Winchcombe were obviously more complex and wide ranging than that. The artificial barrier between 'Swing' arson and supposedly differently motivated arson attacks is well illustrated by the fact that there was an attack near the site of the 'Swing' incident less than two years earlier. In the early morning of 4 March 1829, fire broke out at the farm of William Ireland, at Sudeley Lodge and 'nearly the whole of the property was destroyed, including ricks and out-buildings'. A few days later a box containing phosphorous and matches was found hidden in a rick three miles away at Stanway, 'and it was thereby deduced that the fire at Sudeley Lodge farm was the act of an incendiary'.[21] Within the town itself disorder appears to have been near endemic at times with very frequent reports in both the local press and vestry minutes of large-scale riotous assemblies from at least 1818 onwards. In that year the vestry was considering a plan 'for preventing those riotous assemblies which have of late prevailed in various parts of the town of Winchcombe especially in the evenings of the Sabbath day'. Sundays indeed seem to have been particularly disorderly. In 1832 three Winchcombe beer retailers were each fined 40s. at Gloucester Quarter Sessions for allowing beer to be drunk on their premises on a Sunday, whilst the following year three local labourers were convicted of assaulting John Hooper and his wife and challenging William Kitchen, one of the borough constables, and others to a fight at 11 o'clock on a Sunday night.[22] In the following year a petition signed by 62 parishioners led to a vestry meeting being held 'to take into consideration the present state of the police of the parish'. Several issues were identified including the Sabbath morning being 'ushered in with scenes of regular pitched battles when nearly 100 persons have assembled together'. In addition, beer houses were still open, with noise and disorder therein, during divine

20 I am extremely grateful for the permission of my one-time M.A. student Rob White to use this material.
21 *The Times*, 9 and 16 March 1829.
22 Gloucestershire Archives, Gloucester [hereafter GA], Quarter Sessions /PC/2/51/D/2, 3 and 7; GA, Q/PC/2/52/C/53

service, and 'groups of people meet in various parts of the town, obstruct the footpaths, make use of disgusting language which to persons attending their usual place of worship as well as others is a very great grievance'.[23] Perhaps the worst case of Sunday disorder occurred two years later in April 1836 when two borough constables broke up a disturbance. On arresting the three protagonists the constables were 'violently assaulted' by five men, 'a mob of almost 200 being collected'.[24]

Whilst we could imagine the connections between some of these events and protests in the guise of social crime as somewhat tenuous, there is much less doubt about other incidents in the area. In 1836 the vestry minutes record much discussion about rising crime. Incidents brought to the vestry's attention include 'recent acts of outrage committed in the night time at Longwood and Toddington turnpike gate, highway robbery committed in the vicinity of the town, and the apparently systematic plan of sheep stealing committed almost nightly on the farms in the neighbourhood'. Poaching too appears rife. In a memoir of events of the mid-nineteenth century John Oakey recalled that 'a great deal of poaching was carried on' and this would appear to be both of game and rabbits.[25] This, of course, takes us immediately to the much-debated concept of 'social crime' and questions of, in particular, whether it is possible to delineate such a category at all.[26] For present purposes, however, the more important question centres on whether it is possible to recognise such activities as constituent of social protest. And here at least there would appear to be some element of agreement. Even those commentators, such as Sharpe and Freeman,[27] who are most sceptical of our ability to separately categorise, recognise in poaching (and other activities) at least an element of social protest. The problem remains, however, with any insistence over bracketing off 'social crime', as it does with many other forms of categorisation. Most intriguingly, however, Freeman may have pointed to one direction out of this conceptually blind

---

23 GA, P368/1VE 2/4, Vestry Minutes 31 October 1834.
24 *Gloucestershire Chronicle*, 16 April 1836
25 J. Oakey, *Reminiscences of Winchcombe* (Winchcombe, 1971); GA, Q/SO/ 3-14, Q/PC2/51/A/19.
26 See, for example, E.J. Hobsbawm, 'Distinctions between Socio-political and other forms of Crime', *Bulletin of the Society for the Study of Labour History*, 25 (1972), 5–6; E.P. Thompson, *Whigs and Hunters*, (London, 1975); J. Innes and J. Styles, 'The Crime Wave: Recent Writings on Crime and Criminal Justice in eighteenth-century England', in A. Wilson (ed.), *Rethinking Social History: English Society 1570–1920 and its Interpretation*, (Manchester, 1993); J.A. Sharpe, *Crime in Early Modern England, 1550–1750* (London, 1984).
27 M. Freeman, 'Plebs or predators? Deer-stealing in Whichwood Forest, Oxfordshire on the eighteenth and nineteenth centuries', *Social History* 21 (1996), 1–21.

alley. Drawing on Cronon's exploration of social relations in the forests of New England, Freeman suggests that we must give as much weight to ecological (i.e. nature-culture) relations as we do to the cultural consequences of socio-economic change.[28]

It is perspectives such as these and the important context of general and more widespread disturbances and disorder that a focus only on 'Swing' misses. This, obviously, is not the fault of Hobsbawm and Rudé; rather it is the consequence of their legacy. To move away from this and towards a more holistic perspective may well then be both desirable and rewarding. There remains, therefore, a pressing need to fully re-embrace the dissipated legacy of *Captain Swing* – to critique and build on this legacy – to take 'Swing' forward, in other words. Through the work of people such as Jones and Griffin and through the FACHRS Swing project, an extended, critiqued and nuanced version of 'Swing' and social protest more generally is now emerging. The focus here is on 'local truths' about 'Swing'. It is on the contingent and everyday interactions that provide the critical environment out of which a Swing event could emerge. It is to turn, then, towards fine-grained explorations of local social and parochial relations, and, perhaps most intriguingly, towards the integration of local nature/culture interactions.

In a series of compelling articles, Carl Griffin has done much to alert us to the nuances and complexities of 'Swing' elided by Hobsbawm and Rudé.[29] For the purposes of this present paper, however, the theme we should dwell longest over is his ongoing attempt to explore 'the past geographies of the interconnectedness of nature/culture'.[30] Here Griffin focuses on the malicious damage of trees, something that could take a

---

28 Freeman, "Plebs or predators? 20–21
29 C.J. Griffin, "'There was No Law to Punish that Offence'". Re-assessing 'Captain Swing': Rural Luddism and Rebellion in East Kent, 1830–31', *Southern History* 22 (2000), 131–63; C.J. Griffin, 'Knowable Geographies? The Reporting of Incendiarism in the Eighteenth- and early Nineteenth-century English Provincial Press', *Journal of Historical Geography* 32 (2006), 38–56; C.J. Griffin, 'Protest Practice and (tree) Cultures of Conflict: Understanding the Spaces of 'tree maiming' in Eighteenth- and early Nineteenth-century England', *Transactions of the Institute of British Geographers* 40 (2008), 91–100; C.J. Griffin, 'Cut Down by Some Cowardly Miscreants': Plant Maiming, or the Malicious Cutting of Plants as an Act of Protest in Eighteenth- and Nineteenth-century Rural England, *Rural History* 19 (2008), 29–54; C.J. Griffin, 'Affecting Violence: Language, Gesture and Performance in early Nineteenth-century English Popular Protest', *Historical Geography* 36 (2008), 139–62; C.J. Griffin, 'Swing, Swing Redivivus or Something after Swing? On the Death Throes of a Movement, December 1830–December 1833', *International Review of Social History* 54 (2009), 459–97.
30 Griffin, 'Protest Practice', 93.

variety of forms: trees in private gardens or ornamental trees in the emparked landscape, both of which were relatively low key affairs. Attacks on orchards or timber trees, however, could occur on a much larger scale. In 1796 on Lord Arundel's estate at Ilchester (Somerset) it was reported that thousands of young trees had been destroyed in a series of attacks.[31] Finally, Griffin discusses at length the generally more widely known aspects of attacks on trees, that of wood-taking.

What all these different forms amount to is tree maiming as a form of protest; symbolic or deeply felt attacks on wood as a representation of power. As such Griffin, like many other students of social protest, reveals a tendency to underplay questions of human agency in these events. This, however, is not one of his key aims in this discussion. More vitally this project is also an attempt at restoration of the non-human to studies of the rural past from which it had been banished as part of the reaction against 'traditional' agricultural history. The aim here is to engender explorations of the cultural role of trees (and other flora) in rural life and relationships. As Griffin asserts, attacks on wood 'are also attacks on property ... But whilst the cultural significance ... of machine breaking is well understood ... the role of attacks on the living capital of fauna and (especially) flora remains obscure'.[32] In this cultural history, then, Griffin draws heavily on the views of Owain Jones and Paul Cloke who through their study of orchards, assert that trees must be recognised as equally dynamic partners in giving meaning to space – both figuratively and culturally.[33]

This culturally informed and flora-sensitive methodology could certainly be utilised in any attempt to better understand the complexity of conflict in the Forest of Dean. Here we should pay attention to the role played by vernacular concerns for nature/culture interrelationships and whilst there is not the space to give full weight to such an investigation, a short case study of the Warren James riots may well illustrate the possibilities. Conflict in the Forest of Dean, as with all Royal Forests, was centred around enclosure, deer, trees, mineral extraction and rights of use, or customary beliefs around local environmental relations and natural resource utilisation, in other words. The 1831 riots, the last mass anti-enclosure riots in the Forest of Dean, took place over a number of days in June, and were led by the real, if somewhat hidden from history, Warren James. On 11 June, James and about 80 miners first broke down

---

31 Griffin, 'Protest Practice', 100.
32 Griffin, 'Protest Practice', 98.
33 O. Jones and P. Cloke, *Tree Cultures* (Oxford, 2002); P. Cloke and O. Jones, 'Turning in the Graveyard: Trees and the Hybrid Geographies of Dwelling, Monitoring and Resistance in a Bristol cemetery', *Cultural Geographies* 11 (2004), 313–41.

the enclosure fences surrounding a part of the wood they said that custom dictated should be open. Very rapidly the crowd grew and the action spread. In total about 60 miles of fences were destroyed, the rioters retained control of the area for about four days and were frequently seen grazing their animals on the disputed enclosures. Food and beer to fuel the actions were procured from the local community who, it would appear, were almost unanimously in favour of the actions taken by the rioters.[34] And, as might be expected, the poaching of deer and the taking of wood were both extremely common during this period and for a considerable time afterwards. The latter action was compounded, moreover by the illegal *planting* of fruit trees. As Chris Fisher shows, an 1846 census revealed that 'over the previous 20 years 254 people had planted 2,602 trees on the waste'.[35]

Fisher's work remains virtually the only text to discuss these significant riots in any depth.[36] And whilst the remainder of his thesis is both powerful and convincing, like many commentators who seek to place the study of protest within a broader focus, Fisher's engagement with the riots is significantly less so. Moreover, unlike other commentators on custom,[37] Fisher takes a fairly narrow perspective, focussing only on one of Thompson's two 'paths'[38] which may well have led him to fail to offer much by way of explanation of the Warren James riots. Fisher's is an empirical engagement which largely eschews the full range of interpretations of social protest: from moral economy through to local political negotiation. In one aspect, however, Fisher may well have been right to have been so cautious to move to explanation. In their poaching, in their wood stealing and in their insistence on vernacular ways of utilising the forest, the Dean labouring population may well have been both articulating a set of beliefs not easily encompassed by the established interpretations, and which encapsulate, and come out of everyday interactions between nature and culture.

---

34 Much of the detail of these events has been taken from an anonymously written but contemporaneous biography of Warren James, *The Life of Warren James. The Reputed Champion of the Forest of Dean* (Monmouth, 1831).
35 *Report from the Select Committee on the Woods, Forests and Land Revenues of the Crown*, (Parliamentary Papers, 1889), p. 31; C. Fisher, *Custom, Work and Market Capitalism: the Forest of Dean Colliers, 1788–1888* (London, 1981), p. 36.
36 See also R. Anstis, *Warren James and the Dean Forest riots*, (Coleford, 1986); Wright, I. *The Life and Times of Warren James*, (Bristol Radical Pamphlets 6, no date)
37 See, for instance, B. Bushaway, *By Rite: Custom, Ceremony, and Community in England 1700–1880*, (London, 1982); E.P. Thompson, *Customs in Common*, (London, 1991); A. Wood, *The Politics of Social Conflict*, (Cambridge, 1999).
38 Thompson, *Customs in Common*, p. vii.

If we are looking for an explanatory model with which to explore such interactions, and we really ought to, then one place to look may well be Karl Jacoby's moral ecology.[39] There is no need to dwell over the inspiration and underpinning context of this concept as that is stating the obvious. Nevertheless it is important to note that there is a distinct absence of the Thompsonian Marxist class analysis to Jacoby's approach. This notwithstanding, however, there is much within the thesis which echoes the concerns of students of social protest. It is clear, for instance, that what Jacoby believes he is observing is a clash between two distinct ways of life as made manifest in two widely contrasting sets of 'laws'. From this Jacoby is able to write of 'local resistance [to] the transformation of previously acceptable practises into illegal acts' and of the criminalisation of customary activities. Furthermore, this gave rise, Jacoby asserts, to the rise of the phenomenon of 'environmental banditry' legitimised by support from within local society.[40] Developing this further, in exactly the same way that an earlier generation of historians either ignored 'Swing' altogether or were ideologically hostile to it, early historians of the struggles in America's national parks between conservation and indigenous practises were sympathetic to the ideologies and aims of conservation. As a consequence 'rural folk' came to be understood 'as operating with a flawed understanding of the natural world' and the history of conservation that emerged from this perspective was one reduced to crude dualisms and the triumphalism of the 'unfolding of an ever-more enlightened attitude towards the environment'.[41] This is a view that Jacoby rejects, preferring instead to recognise a much wider and deeper layer(s) of complexity and ambiguity within these tensions, which, from the indigenous population's perspective, is underpinned by a distinct moral universe. In essence, therefore, what Jacoby identifies here is a view of nature from 'the bottom up'. It is this view of nature from within that Jacoby seeks to locate within what he identifies as a moral ecology; essentially an extension of Thompson's thesis to include, and make central, 'vernacular constructions of environmental ethics'.[42] Thus moral ecology can be said to emerge from a combination of local senses of place and vernacular understandings of the interaction of ecology, economy and society.

Jacoby situates this conceptual perspective within three distinct locales: New York's Adirondack Mountains, Yellowstone, and the Grand

39 K. Jacoby, *Crimes Against Nature* (Berkeley, Ca., 2003).
40 Jacoby, *Crimes Against Nature*, p. 2.
41 Jacoby, *Crimes Against Nature*, p. 3.
42 P. Hay, '"Balding Nevis": Place Imperatives of an Invisible Cohort within Tasmania's Forest Communities', *Geographical Research* 46 (2008), 229.

Canyon. Chosen in part to permit a long temporal survey, these were also key sites in the history of the development of the conservation movement in the United States. Furthermore, all three in combination illustrate perfectly the controversies hitherto hidden within wider tropes of conservation. Such controversies, Jacoby feels, are to be found within the fact that conservation 'redefined the rules governing the use of the environment' within the designated areas.[43] What emerges from these various redefinitions at the three sites are squatters, poachers and thieves.

Not content with this, however, Jacoby re-imagines these traditional practices most persuasively. The example of poaching will serve here. As has been long established in the English literature, Jacoby asserts that poaching could be a rebellion against the market or a response to it, or both at once. This, he suggests, reveals a complexity inherent in such actions that is resistant of easy, dualistically-based models of interpretation – a clear message for understandings of Swing and his like. And whilst we must take issue with Jacoby's somewhat lazy formulation of 'rural folk' there is no denying the power of his analysis. What emerges from these local transgressions is an articulation of a 'moral universe' that is of itself derived from and constituted 'the pattern of beliefs, practises and traditions that governed how ordinary rural folk interacted with the environment'.[44] All was underpinned by a robust and long-lived ideology of common rights and a relatively sophisticated ecological code. Moreover, this 'moral universe' provides the important counterpoint to the elite discourse of conservation which, in this reading, emerges not as a neutral act designed to protect a pristine 'wilderness' but rather, through legislation and its enforcement on the ground, as a significant transformative force. As such, conservation represented the triumph of law over custom. A cultural conflict over forest practice was inevitable.

It is, of course, perfectly possible to ask how far moral ecology takes us beyond moral economy and existing discussions of social crime, for here is poaching conceptualised as resistance to social and cultural change and drawing on community support at a time when new social structures have yet to solidify.[45] It is, however, equally, perfectly possible to find an answer to this at a number of different levels. Put simply, Jacoby draws straightforward stealing into his discussion when this, at the very least, was the subject of some considerable discussion amongst students of social crime. There was consequently significant blurring around the boundaries

---

43 Jacoby, *Crimes Against Nature*, p. 5.
44 Hay, '"Balding Nevis"', p. 229.
45 For one of the best and most recent discussions of our understanding of this rather slippery term, see J. Lea, 'Social Crime Revisited', *Theoretical Criminology* 3 (1999), 307-25.

of what constituted social and anti-social crime and whilst this blurring is a reflection of the 'fluidity of social relations in the nascent capitalist society',[46] and part of the lived experience of the emergent working class, it nevertheless reflects also the ever-present problems with categorising and compartmentalising something as dynamic and fluid as disorder. Moral ecology, however, would seem to eschew compartmentalisation and offer up the possibility of bringing together the various forms of social protest into a powerfully holistic analysis that more successfully grounds the decision to protest into everyday experience. In the rural world of 'Swing' and other protest forms, in the limestone uplands of Winchcombe parish as much as in the forest communities of the Dean, interactions between nature and culture, between the human and non-human would have been everyday and taken for granted. The non-human world would have had an active and dynamic role in the cultural world. Vernacular constructions of ecological ethics would have been an integral part of and brought meaning for local people with regard to their everyday and time-rich entanglements with the 'natural'. It is not too big a leap to view such vernacular constructions, conceptualised as moral ecology, as the base from which protest forms emerge. As such, therefore, this opens up the further possibility of readmitting social protest once again onto the stage as a serious and equal player in the 'complex theatre of social relations'.[47] In addition, and perhaps most importantly, the notion of moral ecology allows for the articulation of a much firmer and more convincing link between social relations, protest in the round, and place and space, with the latter taking an active and constitutive role.

The role of place and space as it interacts with, informs and is informed by expressions of moral ecology can be seen most convincingly in the work of Pete Hay. Here Hay, focussing on the politics of place, explores tensions surrounding different ways of life within Tasmania's forest industry. He identifies what he terms as an 'under recognised [third] cohort within Tasmania's forest communities' which, nevertheless have long and deep ties to both people and place.[48] In contrast to the 'productive conservation' ethos of *Timber Communities Australia* those within the third cohort look back to a smaller scale economy, insist on the viability of such an approach and are critical of contemporary production methods. Hay quotes one sawmiller as claiming that 'I could make a year's living out of just one truck load going down there to St Leonards … If they'd drop one log off here on the way to the chip I'd

---

46 Lea, 'Social Crime Revisited', 210–11.
47 A. Wood, *Riot, Rebellion, and Popular Politics in Early Modern England* (London, 2002).
48 Hay, '"Balding Nevis"', 224.

make more money from that one log than they'd make from the rest of the load'.[49] This, however, is emphatically not the romantic and nostalgic articulation of a sense of heritage; rather it is much more reminiscent of the counter-hegemonic possibilities of heritage from below and is an expression of a moral ecology that informs beliefs 'concerning the right and wrong ways of interacting with the natural world'.[50]

Moral ecology, therefore, may well offer a route beyond the somewhat circulatory nature of much of the discussion in a lot of recent work on social protest and the 'Swing' events in particular. This concept places resistance and protest equally 'in place' and allows for a more dynamic relationship between local spaces and protest events than hitherto recognised. Moral ecology also admits place and space as active and constitutive elements as may well be evident in a series of incidents on the River Severn in the late nineteenth century. In 1874 the River Severn Fisheries board, chaired by a member of one of the most successful salmon fishing families, announced a ban on elver (young eels) fishing on the lower reaches of the river below Gloucester. Elver taking was thus criminalised as poaching. Nevertheless, the ban was vigorously resisted by many of the poorer inhabitants of Gloucester for whom the taking of elvers was a time-rich supplement to their diet. Conflict on the riverbank and in the courts followed and such was the extent of the reaction to this ban that the recent historian of these events has been able to label them 'The Elver Wars'.[51] Whilst the title is potentially hyperbolic, it is not hard to imagine this as a conflict over competing attitudes to resource utilisation. The first set of attitudes draws upon a time-rich set of beliefs, patterns and traditions that dictated how ordinary people interacted with the environment while the other is an elite discourse about conservation.

This essay has engaged with the dissipation of the powerful legacy that is *Captain Swing* and suggested that this vital work is both an asset and a liability. Along with moral economy, *Captain Swing* placed the study of rural conflict at the centre of our social histories. And yet, because social protest historians feel the need to constantly return to it, the legacy of *Swing* has been a near marginalisation of (overt, certainly) protest studies. This is unacceptable. To maintain this marginalisation means that the diversity and intensity of events of disorder in and around nineteenth century Winchcombe, for instance, would continue to pass largely unrecognised, for such has been the dominance of the Swing paradigm

49 Hay, '"Balding Nevis"', 227.
50 I. Robertson, 'Heritage from Below: Class, Social Protest and Resistance', in B. Graham and P. Howard (eds), *The Ashgate Research Companion to Heritage and Identity* (Aldershot, 2008); Hay, '"Balding Nevis"', 238.
51 W. Hunt, *The Victorian Elver Wars* (Cheltenham, 2007).

that anything not 'Swing-like' suffers such a fate. This is a regrettable consequence for places such as Winchcombe, suffering as it was from economic decline, have much to tell us about early nineteenth century social relations. Thus it has been suggested here that in their poaching and sheep stealing, in their challenges to 'respectable' society and in their rick burning and rioting, agricultural labourers can be understood as attempting to assert views on resource utilisation at odds to the hegemonic.

There is, therefore, an urgent need to continue the positive work of most recent Swing scholarship and build a new paradigm from which the powerful legacy of protest studies can be reaffirmed. Jacoby's conceptualization of moral ecology offers one possible route towards this. A wider and deeper exploration of the presence (or otherwise) of moral ecological views, moreover, offers the additional possibility of accessing vernacular constructions of ecological ethics in ways most persuasively developed in Hay's exploration of Tasmanian logging communities. For the Forest of Dean in the first half of the nineteenth, just as much as in North America in the latter part of the century and in twentieth century Tasmania, events of protest can be understood as expressive of, and attempts to reassert traditional and vernacular ecological practices. Through their poaching, wood stealing and planting the Dean labouring population may have been articulating a set of beliefs that drew upon their everyday interactions between nature and culture and which are not easily encompassed by the established interpretations of social protest. One aspect of the legacy of *Captain Swing* is that the existence of such beliefs is not regularly contemplated and non-Swing events have been marginalised. To downplay the actions of Warren James and his contemporaries throughout Gloucestershire is to perpetuate the more negative aspects of *Swing*'s inheritance. Building understandings of traditional and vernacular nature/culture relations into our studies of Swing will contribute to a wholly positive legacy that will offer a holistic perspective which pays full attention to both place and space.

The True Life and History of Captain Swing. Rhetorical Construction and Metonymy in a Time of Reform

Peter Jones

In April 1831, the *Poor Man's Guardian* published an anonymous verse which lauded the character and behaviour of a certain Jack Swing. It was to Jack or Captain Swing that the eponymous rural disorders of the previous autumn were attributed:

> Jack Swing is the greatest Reformer,
> The fellow what burns all the hay;
> His reasons got warmer and warmer,
> Till the Slaves of Corruption gave way.
>
> Our tyrants have bred a fine fellow,
> They have foster'd and reared Master Swing;-
> But oh, how the wretches do bellow,
> When fire-balls fly from his sling!
>
> Yet "the Church" (so they tell us) "will smother,
> "The fires that blaze all around;
> "And a SPECIAL COMMISSION, her brother,
> "Will hang every Swing that is found;
>
> "And those who escape from the gallows,
> "Will fall by a General Fast!"
> And these are the means, which (they tell us)
> Will master Jack Swing at the last!
>
> Why, the brains of the tyrants are rotten,
> As sure as Jack Swing is alive;
> 'Twas on fasting that Swing was begotten,
> And on fasting he always will thrive.

> But the Country news, every Post, is
> The best that our wishes could bring;
> That nought, but AGRARIAN JUSTICE,
> Can kill that great Radical Swing.[1]

Jack Swing was certainly a player of considerable versatility. Not only was he a 'great radical' – indeed, 'the greatest Reformer' – but he assumed the guise of an emissary from the revolutions in Europe, he was an 'adept in chymical ignition', and a member of the Catholic Association. A master of disguise, he was sometimes described as a 'defective being, with calfless legs and stooping shoulders',[2] and at others as having the appearance of a farmer and a gentleman.[3] Sometimes he sported 'very large black whiskers', at other times they were red.[4] He travelled on foot or rode a 'sorrel coloured ... Blood Horse with a Switch Tail'.[5] He was often spotted at the scene of an incendiary attack, yet never apprehended and rarely approached. Even those at the very highest levels of government believed that there was substance to the tall tales of conspiracy: barely a week after standing down as Prime Minister, the duke of Wellington wrote to Lord Malmesbury that 'I am sorry to add my conviction that there is a conspiracy in action as well to destroy property and to cause these disturbances', and not seven days after that Malmesbury was in turn moved to tell new Home Secretary, Lord Melbourne, of 'information that I have obtained on this as well as on the other side of the water that Emissaries have been, & are, actively engaged in exciting discontent among our Peasantry, & perhaps in some instances have themselves been engaged in acts of incendiarism'.[6]

In other words, those who wrote the story of the Swing disturbances at the time were clearly alive to the symbolic resonance and dramatic potential of the events of 1830. They identified in 'Jack Swing' a cast of shadowy and dangerous characters, each with his own agenda, and all

---

1. 'Jack Swing' (anonymous), *Poor Man's Guardian*, 2 April 1831, p. 8.
2. E.G. Wakefield, *Swing Unmasked: or, the Causes of Rural Incendiarism* (London, 1831), p. 9.
3. The National Archives, London [hereafter TNA], HO52/11/5, J.P. Bouverie to Home Office, (n.d.).
4. TNA, HO52/6/131, Examination of Susan Day of Berkshire, 28 November 1830.
5. TNA, HO52/6/408, Handbill from Pampisford, Cambridgeshire; Wiltshire and Swindon Record Office, Trowbridge, A1/740/4/1, Anon to Mr Wyndham, Barford St. Martin, 21 December 1830.
6. Hampshire Record Office, Winchester, [hereafter HRO] 9M73/406/2 Wellington to Lord Malmesbury, 20 November 1830; HRO, 9M73/406/24 Malmesbury to Lord Melbourne, 1 December 1830.

entirely explicable within the context of the time. Historians, on the other hand, have tended to describe a much more prosaic set of events. It is now all-but accepted that the so-called Swing risings had very little to do with the metonymical Swing, and that instead they were the result of a variety of structural and influential factors that led agricultural labourers and others in the south of England to take arms against their own particular sea of troubles.[7] True enough, a few have argued for the influence of specific Radicals, and of 'Radicalism' more generally, on the events of 1830. In his pioneering spatial analysis of the disturbances, Andrew Charlesworth suggested as long ago as the late-1970s that 'the mobilisation [of agricultural labourers]...required, albeit loose, a form of organisation', and that 'news from up the road was not enough' to explain the 'contagious' nature of the disturbances. As a result, he argued for the role of 'politically conscious men' in rural communities, who had 'contacts with the outside world', and who took the lead in spreading the conflagration from village to village.[8] Perhaps the best known advocate of the view that there was more to the disturbances than simply rural distress and a breakdown of social relations is Roger Wells who argued that the politicisation of agricultural labourers was much further advanced in 1830 than has been acknowledged elsewhere.[9] He also identified the influence of a cast of characters in and around Battle in Sussex (including Cobbett, on a lecture tour of the south of England spreading word of Reform; Charles Inskipp, a recently resigned and at least partially unhinged London policeman apparently bent on fomenting revolution in the pubs and beer shops of the area; and Treasury Solicitor Charles Maule, charged with suppressing the disturbances who attempted – unsuccessfully – to indict local farmers for inciting the labourers to riot) to rival that of any Georgian melodrama. Nonetheless, neither he nor Charlesworth found any central place in their work for the charismatic Captain Swing himself, Free Irishman, French Revolutionary, arch-Radical, and metonym extraordinaire. This is unfortunate because, as we will see, despite his mythical, manifold identity, he was, in the end, *absolutely central* to the events of Autumn 1830, and in particular to the way that

7   The literature on Swing is extensive, and growing, but for a recent discussion of the historiography, see P. Jones, 'Finding Captain Swing: Protest, Parish Relations and the State of the Public Mind in 1830', *International Review of Social History*, 54 (2009), 429–30, 432.
8   A. Charlesworth, *Social Protest in a Rural Society: The Spatial Diffusion of the Captain Swing Disturbances of 1830–1831* ((Historical Geography Research Series, 1, Liverpool 1979), p. 31.
9   R.G. Wells, 'Mr. William Cobbett, Captain Swing and King William IV', *Agricultural History Review* 45 (1997), 47.

they were understood by contemporaries and mediated by the press and pamphleteers.

By now, it is well known that 'Swing' began life as the signatory of letters sent to farmers at Dover at the beginning of the disturbances warning 'that if you doant put away your thrashings machines against Monday next you shall have a "SWING"'.[10] Thereafter, he put his name to a range of correspondence of varying provenance, and his cause was taken up by the local and national press.[11] It is this last element of his career that is of particular interest to us here, for Swing the synonym quickly became shorthand for events in the country, and the question of how this happened and why it should be the case has been almost entirely neglected by historians. Undoubtedly, the proximity of revolutions abroad and reformist agitation at home were part of the rich mix into which newspapermen dipped their quills in response to the disturbances: as Roger Wells has recently suggested, '[t]he contexts of the insurrection were both long-term conditioners, shorter term developments, and phenomena coincident with the three months of Swing mobilisations'.[12] Nonetheless, even this potent concoction of Radicalism, revolutionary fervour and rural distress does not *in itself* explain the speed and agility with which 'Jack' Swing sprang into the public mind in November and December 1830.

Perhaps the first place to look for Swing's heritage is, as many contemporaries feared, across the Irish Sea. Captain Rock had, after all, been putting his name to threatening letters there for a decade and more by the time the first fires lit up the skies of southern England, and the modus operandi of the two Captains was so similar that reports of Swing's first letter at Dover could not help but make explicit mention of it: 'The whole proceedings,' according to the *Examiner*, 'bear so close a resemblance to Captain Rock that it is impossible not to notice it. Like him, too, the insurrectionary spirit here has taken a *nom de guerre*, and the epithet adopted is "Swing"'.[13] Small wonder, then, that those who should perhaps have known better were drawn in by this simple equation: 'we used to talk of the outrages in Ireland,' wrote John Fitzgerald in November, 'why the very same things are doing close to London ... we must conclude that the people are discontented by agency for concealed

---

10 *The Examiner*, 17 October 1830.
11 Jones, 'Finding Captain Swing', 434–38.
12 R.G. Wells, '1830: the Year of Revolutions in England, and the Politics of the Captain Swing Insurrection' (unpublished), pp.1–2. My thanks go to Professor Wells for his permission to cite this work.
13 *Examiner*, 17 October 1830.

purposes'.[14] But the *proximity* of the actions of Captain Rock is not the only possible explanation for his influence on the rhetorical construction of his English counterpart. During the most intense phase of his epistolary activity, Rock was famously celebrated by the Catholic Romantic Thomas Moore in his 1824 *Memoirs of Captain Rock, the Irish Chieftan, Written by Himself*. In a scholarly introduction to the 2008 edition, Emer Nolan explains that 'the central satiric strategy' of the book (which was published anonymously) 'was to make that well-known name a secret identity by effectively merging the individual and the generic voice in the first-person narrator'.[15] By this means, Moore merged myth with reality, religious and political commentary with rhetorical construction, and in so doing made the kind of narrative sense of the shadowy and multivalent activities of the Rockites (and, for that matter, their proximate counterparts, the Whiteboys and the Molly Maguires) that had probably eluded a genteel English audience at all times previously. As Nolan notes, Rock's *Memoirs* were an immediate publishing success, running to five London editions in 1824 alone, as well as to others in Paris and New York, and being later translated into German and French.[16] By this means Captain Rock was cemented in the public mind as a semi-mythical figure whose works were nonetheless there for all to see.

Of course, Moore's rhetorical construction of Captain Rock was not written in isolation: it mined a rich seam of performance, theatricality and public representation that ran deep within Georgian Britain. As David Worrall notes, throughout the Romantic period 'theatricality was a mode of public being, a representation of the self, which was not confined to dramas performed in the playhouses'.[17] Theatricality, in the form of a subversive popular drama, underpinned the very use of the pseudonym by protesters in Ireland in the first place; how appropriate, then, that their actions should become explicable in the public mind largely through the use of Moore's dramatic conceit in the *Memoir*. All of which is to suggest, of course, that by the time that other subversive signatory emerged on the mainland, a framework already existed within which it was possible for the public, not only to understand his actions, but to describe them, too – hence the speed with which the pseudonymous Swing took root, both in the reportage, and in the public

14 HRO, 44M69/2/1/38, J. Fitzgerald to G.P. Jervoise, 27 November 1830.
15 E. Nolan, 'Introduction' to Thomas Moore, *Memoirs of Captain Rock: the Celebrated Irish Chieftain with Some Account of his Ancestors Written by Himself*, edited by E. Nolan (Dublin. 2008), p. xi.
16 Ibid., p. xi.
17 D. Worrall, *Theatric Revolution: drama, censorship and Romantic period subcultures, 1773–1832* (Oxford, 2006), p. 2.

mind. From the earliest explicit linkage in the *Examiner* of Swing with the actions of the semi-mythical Rock, the papers worked hard to put flesh on the bones. At the end of October, the *Newcastle Courant* stated that 'the outrages of "Swing" continue with great violence' in Kent; at the beginning of November, Hetherington's *Poor Man's Guardian* noted with undisguised approval that '"Swing" continues his triumphant progress without check or fear' across southern England; and a month later the *Hull Packet* noted that farmers were disabling their threshing machines in Oxfordshire 'to avoid a visit from Mr. Swing'.[18] Tellingly, at the end of November, the *Freeman's Journal*, in Dublin, reported the arrest of a 'person of respectable appearance' at Battle, in Sussex, who was supposed to be carrying a number of 'Swing' letters and a 'great quantity of various combustibles' under the headline, 'ARREST OF AN ENGLISH CAPTAIN ROCK'.[19] This personification of Swing continued and strengthened throughout the three months that saw the most intense period of his activities. Yet one fundamental difference between Swing and Rock is of relevance here: in almost all of the reportage of events in the English countryside, Swing is identified simply as 'Mr. Swing', or just plain 'Swing'. He was as yet a civilian, whereas Captain Rock was always keen to declare his military credentials in the letters of protesters in Ireland. Here again, it is difficult not to see the influence of events over the Irish Sea on the elevation of Swing to a military career. By early November, the satirical magazine *The Age* was suggesting that 'you may hang Captain Swing and all his associates tomorrow, and on the day after, Captain Swing the second will make his appearance'; but it did so with Ireland in mind, and its remedy to this proliferation of Swings was (among other things) to 'impose the poor laws upon Ireland, and you will have all England tranquil in a month'.[20] Elsewhere in the same edition, 'Captain Swing' is again alluded to, this time in a skit on a parliamentary exchange between the Irish-born Tory, John Wilson Croker, and Daniel O'Connell.[21] Once again, it was clearly of the utmost importance (or at least, the utmost expediency) for the Tory editor of *The Age*, Molloy Westmacott, to link the goings on in southern England with those in Ireland as directly as he could.

Having once been granted his commission in the press though, Captain Swing's campaign through the satirical journals of the period was swift and decisive. By 14 November, he was headlining at Poet's Corner

18 *Newcastle Courant*, 30 October 1830; *Poor Man's Guardian*, 8 November 1830; *Hull Packet*, 7 December 1830.
19 *Freeman's Journal*, 25 November 1830.
20 *The Age*, 7 November 1830.
21 Ibid., 7 November 1830.

in *Bell's Life in London*; two months later he again played the lead, this time in a verse entitled 'Captain Swing and his Subalterns, or Warm Work for a Winter's Night'.[22] Shortly after his debut he was the subject of a squib in *The Age* aimed at the duke of Wellington, on the occasion of his church pew having been ruined by fire:

> DUKE ARTHUR
> "Who dares to burn my seat of grace
> In such a solemn, sacred place?
> Who the devil has fired my pew?
> Pray tell me, Captain Swing, was't you?
> Oh! If it was you, Captain Swing,
> You did a very wicked thing."
>
> CAPTAIN SWING
> "At such a time, in such a place,
> I little thought 'twould infirm your Grace.
> Arthur, you do deserve the birch;
> You sought t'enslave the British nation;
> I fought to fumigate the church,
> And give you excommunication".[23]

Finally, after the conflagrations in the countryside that bore his name had been largely extinguished by the Special Commissions,[24] Captain Swing finally achieved the recognition he deserved: a biographical account of his life very much in the vein of that accorded to Rock a few years earlier.

The Life & History of Swing, the Kent Rick Burner, written by Himself was, in fact, the work of the Radical Richard Carlile. It tells the story of Francis Swing's decline and fall, from the grammar school-educated son of a small but prosperous farmer to a labourer 'harnessed like a horse to a gravel cart'.[25] Again, the similarities between Swing's ghosted biography and that of Captain Rock are striking: the architects of Swing's downfall are identified as precisely those 'perennial enemies' of the poor identified in Moore's *Memoirs* by Emer Nolan: 'landlords, tithe proctors, large farmers and the like'.[26] But Carlile went even further in his rhetorical

---

22 *Bell's Life in London*, 14 November 1830, 16 January 1831
23 *The Age*, 21 November 1830.
24 Special Commissions, or Assizes, were held to try prisoners arrested during the classical period of Swing in Berkshire, Buckinghamshire, Dorset, Hampshire and Wiltshire. See E.J. Hobsbawm and G. Rudé, *Captain Swing* (London, 1969), pp. 308–9 Appendix 2.
25 *The Life & History of Captain Swing, the Kent Rick Burner, written by Himself* (London, 1830), p. 8.
26 Nolan, 'Introduction' to Moore, *Memoirs of Captain Rock*, p. xi.

embellishment of Swing, bankrolling and staging a successful play based on his life and written by the notorious Robert Turner, also known as the 'Devil's Chaplain'. *Swing: or, Who Are the Incendiaries?* was staged at Carlile's newly opened Rotunda, Blackfriars Road, London, in early 1831.[27] Though clearly an allegory for the distress of agricultural labourers and the corruption of the ruling class, the play nonetheless helped to cement, in the minds of contemporaries, the link between events in the countryside and the rhetorically ubiquitous figure of Swing himself. As Worrall notes, 'the vying for the myth of Swing ... was a site of contestation fought out in pamphlet wars for the minds of the urban, as much as the rural, populace', and Carlile's *Life and History* resulted in at least two alternative versions of Swing's life story, again echoing the literary career of Captain Rock, whose *Memoirs* quickly resulted in the publication of a rejoinder.[28] *The Genuine Life of Francis Swing* is a direct rebuttal of Carlile's account in which Swing blames everyone but himself, beginning with Cobbett and ending with Richard Jones, a mysterious Rotunda-frequenting poacher who has led him into evil ways. It is a cautionary tale worthy of Hannah More in its Millennarian flourishes – no coincidence, then, that it was published by the Society for the Promotion of Christian Knowledge – and in it the lunatic Swing claims still to be throwing inflammatory letters from his gig, concluding: 'I have sold myself to the devil. I am his property ... and so will you soon be if you listen to the blasphemous words of those, my countrymen, who would betray your souls'.[29] Carlile reacted to its publication in typically pugilistic fashion, suggesting in the *Prompter* that:

> It is quite sufficient description of it to say, that the people are advised not to go to the Rotunda, and that the Parson and the rich man make the poor man happy ... This, with a Ghost Story, is the substance at this miserable effort at a trick, a cheat, and a falsehood.[30]

In *A Short Account of the Life and Death of Swing, the Rick-Burner*, addressed directly to 'Carlile, the Fleet Street Infidel' and written by Henry Nelson Coleridge (nephew of Samuel Taylor), Swing is acknowledged as a small farmer who has fallen on hard times, but in this instance the fault is entirely his own. We are told that he invested heavily in 'Cobbett's corn' – which of course failed miserably – and as a result he

27 For a full account of the play's run at the Rotunda, and an brief account of the life of Taylor, see Worrall, *Theatric Revolution*, pp. 340–60.
28 Rev. Mortimer O'Sullivan, *Captain Rock Detected: or, the Origin and Character of the Recent Disturbances* (London, 1824).
29 [H. Nelson Coleridge], *The Genuine Life of Mr. F. S.* (London, 1831), p. 22.
30 R. Carlile, *The Prompter*, 18 January 1831.

became a drunkard and a slovenly worker. In the final analysis, we are told that it was 'intemperance' that led him to a bad end.[31]

The rhetorical reinvention of Captain Swing continued long past his supposed execution by the Royal Commissions, and by the Spring of 1831 he had become a verb, and his name was shorthand for any incendiary activity, actual or metaphorical, that carried a radical or subversive threat. Reporting on fires in the Vendée in France in May, the *Examiner* suggested that 'for a long time past they have carried on a sort of "Swing" warfare there'; for the *North Wales Chronicle*, the second Reform Bill (which was passed in the Commons on 20 April) was promoted by 'incendiary articles in the newspapers, and "Swing" speeches in parliament'.[32] The ongoing narrative of his activities was maintained, in part, by the steady stream of letters bearing his name that continued to be received long past the most intense period of his activities both by the enemies of 'the people', and those of particular individuals. A 'respectable' tavern owner in Plymouth was reported to have received one in January, and the letter is notable for its mischievous flourish, worthy of *The Age's* Westmacott himself:

> Sir, having *smoked* that you have a *tobacco-box* in your house *worked* by *machinery*, this is to inform you, that unless a *stopper* is placed on it, we shall set *fire* to the *tobacco*, and become tobacco *stoppers* ourselves – For the people, Swing & Co.[33]

Mrs. Chandler of Pusey in Wiltshire, on the other hand, was a victim of Swing's notoriety when she was on the receiving end of the attentions of an extortionist keen to cash in on his name:

> Madame – I have to request that you will send me by return of post the sum of 10l., or else your house will be burned to the ground very shortly, as I know you can well afford to spare that sum for a short period until I have the effects to repay it ... [signed] "SWING".[34]

Clearly, the authors of these letters, while motivated by very different aims and hoping for quite different outcomes, were equally alive to the rhetorical strength of Swing and his hold on the public imagination; and this despite the fact that the papers had already confidently reported the arrest and incarceration of the 'real' Captain Swing.

---

31 H. Nelson Coleridge, *A Short Account of the Life & Death of Swing, the Rick-Burner: Written by one Well Acquainted with Him* (London, 1831), p. 25.
32 *Examiner*, 22 May 1831; *North Wales Chronicle*, 31 May 1831.
33 *Morning Chronicle*, 10 January 1831.
34 *Examiner*, 16 January 1831.

On the 23 December 1830 news broke that a man, 'aged around 60, rather under the middle size, thin face, dark eyed brows, prominent nose, and very gray-headed', was in custody having been spotted in the vicinity of Stradishall, Suffolk, throwing letters from a gig.[35] These letters were of an inflammatory nature, spiced with an Old Testament flourish, and all were signed 'Swing':

> England! beware you do not bring Vengeance down upon your heads by robbing the poor. "SWING"
>
> Church of England Parsons, who strain at gnats, and swallow camels, who, (woe), who, who, unto you – you shall one day have your reward! "SWING"
>
> If you do not behave better and give the Poor Man his due I will visit you or my name is not "SWING"
>
> Will you farmers and parishioners pay us better for our labour if you will not we will put you in bodily fear. "SWING"[36]

On further investigation, the man turned out to be Joseph Saville, a Methodist preacher ('or more properly, perhaps, what is called a "Ranter"')[37] from Gamlingay in Cambridgeshire. At his trial, he received the most glowing character references from members of his parish, including the Anglican clergyman, and this seems to have persuaded the court that he was, at heart, a harmless crank. E.P. Thompson agreed, and in 'The Crime of Anonymity' suggested that Saville was lucky 'to have had the loyal backing of his parish … and to have been tried in a county [Suffolk] in which the disturbances were comparatively light', because despite having confessed to dropping large numbers of such letters throughout England, Saville was sentenced to a mere twelve months in prison and a £50 fine.[38] Yet at the time of his arrest his story caused a sensation, both in the press and beyond. The *Morning Chronicle* and the *Hull Packet* both hailed the arrest of the 'real' Captain Swing, and *The Times* reported that his apprehension had 'caused a more than ordinary

---

35 *Examiner*, 26 December 1830.
36 *Jackson's Oxford Journal*, 1 January 1831; *Examiner*, 26 December 1830; TNA, HO52/10/91 Correspondence from John Garey, n.d.
37 *Examiner*, 26 December 1830.
38 E.P. Thompson, 'The Crime of Anonymity', in D. Hay, P. Linebaugh, J. Rule, E.P. Thompson and C. Winslow, *Albion's Fatal Tree. Crime and Society in Eighteenth-century England* (London, 1975), p. 289.

sensation in the area', and that it was rumoured that he was 'the actual and original "Swing"'.³⁹

Saville's case is of particular interest to us for a number of reasons. The details varied considerably between reports, and changed significantly over the brief period between his arrest (on the 16 December) and his trial (on the 15 January). At first, he was simply described as 'a person travelling in a gig', and 'a traveller in the straw hat line'.⁴⁰ On his arrest, he was reported as having a number of further 'Swing' letters in his possession, as well as the sum of £580. Soon after, though, he was being described as 'a man of rather gentlemanly appearance', and 'a respectable looking person' who was travelling in a 'neat, nearly new gig' which was being pulled by 'a beautiful grey horse', and that he had up to £700 and many hundreds more letters about his person.⁴¹ Crucially, *The Times* was even more specific about his mode of transport, reporting that it was 'a green gig', and it went on to remind its readers that 'it will be recollected that that there was a person, who fled in a green gig, detected in the act of setting fire to some stacks near Cambridge'.⁴² These details are important in terms of the invention, and rhetorical *re*invention, of Captain Swing, and Joseph Saville's place within it, because within the general atmosphere of conspiracy and intrigue he seemed to tick all the relevant boxes. From as early as the beginning of November, reports had been circulating in the newspapers of 'strangers' who were responsible for inciting – and even igniting – the fires that lit up southern England. The *Morning Chronicle* reported that 'Two respectably dressed men, who were travelling in a barouche [near Bedfont] stopped a boy in the road, and one of them said: "Who is your Master, Boy?" The boy replied, "Master Sherwin, Sir." "Oh tell him to keep a look out" [they said] and drove on'. The report concluded darkly that 'about ten o'clock ... the same night, [Sherwin's] two barns, several outhouses, and stabling were discovered to be on fire'.⁴³ Similarly, *The Times* reported on 'a man, dressed in shabby genteel, but of manners apparently above the ordinary class', who had been spotted close to fires at Battle in Sussex; whereas the *Examiner* reported that 'previous to several of the late alarming fires in Kent ... a post chaise had arrived in the neighbourhood, and after staying a short time, had gone away again ... a fire has invariably happened the same night'.⁴⁴

39 *Morning Chronicle*, 23 December 1830; *Hull Packet*, 28 December 1830; *The Times*, 23 December 1830.
40 *North Wales Chronicle*, 25 December 1830; *Newcastle Courant*, 25 December 1830.
41 *Jackson's Oxford Journal*, 1 January 1831; *Examiner*, 26 December 1830.
42 *The Times*, 23 December 1830.
43 *Morning Chronicle*, 11 November 1830.
44 *The Times*, 19 November 1830; *Examiner*, November 1830.

Moreover, as we have seen tales of 'gentleman conspirators' were not confined to the press. Correspondents to the Home Office felt it important to note that in Berkshire, Richard Jordan had seen 'two persons in a gig who were with the mob nights and mornings', and that Susan Day had been accosted by 'a man in a [green] gig' who 'was dressed in a dark brown great coat' and asked her about the barns belonging to her employer, Mr. Gibbs.[45] Once again, the green gig makes an appearance: in Essex, too, it was seen near Lambridge, the carriage of a man who had been observed 'in the act of setting fire to a stack', and who was observed to escape with a companion.[46] Unsurprisingly, the men in the green gig were never identified, but when Saville made his appearance on the scene, having confessed to dropping inflammatory letters the length of England, from Yorkshire to the Wash and beyond, even those in high office must have felt they had their man. Indeed, judging from the correspondence of the investigating officer Barton it becomes obvious that Melbourne, the Home Secretary, was instrumental in seeking further information with which to incriminate Saville.

Contrary to E.P. Thompson's later dismissal of Saville as a crank, Barton described him as 'a clever, specious person ... apt to assume the cloak of religion to forward his beliefs'. Again, clearly under the direction of Melbourne himself, Barton searched Saville's house in Gamlingay for evidence that he was directly connected with a fire at Blundisham where, he wrote, 'a person answering the same description [is] suspected as [being] concerned in setting fire to a straw stack'.[47] Curiously, despite the fact that no evidence was offered at his trial linking Saville to the fire at Blundisham, the self-confessed signatory of a thousand 'Swing' letters is known to have been there on the day that it occurred, and even, to an extent, incriminated himself in a letter that he sent to his wife, and that was later copied by Barton. Having arrived in the village in the early evening, Saville was roused by 'a cry of fire which made the village naturally in a bustle indeed'. He noted that the fire was in a hayrick down the street from his lodgings, 'very near many thatched Barnes', and that it might have taken 'a whole row of houses down'. He writes that he went out to watch the fire, but rather than helping to extinguish it, 'placed myself in a stable, rather seeing the straw in a blaze', whereupon he was accosted by a local gentleman who questioned his identity: 'A stranger I replied. Pray Sir says he, May I ask where you are from? Yes Sir I am at Mr

45 TNA, HO52/6/128, 131 Depositions of Richard Jordan of Langeat and Susan Day of East Lockinge, n.d.
46 TNA, HO52/7/373, Correspondence of R.G. Ward of Harlow, 8 December 1830.
47 TNA, HO52/10/94, Correspondence of J. Barton, 20 December 1830.

Paters [his lodgings] by which answer he was appeased'. He finished his account by stating ominously, '[t]his is something like Eliza's foretelling, but I am at liberty yet'.[48] Whatever the reason for Saville's light treatment, and the fact that the authorities chose not to pursue him for the Blundisham fire, his appearance at the scene and his curious activities as an acolyte of 'Swing' fed the feverish appetite of those in government, in the offices of the local and national press, and in the drawing rooms of southern England for tales of conspiracy and intrigue.

With Saville's case firmly in mind, and with the clarity of two centuries' distance, we can see that Captain Swing had a strange and symbiotic relationship with the events in the countryside in the autumn of 1830. Starting life as an anonym (first around Dover, and then countrywide) he quickly became both a synonym and a metonym for those who wrote the story of the disturbances as they took place. 'Swing' functioned both to simplify and to make a kind of narrative sense of those elements of the story that were otherwise too perplexing to understand or too concerning to contemplate, and in particular the widespread resort to arson. Amid the pre-reform fervour of 1830, radical agitation and nearby revolution seemed to be everywhere, and in many ways it made more sense to see the hidden hand of conspirators in green gigs – at least, in the offices of Whitehall and the overstuffed parlours of Kensington – than it did to recognise that long-term structural change could be the catalyst for such profoundly destructive (and, to many, fundamentally un-English) activities among ordinary agricultural labourers. For those closer to the action, though, it was a very different story: no matter how avidly they followed the melodrama of Swing as it unfolded in the press, they were under few illusions about the long-term effects of deprivation, denial and distress.

Thomas Whittet of Bourne was clear that the disturbances were due to: '[t]he poverty which compelled the farmer to use the threshing-machine [and] bore down the labourer to unprecedented distress, and drove him to desperation'; T. Baker of Whitburn near Durham was clear, even some distance from the centre of events, that 'I believe the refusal of Parliament to listen to the voice of the Poor combined with Parochial Tyranny, to have been the cause of the heartburnings and rick-burnings of 1830 and 1831'.[49] Some local commentators were even more precise in their diagnosis, such as Mr. Rolph, the Surgeon of Rochford, Essex:

48 TNA, HO52/10/100–1, Joseph Saville to Mary Saville, 13 November 1830 [copied by J. Barton].
49 *Report from the Select Committee on the Poor Laws*, 1834, Appendix B1, 'Rural Queries', Part 5, Question 8, pp. 50, 165.

> The use of thrashing-machines threw many Labourers out of employment at that period of the year when they used to be employed in the barns instead of the fields. Low and insufficient wages were also the result of this machinery. They had no land or garden of their own to cultivate. They were made solely dependent for their subsistence on the wages of their daily labour, or the Poor Rates. The waste and poor grounds were entirely monopolised. Land had become so valuable that even the Commons were taken from the poor, and inclosed. They thus became entirely destitute. A general spirit of insubordination and outrage seized them. They demolished those machines which they thought superseded human labour, a separation of interests and affections took place between the rich and poor, and all the bitter hatred and revolting circumstances of a servile war ensued.[50]

It took the authorities, no less than the majority of popular opinion, a considerable time to accept the Surgeon's diagnosis, but eventually even they were forced to abandon tales of Irish patriots and French revolutionaries in the face of overwhelming evidence to the contrary.

Of the 1,976 men tried at the five Special Commissions (and the many hundreds more tried at the county assizes) none was found to have been a major conspirator or to have been motivated by anything more than the most basic political inclination.[51] Yet this is not to say that the political ferment that saturated the press – radical and reactionary alike – was without influence. Notwithstanding the lack of evidence to suggest a *direct* connection between radical agitation and events in the countryside, contemporaries of all persuasions agreed that the general clamour for reform was nonetheless a factor in the disturbances. George Wrotham of Kent suggested that 'much harm was also done by the press, by the writings of the Cobbetts and Carlisles [sic]', whereas the Rector of Michaelmersh, Hampshire, believed it was down to 'inflammatory publications, and grievances from denial of customary indulgences and vexatious lowering of wages'.[52] This view was articulated most succinctly by Edward Gibbon Wakefield, in his celebrated postscript on the career of Captain Swing, when he wrote that: 'The first main cause of the crime is misery ... [but] Partial instruction, and great political excitement being added to misery, the effect is produced'.[53]

---

50   Ibid., p. 184.
51   See Hobsbawm and Rudé, *Captain Swing*, pp. 253–64.
52   Ibid., pp. 268, 423.
53   E. Gibbon Wakefield, *Swing Unmasked: or the Causes of Rural Incendiarism*, cited in the *Leeds Mercury*, 4 January 1832.

As contemporaries came to terms with the true complexity that lay behind the disturbances, Captain Swing underwent a further transformation, and as the memory of the main events of October and November 1830 faded he shifted from being a useful synonym for all that was confusing and most disturbing about the work of rick-burners to something of a spokesman for those who opposed the remnants of 'Old Corruption'. In February 1832, *The Satirist* published 'The British Silk Weaver's Lament', aimed at those who continued to resist reform at any price:

> While ELLIS, LAWSON, GLADSTANES, too,
> Make merry with the thought,
> Let them with cruel SEWELL view
> The mis'ry they have brought;
> To deathless fame while they aspire,
> Time, on the constant wing,
> Will puff such fame to endless fire,
> Cooked up by CAPTAIN SWING.[54]

A year later the *Morning Chronicle* reported a parliamentary debate on the Corn Laws in which Mr. Duffie was quoted as saying:

> Philosopher Swing – the greatest philosopher of modern times, would give them the best reason [for repeal]. He would not destroy the peasantry. He would do all to improve them, for he has not forgotten the words of Goldsmith –
>
> "A bold peasantry, their country's pride,
> When once destroyed can never be supplied".[55]

Clearly, for those in the mainstream for whom 'reform' turned out to be more of a frustration than a triumph, 'Philosopher Swing' was a lot more than just as a pantomime figure with a fire ball and a hidden hand, and by 1834 even they could see some merit in his actions.

Unsurprisingly, Swing continued to shift and change his identity long after the events that gave him life faded to a distant memory. Within a few years, he was a 'predial Chartist'; within a few more, he was the subject of a tame Edwardian thriller based on the disturbances.[56] In more recent times, he was the subject of an agitprop play in the 1970s, appeared

54 *The Satirist*, 5 February 1832.
55 *Freeman's Journal*, 28 February 1833; *The Morning Chronicle*, 1 February 1834.
56 *The Labourers' Friend Magazine, for Disseminating Information on the Advantages of Allotments of Land to the Labouring Classes* (London, 1840), p. 54; C.H. Avery, "*Captain Swing*": *A Tale of the 1830 Riots* (London, 1907).

eponymously on a successful album in the 1980s, and is currently masquerading as a five-piece band on the folk-roots circuit.[57] But it is as the rhetorical embodiment of the fears, hopes and expectations of the public mind at a time of great excitement that he really came to life, a metonymical figure that gave shape and substance to so much that was otherwise unintelligible. Swing undoubtedly became the puppet of propagandists on both sides of the ideological divide, from Charles Molloy Westmacott to Richard Carlile, and from the Henry Hetherington to the SPCK, but in the end he had a much wider application even than that. He was a protean figure, available to newspapermen and pamphleteers, but also to ordinary members of the concerned middle classes who craved a rational explanation for the events of Autumn 1830. In other words, though peripheral to the actual mobbings and attacks of arson, he was absolutely central to how they came to be described and understood: in the final analysis Jack Swing was not only the 'greatest Reformer', he was anything the public wanted him to be.

57 P.A. Thompson, 'Captain Swing at the Penny Gaff' (unpublished, first performed at the Unity Theatre, London, 1971); Michelle Shocked, *Captain Swing* (Mercury Records, 1989); for the band Captain Swing, see http://www.captainswing.pwp. blueyonder. co.uk/ (accessed 16 November 2009).

'The Owslebury Lads'

Alun Howkins

On 23 November 1830 in the Hampshire village of Owslebury a 'large crowd' of men broke agricultural machinery on several different farms. They also demanded a raise in wages; that farmers' rents and tithes be reduced; bread, beer, and payment for their work in breaking the machines.

Nearly seventy years later, in March 1906, the folk song collector George B. Gardiner took down a song called 'The Mob Song' or 'The Owslebury Lads' from a 68 year old man called James Stagg in Winchester. Shortly after this his collaborator H.E.D. Hammond noted the same song from the same singer.[1] This song is unique in that it is the only one about Swing which has survived in the oral tradition.[2] Unknown to Hammond or Gardiner the song (without a tune) had already been noted down by the Rev. T.E. Roach, Vicar of Twyford about 4 miles from Owslebury, and published in a local antiquarian journal.[3]

The version common to Hammond and to Gardiner runs as follows:

---

1 There are two versions of the song in the Vaughan Williams Memorial Library, Cecil Sharp House, London [hereafter VWML]. They are identical. The one collected by Gardiner is in VWML, George B. Gardiner MSS, H204. It was also collected from what seems to be the same man by H.E.D. Hammond, VWML, Hammond MSS, H333.

2 The Round Index shows none in any of the major collections. More interestingly, and perhaps surprisingly, there appear to be no printed broadsides. The only references I can find to 'Swing' are in three 'topical catalogue songs' in the Harding collection in the Bodleian Library, Oxford. One, with no printer, 'Odds and Ends of the Year 1830', (Harding B25 (1390)) contains the verse : What do you think of bold Captain Swing/I think through the country he has done a wicked thing/He has caused great destruction in England and France/If justice overtakes him on nothing he'll dance'. The same verse occurs in 'The Odds and Ends of the Present Date, 1831' printed by J.V. Quick in Clerkenwell. (Harding B 13 (293)). A third ballad printed by Catnach at Seven Dials, 'Something or other Starts New Everyday' contains the lines: 'It would be something to lay hold of great Captain Swing/In summer, or autumn or winter, or spring....' (Firth c. 16 (34)). My thanks to Vic Gammon for guiding me to these.

3 [Rev.] T.E.Roach, 'The Riots of 1830', *Hampshire Notes and Queries* 8 (1896), 98.

> The thirtieth of November last eighteen hundred and thirty,
> Our Owslebury lads they did prepare all for the machinery,
> And when they did get there, my eye, how they let fly
> The machinery flew to pieces in the twinkling of an eye.
>
> Chorus: The mob, such a mob you never had seen before.
> And if you live for a hundred years you never will no more.
>
> Oh, then to Winchester we were sent our trial for to take,
> And if we do having nothing said our counsel we shall keep,
> When the judges did begin, I'm sorry for to say,
> So many there were transported for life and some was cast to die.
>
> Sometimes our parents they comes in for to see us all,
> Sometimes they bring us 'bacco or a loaf that is so small,
> Then we goes into the kitchen and sits all round about,
> There is so many of us that we are very soon smoked out.
>
> At six o'clock in the morning our turnkey he comes in,
> With a bunch of keys all in his hand tied up all in a ring,
> And we can't get any further than back and forward the yard,
> A pound and a half of bread a day and don't you think it hard.
>
> A six o'clock in the evening the turnkey he comes round,
> The locks and bolts they rattle like the sounding of a drum,
> And we are all locked up all in the cells so high,
> And there we stay till morning whether we lives or dies.
>
> And now to conclude and to finish my new song,
> I hope you gentlemen round me will think that I'm not wrong,
> For all the poor of Hampshire for the rising of their wages
> I hope that none of our enemies will know for the want of places.[4]

This is a triumphant song – a fact emphasised by its up beat tune and the repetition of the phrase 'the mob' as a chorus. It has little in the way of sorrow, regret or repentance which so often characterise crime/confession ballads,[5] or other materials associated with Swing. For example the simple titles of the 'True Account of the Life and Death of Swing the Rick Burner', which also contained the 'Confession of Thomas

---

4   VWML, H.E.D.Hammond MSS, H33, George B.Gardiner MSS, H204
5   For a discussion of these in an earlier period see J.A. Sharpe, '"Last Dying Speeches" Religion, Ideology and Public Execution in Seventeeth-Century England', *Past & Present* 107 (1985).

Goodman' speak volumes for their tone.[6] In contrast the very title given to Hammond's version 'Mob-Song', like its chorus is an evocative assertion of the power of the crowd. The last verse, in common with many popular ballads of the period ends with the hope of better times (the raising of wages) and obscure wish that our enemies might 'know' for the want of places (Roach's version has 'live'). It also identifies both the singer via the first person narrative and the listener via the inclusive 'our' with the cause of the mob.

Even in all this the song is unusual, but it becomes more so. There are hundreds of nineteenth-century songs about 'real' events, and many of those are about radical moments, for example Peterloo and most notably 'General Ludd'.[7] These were mostly printed as broadsides in urban areas either by radical printers or by the ordinary traders simply seeking to make a few shillings. They were normally written by 'wordsmiths' for a penny a line or less. However the 'Owslebury Lads' is not like that at all. The song has never been found in printed form anywhere, nor does it appear, despite Gardiner's wish to link it to 'The Lancashire Boys', as a local variant of a different text from elsewhere in Britain. This suggests it is a very local product. Unfortunately we cannot ask James Stagg, and Hammond and Gardiner, like most early folk song collectors, had little interest in their informants and he was no exception. Gardiner gives Stagg's age as 68. This means it is likely that he was James Stagg born in Morestead, about three miles from Owslebury, in 1841. He lived all his life within a few miles of Owslebury, starting his working life as a living-in farm servant aged ten and ending it as a farm labourer and lodger. He never married. Having been born 10 years after Swing, and in an area where there were a number of riots in November 1830, he must have known the song's significance – the text after all is hardly ambiguous – and been able to relate it to his community's history.

Oddly the Rev. Roach is more interesting. His version of the song, which differs in slight but unimportant ways from that collected by Hammond and Gardiner, he says he took down 'from the lips of an old man, now bedridden, who, as a lad of seventeen was present on the occasion referred to in the first line'. This kind of statement, used to give credibility to the song and singer, is commonly made about singers of songs of 'real' events. However, the old man who gave his initials (M.H.) but not his name to Roach gives a very accurate account of the 23 November, and its aftermath. He also claimed his brother, who had also

---

6 Reproduced in I. Dyck, *William Cobbett and Rural Popular Culture* (Cambridge, 1992), pp. 172–73.
7 On Ludd, see K. Binfield. *The Writings of the Luddites* (Baltimore, 2004).

been present, wrote the song. M.H. said that in later years that he 'has had many a pot of beer from singing it'.[8]

I

I want to take the song as the starting point for a wander across Owslebury's 'Downs' and still unenclosed Commons, and to follow the 'Owslebury Lads' down some rather odd and unlikely lanes and bye ways. To call this a study in micro history is a bit grand but I do think in this one case, albeit a very unusual one, we can see some of the bigger 'problems' of 'Swing' and popular disturbance which a new generation of scholars, well represented in this collection, are addressing in such innovative ways.[9] As we shall see the 'case' of some of those involved at Owslebury has attracted some notice from historians in that the events in the village have been singled out as ones in which farmers were especially involved. That is certainly the case, but even that is much more complex than we have hitherto thought. To an extent this is a function of the sources we rely on for 'Swing' which, as we shall see, tend to refer to most 'rioters' as 'clowns' or 'the mob'. However, the song – for all its limitations as a source – suggests some of the motives for the behaviour of those whose voices are seldom heard in the standard sources.

The events which took place in Owslebury were part of a series of outbreaks in that area of Hampshire over 22 and 23 November 1830, the two most disturbed days in the county. The village sits on high ground more or less in the middle of a kind of Swing epicentre bordered by the modern A272 to the North, the A31 to the East, the A27 to the South and the M3 to the West. In this area, between 19 and 28 November, there were ten outbreaks of various kinds which came to the notice of the authorities. It is possible there were outbreaks in Owslebury on two days, the 22 and 23 November, but I can find no direct evidence of this at present. Certainly there were 'problems' on 23 November. The spark was probably a wage riot and demand for tithe and rent reductions at Corhampton about 5 miles away on the 22nd, as a labourer Nicolas Freemantle was charged for offences at both Corhampton and Owslebury.

The 'Owslebury Lads' began their work early on the 23 November. Between 9 or 10 in the morning of 23 November Richard Rest was 'at plough', when he saw 'a mob of 20 persons coming towards him ... they

8   Roach, 'The Riots of 1830', 96.
9   In addition to pieces in this collection I think the work of Katrina Navickas on Luddism is especially interesting: see her 'The Search for General Ludd: the Mythology of Luddism', *Social History* 30 (2005) and 'Moors, Fields, and Popular Protest in South Lancashire and the West Riding of Yorkshire, 1800–1848', *Northern History* 46 (2009).

took his horses from the plough, and ... said that he should go along with them'.[10] However, by that time it seems likely they had already broken machines at Farmer Young's, who was a substantial farmer of 200 acres employing eight men, Mr Deacle's, at Marwell Farm, Mr Smith's at Hurst Farm and a Mr Lownde's farm. At some point James Knight at Baybridge was 'robbed,' presumably the victim of a demand for money and or food. Between 11 and 11.30 they arrived at the most substantial house in the parish, Marwell Hall. This belonged to Lady Mary Long and although she was in the house their demands for 'money and victuals' were dealt with by her butler. By now the mob had grown to 'more than 100 persons'. These included significantly two farmers. Mr Deacle, who farmed Marwell Farm as a tenant, and John Boyes who was a copyholder of 50 acres on Colden Common to the north west of Owslebury. They left Marwell and went to Mr Debenalls (this is probably Mr Dipnall described in 1841 as a yeoman) at then to Longwood House where they arrived at about 3 o'clock.

Longwood House was the Hampshire seat of Lord Northesk. He had been third in command to Nelson at Trafalgar, but in 1830 he was in London where he was to die in May 1831. Here the mob was met by Moses Stanbrook, the fifty-year old steward of Lord Northesk. Stanbrook told the Special Assizes at Winchester, 'he heard a great noise, and going up stairs, he saw a mob of men, amongst whom were Adams and Freemantle ... Adams said, "Have you any machinery?"'[11] They were told that there was only an old winnowing machine which was 'no use', but they still insisted on destroying it. They then asked for payment for their work – five sovereigns. Stanbrook told them that Lord Northesk was not at home so any money paid would be his, and that he did not have that amount in cash. After some arguments they agreed to take a £5 note. Stanbrook said he had paid the men because he was afraid that if he did not 'damage would be done to the property'. This view was supported by a servant, Grace Nott, who told the court that 'they declared they if they had not got the money they would break all our windows'.[12] It was for the events at Longwood that most of the 'Owslebury Lads' were initially charged.

After collecting their money the mob left Longwood and went to Owslebury Downs. Here they met with 'a party of men from Upham and Waltham (nearby villages) all of whom declared their intention of sharing the money'.[13] They were then drawn up 'by the score' over 100 in

10   *The Times*, 30 December 1830.
11   *Hamphire Telegraph and Sussex Chronicle*, 3 January 1831.
12   *The Times*, 30 December 1830.
13   *Hampshire Telegraph*, 3 January 1831.

all, and the money was shared out – 2s. for each. They then dispersed with many of them going to a public house remembered in 1897 as 'an old posting house on the road between Winchester and Bishops Waltham, now the farm of White Flood', which still stands.[14]

II

In all 17 men and one woman were charged as a result of Captain Swing's visit to Owslebury, mostly for the breaking of the winnowing machine, 'robbery' and an assault on Moses Stanbrook at Longwood House. We can reconstruct something about most of those charged and their 'victims', and that basic material is presented here in tabular form.

Looking at Table I, there are ways in which the 'Owslebury Lads' fit closely with what we know of Swing rioters, but there are others in which they differ radically. Holland et al estimate 61 per cent of Swing offenders were agricultural labourers which is the exact figure at Owslebury if we assume all the 'unknowns' were labourers which seems likely. However then it goes wrong . We have also one tradesman, a carpenter, a shepherd, three farmers and a farmer's wife. Since Holland et al have only five farmers and no farmers' wives, and only three shepherds in their national sample, Owslebury starts to look very odd indeed. This is compounded by the age range. The national sample very clearly shows a clustering of offenders aged between 19 and 25. At Owslebury only five were in that age range, while seven were over thirty.[15]

It seems likely that these unusual features did not go unnoticed by the authorities. Although timing is a bit unclear, it seems probable that the three farmers Boyes, Deacle and Smith were all arrested on 24 or 25 of November, and eventually bailed. Of the seven who appeared in the first case only James Fussell and John Hoare were under 30. Also included in that group were the carpenter, William Barnes, who was also Parish Clerk of Owslebury and the shepherd William Adams. All this suggests a fairly selective initial policy of arrest directed at parish 'leaders'. Indeed Mr Sergeant Wilde, who prosecuted Boyes, said he 'believed (him) to have been mainly instrumental in fomenting much of the riot and disorder which had occurred in the county'.[16] Only later it seems were more 'ordinary' Swing offenders taken.

We can see this even more clearly in the case of the two farmers John Boyes and Thomas Deacle. John Boyes already has more than a footnote

14 Roach, 'The Riots of 1830', 98.
15 See M. Holland (ed.), *Swing Unmasked. The Agricultural Riots of 1830 –1832 and their Wider Implications* (Milton Keynes, 2005).
16 *House of Commons Debates*, 21 July 1831, vol. 5, cc. 158 –59.

to history. In the Hammonds' *Village Labourer* he appears as an independent small farmer who stands up for the labourers against parson and squire – and there is a good deal of truth in that judgement.[17] In November 1830, he was nearly 50 years old, and a farmer of 50 acres at Colden Common in the north west of Owslebury parish. However, his land was held by copyhold, an ancient form of tenure, which gave many of the rights of freehold but could be taken back in certain circumstances by the lord of the manor. Such tenures were rapidly being extinguished during the eighteenth and nineteenth centuries as part of the rationalisation of capitalist agriculture. His copyhold, with its sense of an older world, as well as his small farm on the edge of the still unenclosed common, gives Boyes the aura of the independent yeoman so beloved of Cobbett, and reproduced in the Hammonds' account.

In 1831, Boyes was married to Faith, who had been born in London, and had 10 children, the youngest aged six. He also had some standing in his community. The three character witnesses at his trial were all farmers. Thomas White of Bishop Stoke, Caleb Howton of South Stoneham and Charles White, a farmer and innkeeper of Owslebury who was one of the 'victims' of the 23 November. All had known Boyes for many years and testified to his honesty and industry, as well as stressing that he owned his own land.[18] He was also a member of Owslebury vestry.

Boyes joined the 'Owslebury Lads' at Farmer Smith's. He was, he said 'going (along the Marwell Road) with some sacks to be mended, when he heard a great noise being made by the mob, who were breaking a machine at Mrs Smiths'.[19] When Boyes arrived Mrs Smith asked him to come to the house and explained that she was frightened that the mob would 'do more injury than they already effected unless something was done'. Thomas Deacle (called Diggles in *The Times* and Dagle in the *Hampshire Telegraph*) was already in 'Mrs Smith's parlour'. He, Boyes and Mrs Smith then drew up 'a piece of paper' which they all signed.

17 J.L. and Barbara Hammond, *The Village Labourer* (London, 1966) pp. 282 –83. The Hammonds call him Boys as do some other contemporary accounts. Others refer to him as Boyce, see *Cobbett's Political Register* (90 vols, London, 1802 –36), 24 September 1831.
18 *The Times*, 30 Dec 1830; *Hampshire Telegraph*, 3 January 1831
19 *Hampshire Telegraph*, 3 January 1831.There is some confusion here. *The Times* reports refer to 'Farmer Smith' and a substantially similar account to the one used above changes everything to 'he' and 'Mr'. There is a Smith on the 1841 Census described as Yeoman – 65 year old John Smith of Hurst Farm who has a wife Phoebe aged 60. I am assuming because the *Hampshire Telegraph* material is more detailed that it is correct in referring to Mrs Smith. It also makes more sense of the appeal to Boyes as a man as well as somebody known to the labourers

Table 1: The 'Owslebury Lads'.

Name	Age	Occupation	Address	Offence	Sentence	Other details
Adams, Wm.	35	Shepherd	Whites Cottage Owslebury Down	Robbery/assault/riot	Death recorded. Transportation for life.	Wife alone in 1841. 7 children ?
Barnes, Wm.	42	Carpenter	Pitcroft(?) Lane	Robbery	Acquitted	Parish Clerk Prosecution witness
Batchelor Benj.	32	Agricultural Labourer	Fish Pond Colden Common	Robbery assault/theft	Acquitted	
Batchelor John				Conspiracy to raise wages	Not apprehended	Tried with Deacle, Lent 1831 'copyholder' Signed paper tried twice
Boyes, John	49?	Farmer	Colden Common/ Henshing		7 years transportation	Tried twice
Boyes, Wm.	24	Agricultural Labourer		Robbery/assault/ Riot	Acquitted	
Churcher, Chas.	29	Agricultural Labourer	Droxford?	Robbery/assault	Acquitted	
Deacle, Thos.	31?	Farmer		Riot/conspiracy/	Acquitted	Sues magistrates Signed paper
Deacle, Caroline		Farmer's wife		As above but charge dropped before court	No bill	
Freemantle, Nicolas	30	Agricultural Labourer?	Roughhay Lane	Robbery/assault	Death recorded. Transported for life	Also active at Corhampton 'genteel looking'
Fussell, James	29	Unemployed		Robbery	7 year	

Name	Age	Occupation	Address	Crime	Outcome	Other
Hayter, Benj.	19			Machine breaking	acquitted	
Hayter, John	24			Machine breaking	Acquitted	
Hillier, George	25			Machine breaking	Acquitted	
Hoare, John	19	Agricultural Labourer	Braybridge	Demanding money	Acquitted	
James, Orton					Not apprehended	Tried with Deacle Lent 1831
Smith, Robert	55	Farmer		Conspiracy to lower rents and tithes	No bill	Tried with Deacle Lent 1831 signed paper

Table II: The Owslebury Victims

Name	Age	Occupation	Address	Crime	Other
Deacle, Thos.		Tenant farmer	Marwell Farm Owslebury	Machine Broken	Urged its destruction. Signed paper
Debenhall or Dipnall ?		Farmer	Greenhill	Machine broken	
Knight, James		Independent means	Baybridge? Greenhill	Assault/robbery	
Long, Lady Mary		Independent means / rentier	Marwell Hall	Robbery	Signed paper
Lownde				Machine broken?	Signed paper
Smith (Mrs)		Farmer		Machine broken	Signed paper
Stradbrooke Moses	50	Steward	Longwood House	Machine broken/robbery/assault	Signed paper
White, Charles		Farmer/innkeeper			
Young, Henry	64	Farmer 206 acres	Owslebury Street	Machine broken	Signed paper

The piece of paper was an agreement to be signed by all farmers and landowners in the parish. It read: 'We, the undersigned, are willing to give 2s. per day for able bodied married men, and 9s. per week for single men, on consideration of our rents and tithes being abated in proportion'.[20] All farmers who were visited by the mob after Mrs Smith were asked to sign the paper, and landlords were asked to sign it 'on the other side to lower (their) rents'. Boyes was asked by Deacle and Mrs Smith if he would go with the mob and present the letter to farmers asking them to sign. This they argued would control the mob's violence and help to resolve what they appeared to believe were legitimate grievances. Boyes agreed and went with the crowd to Marwell Hall and to Rosehill (Longwood House) and possibly elsewhere. This, Boyes said at his trial, was the only role he had taken in the events; above all he insisted he had had no part in demanding money. Furthermore, he argued that his presence had controlled the group and prevented real violence on their part. At the end of the day at the Old Posting House he told the court that:

> The mob came there. After staying there some time, one of them said "We'll meet again tomorrow morning, and get some more". I said, "you have got too much, I am afraid already". Many of them said, "we have; I'll go to my work to-morrow".[21]

As a result of this intervention Boyes claimed the 'mob' did not meet the following day, and there were no further incidents in Owslebury.

Like many of those tried he was, we assume, arrested later, possibly the next day, after somebody had named him. Deacle claimed that those who gave evidence against him were actually rioters:

> (William) Barnes, a carpenter ... stated that during the trials under the Special Commission, ... the jailor (sic) Beckett called him out, and took him to a room where there were Walter Long, a magistrate, and another person who he believed to be Bingham Baring, who told him that he should not be put upon his trial if he would come and swear against Deacle.[22]

Certainly most evidence against Boyes, apart from that given by the 'victims', came from John Smoker, who although a 'rioter' was not

---

20 *The Times*, 30 December 1830.
21 *The Times*, 30 December 1830.
22 Hampshire Record Office (hereafter HRO) 92 M95/F2/10/1 'To the Honourable the Commons of the United Kingdom of Great Britain and Ireland, in Parliament assembled - The Humble Petition of Thomas and Caroline Deacle of Marwell farm, in the Parish of Owselbury (sic), in the County of Hants...'

charged, so we assume had been given immunity or was actually acquitted.

Whatever happened around the arrest and initial interrogation of Boyes he was given bail, probably because of his status as a small farmer. However, his bail did not stop him pushing the cause of wages. Following the same beliefs which had led him to go with the mob on 23 November, on 9 December he attended the vestry meeting in Owslebury and, with other farmers, he agreed that the wages in Owslebury should be 10s. a week over the age of 20, 7s. per week for 17–20 year olds and between 4s. and 5s. a week for 13 –17 year olds. In addition married men with more than three children were to be given 6d and a gallon loaf a week for each child. However the vestry saw this settlement as final and said that 'they will not yield to threat or intimidation on the part of any of the men, but will prosecute to the utmost extent of the law, such base conduct'.[23]

While the involvement of farmers in Swing riots has frequently been noticed, trials and convictions of farmers are very unusual and so the involvement, and prosecution of two, Thomas Deacle as well as John Boyes is unique. Deacle is (and was) something of an enigma.[24] In 1831 he was about 30 years old, married to Caroline Deacle and living at Marwell Farm, Owslebury, and since he had a machine destroyed one assumes he was farming it. This is supported by a letter to *The Times* in 1831.[25] In 1851 Marwell Farm consisted of 500 acres and employed 10 full time workers – a substantial holding by any measure.[26] Deacle, in common with most Hampshire farmers, was a tenant.

However, his background was not that of most ordinary farmers. His father, he claimed, was the Rector of Uphill in Somerset, and there certainly was a Thomas Deacle who held that living in the 1820s, while

23 HRO, Top 248/3/10. For a discussion of this kind of action by farmers and others, see A. Randall, *Riotous Assemblies: Popular Protest in Hanoverian England*, (Oxford, 2006), chapters 4, 7, and especially 12.
24 Deacle occurs in the Hammonds who call him both 'a well to do gentleman farmer' (correct) and ' a small farmer' (incorrect). Hammonds, *The Village Labourer*, pp. 278, 287. Ian Dyck gives him more coverage but still appears to believe he was a small farmer, *William Cobbett and Rural Popular Culture*, pp. 178, 181. He occurs more substantially in A.M. Coulson, 'The Revolt of the Hampshire Agricultural Labourer and it's Causes, 1812 –1831', unpublished University of London thesis (1934), pp. 236 –54. Roger Wells in an unpublished paper also refers to him as a 'small farmer' and accepts Baring's assertion in a letter that he was linked to Sutton Scotney, the well known hive of village radicalism. He does not occur in Hobsbawn and Rudé, *Captain Swing* or Holland (ed.), *Swing Unmasked*.
25 *The Times*, 19 July 1831.
26 The National Archives, London, Census Enumerators Books, HO 107.1675 Owlesbury.

his brother was also a clergyman with an income of £2000 a year. 'He himself', he told the court was 'of independent circumstances, and has graduated in the University of Oxford'.[27] Again this seems to have been true. Throughout his trial and subsequently he was referred to as a 'gentleman' or even 'country gentleman' and his wife as a 'lady', and a Thomas Deacle, son of the Vicar of Uphill, was at Lincoln College, Oxford from 1818 to 1821.[28]

He also had at least one very interesting friend – Gideon Mantell, one of the founders of modern geology and a key figure in the early study of fossil remains.[29] Mantell's support for the Deacles, when the latter was brought to court, prompted comments from his friend Charles Lyell in a letter of September 1831: 'Pray let me hear what you had been doing besides writing letters about the Deacles to the great scandal of my tory friends'. The Deacles also attracted further support among Mantell's circle. In a letter to Mantell dated 5 September 1831, the geologist Robert Bakewell commented: 'I was greatly rejoyced to see your hand lifted in the cause of the Deacle's. A more violent outrage was scarcely ever committed & yet they were to be born down by the character of the Barings against direct evidence'. According to the footnotes to the University of Sydney manuscript edition of the Mantell/Lyell correspondence, 'there are several references in Mantell's *Private Journal* during the period 1830 –32 indicating that he was on friendly terms with a Mr Deacle who lived in the Lewes neighbourhood'.[30] All this suggests the Deacle moved well outside the local circle of the ordinary farmers and the county hunt.

What is at first striking is that Deacle's role, and what is more interesting, that of his wife, seems to have been much greater than that of John Boyes. Deacle had his machine broken quite early in the morning of the 23 November, and whether forced or not Deacle then joined the mob. According to a witness he 'gave two sovereigns to the men. A boy in his service was blowing a horn or trumpet along with the crowd, and Deacle called on him to blow up'.[31] Certainly several of the defendants from 23 November named Deacle as their leader. William Adams, said 'Mr

27 *The Times*, 7 March 1831.
28 J. Foster, *Alumni Oxonienses: The Members of the University of Oxford, 1715–1886* (Oxford, 1888).
29 See letter to *The Times*, 19 July 1831
30 *Charles Lyell and Gideon Mantell, 1821 – 1852: Their Quest for Elite Status in English Geology*, ed. A.J. Wennerbom, No. 87. University of Sydney Library, http://ses.library.usyd.edu.au/bitstream/2123/380/2/adt-NU1999.0011whole.pdf. Accessed 23 Nov 2009.
31 *The Times*, 22 July 1831.

Diggles (sic) the farmer, was the man who gave all the orders' and Nicolas Freemantle said 'Diggles ordered me to go to Mrs. Long and demand £10 from them'.[32] Even more unusual was the fact that it was suggested that Deacle's wife Caroline was involved, although the charges against her were withdrawn before their trial. Freemantle said she was present on horseback at another farm where, it was alleged, he had threatened the farmer that if he did not pay and send his men with the mob, 'we shall have a fire'. The 'housekeeper' of the earl of Northesk, recalling the events at Longwood House, claimed that 'a lady on horseback, whom she understood to be Mrs Deacle, accompanied a crowd of peasantry, when they broke a winnowing machine the property of his Lordship'. It was also alleged (by the informer John Smoker) that Mrs Deacle stayed with the mob all day and was present at the dividing up of the money.[33]

There are problems with this evidence, not least that it was never tested in court, but the old man who sang 'The Owlesbury Lads' to the Rev. Roach, and had been with the mob, remembered the person he called 'Mrs D.' who had been out that day and in the evening was at the Old Post House. As they drank their beer she 'was riding up and down and exhorting the men to break their cups if they were not full measure'.[34] Against this Deacle asserted that he, like Boyes, 'was far from giving any encouragement to the mob (and) that he had exerted himself a good deal to prevent the destruction which they had committed'.[35]

The Deacles were arrested on the afternoon of 24 November by two constables and six magistrates in circumstances which, as we shall see below, were to become a national *cause célèbre*, and were bailed on 27 November. However they were not to stand trial with the first lot of the Owslebury men at the Special Commission. Instead they would be tried at the Lent Assizes in 1831.

We know, or can work out quite a lot about Boyes and the Deacles – but what of the rest of the 'mob', those described at Boyes' trial as 'clowns'.[36] All, with the exception of William Adams and William Barnes were described as agricultural labourers. Barnes was a carpenter and parish clerk of Owslebury and spent a great deal of his case insisting he had been 'pressed' by the mob and seeking support from others for his innocence during the trial.[37] He also gave damning evidence against several of his fellows. During the course of the trial many claimed that they were either

32 Ibid
33 Ibid
34 Roach, 'The Riots of 1830', 97
35 *The Times*, 7 March 1831.
36 *The Times*, 30 November 1830.
37 Ibid.

forced by threats or appeals to communal solidarity to join the growing mob – a defence frequently used through out the Swing hearings. For example, William Adams said he was 'at work when I was called away by the mob'. Adams does not say where he was at work but by the time the 'mob' had got to him, they were 100 strong, and were breaking a machine in the field belonging to Mr Deacle. William Boyes said that 'a man came and told me I must go with the mob; if I did not go willingly, they said they would press me and it would be the worse for me'.[38]

In summing up the case against the Owslebury rioters the Judge was at great pains to separate John Boyes from the others arrested. He was, Mr Justice Parker said, 'in a very different station from the rest. He was not a labouring man but a farmer', who was using the mob for his own ends – reducing rents and tithes. The implication was that Boyes was also a leader 'moving in a higher rank of life than the clowns by whom he was surrounded'. Parker ended his summing up by saying that Boyes 'had been sufficiently present to be guilty of robbery, provided the jury should be of the opinion that his presence was a guilty presence'. As clear a direction to find him and the others guilty as one could get.[39]

However, the 'Owslebury Lads' were still being tried by a jury and the jury found Boyes not guilty. It also found the informers William Boyes and William Barnes not guilty as well as Fussell, and Hoare. Only William Adams and Nicholas Freemantle were found guilty of felony for the assault on Moses Stanbrook and the theft of a £5 note from him. They were sentenced to death.[40] Freemantle had already been convicted for offences at Corhampton on 22 November.

But it was not over. Mr Serjeant Wilde, one of the prosecutors at Winchester and later M.P. for Newark-on-Trent was outraged at Boyes acquittal, which he put down to the Jury's 'sympathy for the state of life in which he was placed ....' He wrote that evening to the Attorney General who was sitting in the other court:

> Stating in his opinion, that a man who he believed to have been mainly instrumental in fomenting much of the riot and disorder which had occurred in the county should not be allowed to escape, as there were other indictments brought against him. In this the Attorney General concurred, and by his advice Boyce (sic.) was brought before another jury in another Court.[41]

38 Ibid.
39 Ibid.
40 HRO, 14M50/4. Sentences of Prisoners tried at the Special Commission, Winchester, December 1830.
41 *House of Commons Debates*, 21 July 1831, vol. 5, cc.158–59.

Boyes was tried a second time the following day along with James Fussell, who had also been aquitted earlier. On this occasion Boyes and Fussell were charged with robbing Lady Mary Long at Marwell Hall. Even after the near 200 years since that day at Winchester one has a sense of the desperation of the two men hidden in the single line in the press report, 'the prisoners made no defence',[42] and indeed, one might ask, what would have been the point?

Boyes and Fussell were sentenced to seven years transportation. Fussell, however, had his sentence commuted to imprisonment almost immediately, but, as if to further mark out Boyes, he was swiftly sent to Southampton and put on board the convict ship the 'Eliza'. He arrived in Van Diemen's Land on 28 May 1831.[43]

Thomas Deacle was brought to trial at the Lent Assizes in March 1831.[44] It is not clear why the case was delayed but it gave the judiciary a chance to retry, at the same time, two more of those found innocent by the jury at the Special Commissions – William Boyes and John Hoare. It also brought to the bar the 'respectable farmer' Mr Smith, presumably the farmer in whose parlour the 'piece of paper' had been drawn up on the 23 November and so we can only assume this was an attempt to punish the last of the farmers involved in Owslebury. However, no bill was found against him and he was acquitted. There was also no bill found against Caroline Deacle. But it was to go even more badly wrong in court. William Boyes turned king's evidence and was acquitted, leaving only Deacle and Hoare. However, during the examination of witnesses the 'Counsel for the prosecution said he did not wish to press the case further, the evidence not being in his opinion sufficient to support the indictment'. The reasons here are complex, but in July 1831, under the protection of Parliamentary privilege, Wilde spoke about Deacle as he had about Boyes:

> Looking at the informations against Deacle, at his station in life, and the part he was described to have taken in these proceedings, he thought that he ought to be prosecuted, and in this the Attorney General concurred; ...that the prosecution had not been gone into, he could only attribute to the speedy pacification of the county which followed the first steps taken to bring the guilty parties to justice.[45]

---

42 *Morning Chronicle*, 3 January 1831
43 Archives Office of Tasmania, Convict Records Online: Conduct Books, Con 31-1-4/116. http://search.archives.tas.gov.au/default.aspx?detail=1&type=I&id=CON31/1/4
44 For what follows, see *Hampshire Telegraph*, March 1831
45 *House of Commons Debates*, 21 July 1831, vol. 5 c. 159.

It is also possible, indeed likely that the authorities were no longer happy with proceeding in a case (the one against Deacle at least) which was already causing 'discussion' in Hampshire, and which, in the next few months, was to blow up into a national *cause célèbre*.

In July 1831, Deacle brought a private prosecution against four magistrates and an attorney-at-law for wrongful, aggravated and violent arrest as well as trespass. Among those summoned by Deacle were two members of the Baring family, Francis M.P. for Portsmouth and his cousin Bingham Baring, whose tireless and vengeful pursuit of Swing rioters had made him notorious at least in radical circles. This is not the place to go into the Deacle case in any detail. Very briefly he won but was only awarded £50 damages which were widely regarded as at best an outrage and at worst (and probably correctly) an example of the ruling class looking after its own.[46] Deacle then petitioned Parliament for a Select Committee to examine his treatment and his charges of 'magisterial oppression'. He lost but the debates on his petition in July and September –October 1831 give a fascinating insight into attitudes to Swing, the rioters and the state of the countryside in late 1830.

What is clear is that many, including Serjeant Wilde, the Attorney General and the Barings regarded Boyes and Deacle as ring leaders who had planned the events at Owslebury. However, as Cobbett pointed out,[47] they were only willing to say so publically under Parliamentary privilege. For example, Sergeant Wilde said of Boyes:

> In the course of those investigations, he found, that a certain number of farmers had met together and drawn up a paper addressed to landlords and clergymen, for the purpose of inducing them to lower their rents and tithes. At this meeting there were several whose names were stated, and amongst others this Mr. Deacle, and a man named Boyce. Soon after this, some of the same parties met again, attended by a considerable number of labourers, who pressed others to join; so that, at last, they became formidable in numbers, and proceeded to the houses of several gentlemen in the neighbourhood, at first insisting that the paper for lowering rents and tithes should be signed, then demanding money, and also destroying machinery.[48]

46 For a cogent argument on these lines see *Cobbett's Weekly Political Register*, 23 July 1831. For an account of the case see *The Times* 15 July 1831; *Cobbett's Political Register*, 23 July 1831. See also Deacle's Petition to the House of Commons. There is a copy in HRO 92 M95/F2/10/1
47 *Cobbett's Political Register*, 30 July 1831.
48 *House of Commons Debates*, 21 July 1831, vol. 5, c. 158.

Francis Baring, one of those sued by Deacle and, like Bingham Baring, an indefatigable hunter of peasants, spoke at length on Deacle under the same privilege:

> A good deal had been said of the station of the Deacles. He was willing to allow, that they were much above the ordinary condition of the farmers in that part of the country; he was quite willing to admit, that their station was much above the class of those who had been charged with the proceedings which were unhappily, at that time, going on in this part of the county; but that only made their conduct the more reprehensible. He had seen, with pain, and with sorrow, the ignorant and deluded labourer guilty of acts which required the immediate interposition of the strong arm of the law; but when he found a person like Mr. Deacle, a man above the common rank of farmers, employing his influence to encourage the commission of the offences of which the poor labourers had been guilty – inciting them to frame-breaking, encouraging them to demand the reduction of rent and tithes, and accompanying them to demand money, ... when he saw all this, he thought, that such a person was deserving of the immediate attention of the Magistracy, ... It was with that view the arrest took place, under the circumstances which had been described; and he was bound to say, that after the execution of the warrant against the Deacles, they heard no more of any outrages in that part of the country.[49]

We are now a long way from Owslebury Moor – but we will go further yet. Immediately following that debate Deacle and then Boyes gained a new ally – William Cobbett. On 23 July the *Political Register* published a lengthy account of the Deacle case and the subsequent debate in the Commons written by Cobbett'.[50] In the following week Cobbett continued his fight for Deacle but now he had heard of 'Farmer Boyes' and 'the infamous libel' which had been published against him.[51] But Cobbett's involvement was more than simply support through the pages of the *Political Register*. As Ian Dyck has shown Cobbett was in touch with Deacle certainly from July to October 1831. He had a hand in drawing up the Deacles' petition to Parliament of 29 July 1831, helped with public statements and arranged for their legal support.[52] It is also likely that he had a hand in the 20 petitions which were sent to the Commons asking for a Select Committee to investigate the Deacle affair between July and October 1831.[53]

49 *House of Commons Debates*, 21 July 1831, vol. 5, cc. 151 –52.
50 *Cobbett's Political Register*, 23. July 1831.
51 Ibid., 30 July 1831.
52 Dyck, *William Cobbett and Rural Popular Culture*, p. 181, see also fns. 100, 101.
53 These can be traced through the *House of Commons Journal*.

The Deacles' petition was finally debated in the House of Commons at the end of September 1831.[54] Despite some support it was clear that the Government was against a Select Committee and the motion to set one up was defeated by 78 votes to 31. Following this defeat the petitions for the Deacles come to an end, but Cobbett continued to press their case until at least July 1832 as part of his continued struggle with the Barings. However, Deacle seems to have had enough. Cobbett suggested in 1832 that Deacle was considering going to America, a course already hinted at by Mantell, and a possibility which Cobbett declared would be a disaster, not only for Deacle but for justice and liberty.

The ending, if that is what it is, is bizarre. In 1835 Thomas Deacle appeared before the magistrates in Taunton charged with challenging to fight the rector of his parish over the alleged seduction of his wife Caroline. The bench ordered him to keep the peace and he was fined one shilling.[55] Stranger still was the career of Caroline Deacle. In April 1836 the *Manchester Times* carried the following report from a Bristol paper:

> The young lady who recently made her début at our theatre is the Mrs Deacle whose case with the Barings, about four years since, excited so much interest throughout the kingdom in the House of Commons.[56]

During the next 5 to 6 years, Caroline Deacle made regular appearances as an actor in melodrama throughout the English provinces, and briefly in London. In 1844 *The Era* reported that she was in India where she had recently married Captain Andrews of the 52nd Regiment of Native Infantry and continued that 'they were going to Bombay to undertake the management of the theatre there'.[57]

What then of Thomas? It is possible he went to America, and Caroline claimed he was dead in order to marry Captain Andrews. However, given she was sufficiently well known in the theatre to be regularly reviewed that seems unlikely. More likely is that Thomas is the Tomas Deacle who died in or possibly before 1843 in Newton Abbott, Devon. His death and her move to India might account for why neither appears on the 1841 census.

The subsequent history of John Boyes was less colourful if more harrowing. As at his trial, the local elite continued to hunt him down. He was, as we saw above, a copyholder. This meant that in certain circumstances the lord of the manor could have the copyhold refused and the holder evicted. At the manorial court at the end of 1831, the lord of

---

54 *House of Commons Debates*, 27 September 1831, vol. 7, cc. 678–701.
55 *Hampshire Telegraph*, 3 April 1835.
56 *Manchester Times*, 2 April 1836.
57 *The Era*, 1 September 1844.

manor, Lady Caroline Mildmay argued that that since Boyes' was a felon his property was 'escheated and forfeited' to the manor – that was to herself. Arising from this a petition signed by 'owners and occupiers in the county of Hampshire' was presented to the King in August 1833. Interestingly this petition argued for Boyes' innocence on exactly the same grounds that had been used earlier to condemn him – that he had been misled by his 'more opulent neighbours'. It also repeated his claims at his trial that he had gone with the mob to control them. On that basis the petition 'begged' that Boyes should be pardoned and returned to the 'arms of his disconsolate wife and family ...'[58]

It is unclear what happed to the petition despite the high hopes held for it, but Boyes was pardoned, along with many other Swing rioters, in October 1834 through, the *Hampshire Telegraph* claimed, the good offices of Lord Palmerstone.[59] The 1841 Census shows John Boyes living in Owslebury, while that of 1851 shows him as living in Colden Common as a famer of 50 acres employing five men.

Of the rest of the 'Owslebury Lads', William Adams and Nicolas Freemantle were sentenced to death, and John Fussell to prison for seven years. According to the available evidence, it seems that John Bachelor and James Orton was never caught. The rest were acquitted. The sentences against Adams and Freemantle were commuted to transportation for life. Here, for now at least, we lose sight of Freemantle. It is a common name in the area, but he is not on any of the convict registers I have been able to check. Of Adams we know more as he occurs in Kent and Townsend's fine study of the men of Wessex who were transported to New South Wales after Swing.[60] Adams was sent to Portsmouth in early February 1831 and then to the convict ship the 'Eleanor' which arrived in New South Wales on the 25 June. As the judge had promised him, he remained there for the rest of his natural life. On arrival he was assigned to Thomas Bartie who had 2560 acres of virgin land on the Williams River. By 1837 he seem to have been working as a 'free' worker, which would fit the fact that many Swing rioters received pardons after 4 or 5 years. He died in 1887 far from Hampshire where he had started – but he had his own land something he could never have dreamt of in Owslebury.

---

58 *Morning Chronicle*, 12 August 1833.
59 *Hampshire Telegraph*, 20 October 1834.
60 D. Kent and N. Townsend, *The Convicts of the Eleanor. Protest in Rural England. New Lives in Australia*, (Sydney, 2002). What follows is based on their account.

III

This journey of five years has taken us a long way from Owslebury and its song – but I want to return to that now by way of a kind of conclusion. At the most simple level, what is the relationship between the song and what happened in Owslebury? The first answer has to be nothing at all. The song does not mention Boyes or Deacle, lowered rents or lowered tithes – it talks instead of the mob, of their experience and in the end of their hopes. It not a song for or about Boyes or Deacle, but a song of the mob – of the young men – of those, who wanted to have a pint and toast all ' the poor of Owslebury', 'the raising of their wages' and some obscure damnation to their enemies. It is striking that in the song's lyrics it is 'parents' not wives and families who visit the prisoners in Winchester. This is the voice of the 'Owslebury Lads', not the farmers or the old and respectable caught by desperation in a social war they didn't want, but the young and the devil-may-care. We can still hear it there in the song – the voice of Little Devil Dout from the Mummers Play taken from house to house round the Parish every winter – raising a few pence in hard times – very like the processions of 23 November 1830.

> In comes I Little Devil Dout
> With My big broom I'll sweep you out
> Money I want and money I crave
> Else I'll sweep you into your graves.

But we can also hear a different voice – the voice of the betrayal of young men sent to Winchester, transported or even hanged for something nobody had told them was even a crime. 'M.H.', who gave the song to the Rev. Roach, seems to say that his brother who wrote the song was caught but not transported in October 1830. So who do we have as our 'Owslebury Lad'? Perhaps John Hoare or Benjamin Hayter, both the right age, both arrested and acquitted, although they probably spent at least some time in Winchester Gaol, but not John Boyes or Thomas Deacle.

Yet Deacle and Boyes were there, and almost certainly played some kind of leadership role – even if they were very different. Here we find another Swing, one perhaps familiar through the writing of Roger Wells, who has argued for some thirty years for the Swing rising to be seen as much more political, in a conventional and radical sense, than most of those who have written on the riots. Wells has noticed Deacle, but like the Hammonds he refers to him as a small farmer.

Intriguingly, Wells argues that Deacle was involved in petitions from the Sutton Scotney area before the Owslebury outbreaks. However the evidence for this is from Bingham Baring who sought to discredit Deacle by tainting him with radical conspiracy on all occasions, so this should perhaps be treated with caution.[61] However, Deacle's friendship with the radical Gideon Mantell, and clear contacts with Cobbett, by, at the latest in July 1831, point to a possible history of radicalism. There is also something oddly bohemian about Deacle, with his considerable wealth and his actress wife which smacks of some aspects of the libertarian London radicalism written about some years ago by Ian McCalman.[62]

As to the role of the Deacles, Thomas and Caroline, I think there can be little doubt that while they were not instigators in any formal sense, on 23 November they played a key role in organising and marshalling the 'Owslebury Lads'. The consistency of the accounts, even if we ignore the biased testimonies of Bingham Baring and Serjeant Wilde, show Deacle giving money to the mob, going along with them, providing them with a trumpeter and helping draw up their 'demands'. Nobody denied that Caroline Deacle was with the mob all day on horseback, or that she appeared to enjoy the occasion, nor that she was present at the Old Posting House at the days end.

John Boyes was different. Again it is clear he played some leadership role, but in his case one deeply set within the tradition of the moral economy.[63] Boyes was a famer but one much closer to the 'Owslebury Lads'. He was a small man working bad land, he also appears from a statement of character given in the 1833 petition for his pardon, to have been a wage labourer as well as farmer, which would fit with what we know of the 'English peasantry' as well as the more tragic figure of William Wall hanged in 1830 for inciting incendiarism.[64] His involvement in the vestry and their decision to impose wage rates in the parish fits well with a traditional and paternalist world view as does the vestry's insistence that this was the final offer and should mean the end of

61 R. Wells, '1830: The Year of Revolutions in England and the Politics of the Captain Swing Insurrection', p. 33 at http://www.canterbury.ac.uk/arts-humanities/history-and-american-studies/history/Documents/PoliticsOfCaptainSwing.pdf accessed 25 November 2009.
62 I. McCalmain, 'Unrespectable Radicalism: Infidels and Pornography in Early Nineteenth-Century London', *Past & Present* 104 (1984). This includes an engraving of the infidel pornographer Benbow's London shop showing an advertisement for Cobbett's *Political Register*, ibid., 79.
63 I am using the term here in the broad sense adopted by Randall, *Riotous Assemblies*, especially Chapter 12.
64 See A. Howkins, 'An English Peasantry Revisited 1800 –1900' in J. Broad (ed.), *A Common Agricultural Heritage. Revising French and British rural divergence*, Agricultural History Review Supplement Series 5 (2009). On William Wall see S. Poole, '"A Lasting and Salutary Warning": Incendiarism, Rural Order and England Last Scene of Crime Execution', *Rural History*, 19 (2008).

threats. In view of this it seems likely he had a key role in drawing up the demands on the paper carried by the mob, although of course none of the 'farmer's demands' were included in the vestry decision.

Boyes, unlike Deacle, returned to Owslebury and was clearly able to draw on local support in a way Deacle could not. The petition of August 1833 was described as having been 'numerous and respectably signed' and gave a version of the events of less than two years earlier which was entirely drawn from Boyes' own account.[65] The attacks by Wilde and Baring are completely ignored. In contrast the only petition to the Commons in Deacle's case which came from Hampshire was one attacking him and supporting Baring.[66] Further when Boyes was finally pardoned the *Hampshire Telegraph*, which had been extremely hostile to him in 1830 spoke of his being 'accidentally' among the rioters and continued that it was 'mainly owing to his influence and persuasion' that there was no further rioting'.[67]

What happened at Owslebury on 23 November 1830 was a great deal more complex than the initial accounts suggest, and indeed than I thought when I started to look at them. At work on that day were not one Captain Swing but at least three – the 'mob', probably following the traditional rituals of protest; Farmer Boyes acting the role of the local spokesman in the complex liturgy of the moral economy; and Thomas and Caroline Deacle representing an external, politicised and, perhaps even, urban radicalism. For all of those reasons I cannot believe what happened at Owslebury was typical of the course of Swing, and so therefore it perhaps has little relevance as micro-history, but it does raise a few questions about quite who the 'Owslebury Lads' and their mates all over the south of England were, and just what they thought they were doing.

65 *Morning Chronicle*, 12 August 1833.
66 *House of Commons Debates*, 27 September 1831, vol. 7, c. 678.
67 *Hampshire Telegraph*, 20 October 1834.

Tumult, Riot and Disturbance: Perspectives on Central and Local Government's roles in the Management of the 1830 'Captain Swing Riots' in Berkshire and adjoining districts*

Margaret Escott

I: Introduction

Forty years ago, Eric Hobsbawm and George Rudé delved into the lives and living conditions of the labourers and artisans of southern and eastern England who became followers of Captain Swing and analysed their motives for doing so. They suggested explanations for the rioters' conduct, the authorities' eventually harsh response and the geographic diffusion, timing and distribution of the disturbances; and prefaced their account with a working analysis of regional farming, poverty and poor-relief practices that highlighted the importance of parish politics, long before David Eastwood complained that most 'historians of Hanoverian England had not fully appreciated how the development of the parish as a political unit was predicated on the parallel development of a distinctive parochial political culture'.[1] Later research has built on and occasionally questioned Hobsbawm and Rudé's findings.[2] For example,

---

*   My thanks go to the staff of Berkshire Record Office, The National Archives, the Museum of English Rural Life and the National Library of Wales who made this study possible. I would also like to thank Elmar Torenga for drafting the map.

1   E. Hobsbawm and G. Rudé, *Captain Swing* (London, 1988); D. Eastwood, *Government and Community in the English Provinces, 1700–1870* (Basingstoke, 1997), preface.

2   For example, C.J. Griffin, 'Swing, Swing Redividus or Something after Swing? On the Death Throes of a Movement, December 1830 – December 1833', *International Review of Social History* 54 (2009), 459–97; S. Poole, '"A Lasting and Salutary Warning": Incendiarism, Rural Order and England's Last Scene of Crime Execution', *Rural History* 19 (2008), 163–77.

we now know that certain parliamentary papers of the early 1830s, including the report and evidence of the 1833 select committee on beer sales, and responses to the rural queries (published in 1834) which inquired about the riots and poor law administration, were self- or pre-selected.[3] Allowing for important regional variations, it is also possible to detach the endemic social crimes of arson, poaching, plant and animal maiming, from the milieu of collective rural protest and machine breaking associated with 'Swing'.[4] *Captain Swing* dwells on tensions within parishes and differentiated between the roles played in the disturbances by craftsmen, who were assumed to be literate and politically aware, and labourers, who were not – a distinction pressed throughout the trials by the reporters of the *Times* which deemed the former culpable and the latter for the most part vulnerable or unfortunate.[5] *Captain Swing* skims over or understates the pressure that the disturbances and precipitate prosecutions by special commission placed on government departments and individuals at all levels of county government – from parish constables to magistrates and their clerks, gaolers, clerks of the peace, county sheriffs, lords lieutenant and the yeomanry. In Berkshire the latter had in any case been disbanded in 1828 when, implementing the late Goderich administration's decision, the duke of Wellington's ministry withdrew government funding from small county corps. This left hurriedly improvised peace-keeping forces, often lacking legal sanction and suitable weapons, to fill the gap during the 1830 Swing riots.[6] As

3   *Parliamentary Papers* [hereafter *PP*] (1833), XV(i), 1–260; (1834), XXX, App. B.1.; M. Blaug, 'The Poor Law report re-examined', *Journal of Economic History* 24 (1964), 229–45. See also on this point, M.A. Lyle, 'Regionality in the late Old Poor Law: the treatment of chargeable bastards from Rural Queries', *Agricultural History Review* 53 (2005), 141–57; N. Verdon, 'The Employment of Women and Children in Agriculture: a Reassessment of Agricultural Gangs in Nineteenth-century Norfolk', *Agricultural History Review* 49 (2001), 41–55.
4   C.J. Griffin, 'Protest Practice and (tree) Cultures of Conflict: Understanding the Spaces of 'tree maiming' in Eighteenth- and early Nineteenth-century England', *Transactions of the Institute of British Geographers* 40 (2008), 91–108; C.J. Griffin, 'Knowable Geographies? The Reporting of Incendiarism in the Eighteenth and early Nineteenth Century Provincial Press', *Journal of Historical Geography* 32 (2006), 38–56. Note the contrasting portrayals of T. Shakesheff, *Rural Conflict, Crime and Protest: Herefordshire, 1800–1860* (Woodbridge, 2003), and J.E. Archer, *"By a Flash and a Scare": Incendiarism, Animal Maiming and Poaching in East Anglia, 1815–1870* (Oxford, 1990).
5   The National Archives, London [hereafter TNA], HO52/6, f. 178; *The Times*, 29 December 1830.
6   TNA, HO52/6, f. 67, John Pearse, of Chilton Lodge, Hungerford, M.P. for Devizes to Lord Melbourne, 25 November 1830. 'I cannot refrain from lamenting that the most injudicious disbanding of the yeomanry corps – the expense was petty compared to its

Roger Wells, Carl Griffin and others have demonstrated the transition from Wellington's ministry to the second Lord Grey's in November 1830 caused no major political or strategic change in central government's handling of 'Captain Swing'.[7] Within individual counties the picture is less clear. Recent government initiatives on poverty and policing had tended to prioritize the parish at the county's expense;[8] and attitudes to labour rates, allowances and fixing winter wages – the magisterial interference on the price of labour often locally allied to 'Swing' – were divided and divisive.[9] This was evident in Berkshire where the king's residence at Windsor Castle and the cross-border estates owned by Wellington (prime minister until 16 November), the radical Sir Francis Burdett, Bt. (1770–1844) and William Pleydell-Bouverie (1779–1869), 3rd Earl of Radnor generated contemporaneous interest.

Just as the rioters did not confine themselves to a single parish, so too many of the magistrates, landowners and attorneys dealing with them had property and practices in more than one petty sessions' division or county and faced simultaneous calls for action from each. In tranquil times inter-county (and divisional) variations in practices and fees or any awkward scheduling of meetings were trivial matters, commonly resolved by requests to county clerks of the peace and reference to the latest edition of Richard Burn's *Justice of the Peace and Parish Officer* and the magistrates order books. During and immediately after the 'Swing' riots these

      value. It hurt and insulted the feelings of the yeomanry in all those counties where the troops were not preserved. It created an illiberal comparison with those where they were, & most assuredly if the whole had existed all these riots would have been quelled instantly by the ready means that could have been thus supplied on the spot'.

7 C.J. Griffin, 'Policy on the Hoof: Sir Robert Peel, Sir Edward Knatchbull and the Trial of the Elham Machine Breakers, 1830', *Rural History* 15 (2004), 1–22; C.J. Griffin, '"There was No Law to Punish that Offence". Re-assessing 'Captain Swing': Rural Luddism and Rebellion in East Kent, 1830–31', *Southern History* 22 (2002), 131–63; R. Wells, 'Mr William Cobbett, Captain Swing, and King William IV', *Agricultural History Review* 45 (1997), 37–38; R. Wells, *Politics of Captain Swing*, Canterbury.ac.uk web publications (2007). For a review of earlier publications see J. Stevenson, 'An Unbroken Wave?', *Historical Journal*, 37, 3 (1994), 683–95.

8 J. Innes, '"Central Government 'Interference'": Changing Conceptions, Practices, and Concerns, c. 1700–1850', in J. Harris (ed.), *Civil Society in British History* (Oxford, 2003), pp. 45–49, 53.

9 D. Eastwood, *Governing rural England: tradition and transformation in local government 1780–1840* (London, 1994), pp. 161–63, 181; A. Randall and E. Newman, 'Protest, Proletarians and Paternalists: Social Conflict in Rural Wiltshire, 1830–1850', *Rural History* 6 (1995), 205–27; TNA, HO52/11, ff. 127–29, Charles Ashe A'Court to Melbourne, 30 November 1830. A'Court warned that the Devizes magistrates' ruling on wages would incite further trouble by 'interfering in the most direct manner with the price of labour'.

differences caused problems which have been understated or conveniently overlooked.[10] Buckinghamshire's correspondence with the Home Office during the 'mobbings' reveals the competing interests of the agricultural and manufacturing districts, of boroughs and county,[11] of the county M.P. Lord Chandos[12] (the lord lieutenant's son and vice) and the high sheriff Sir Richard Howard Vyse.[13] While it is evident from the Berkshire letters, that the lord lieutenant and custos rotulorm Montagu Bertie, 5th Earl of Abingdon was, through ill-health, a London-based absentee, who resisted Home Office suggestions that he should appoint a vice-lieutenant, and returned to his county only after the rioting had subsided.[14] Meanwhile a deputy lieutenant, Frederick Page of Speen, apologized repeatedly to the Home Office for acting 'before taking his dedimus' as a magistrate.[15] M.P.s were granted leave of absence by the House of Commons to return to their disturbed neighbourhoods,[16] and, taking the initiative, mayors, town clerks, county deputy lieutenants and magistrates corresponded directly with the Home Office, the department responsible for law and order. There, their reports were corroborated and often anticipated by intelligence from district postmasters and postmistresses, forwarded by the Secretary to the Post Office Sir Francis Freeling in a well honed operation. Within individual counties, the chains of communication were often less efficient. In Berkshire communications with the magistrates of the eleven divisions, the sheriff and the clerk of assize were channelled through the offices of the clerk of the peace William Budd in Speen, near Newbury, and the under-sheriff John Roberts in Wokingham – a cumbersome process if the county was 'disturbed'.[17] Wokingham was also the

10 'Return of the orders and regulations made by magistrates in the several counties of England and Wales' *PP* (1833), XXXI, 375–424. See also the procedural regulations for individual county courts e.g. *Resolutions, Rules, Orders & Regulations of the Court of General Quarter Sessions of the Peace of the County of Somerset (with appendix)* (Taunton, 1817), and the papers of the Hungerford attorney William Robert Hall, clerk to the magistrates of the Hungerford (Berkshire) and Ramsbury (Wiltshire) divisions (Berkshire Record Office, Reading, [hereafter BRO] D/EPG/01/4/... & D/EPG/01/5/...), currently being edited for *Berkshire Record Society*.
11 TNA, HO52/6, ff. 257–316.
12 Richard Plantagenet Temple Nugent Brydges Chandos Grenville (1797–1861).
13 Maj-Gen. Sir Richard William Howard Vyse (1784–1853) of Stoke Poges.
14 TNA, HO52/6, f. 93.
15 TNA, HO52/6, f. 30; J. Pellew, *The Home Office, 1848–1914* (Oxford, 1982), p. 3.
16 38 M.P.s received leave to return to their disturbed neighbourhoods for periods ranging from ten days to a month, 22 November – 6 December 1830 (*Commons Journals*, volume 86).
17 TNA, HO52/6, ff. 4–136; 'Sir Francis Freeling (1764–1836)' in H.C.G. Matthew, B. Harrison *et al* (eds), *Oxford Dictionary of National Biography*, (Oxford, 2004–); BRO, D/EPG/01/04/3, 39.

Tumult Riot & Disturbance
Berkshire 1830

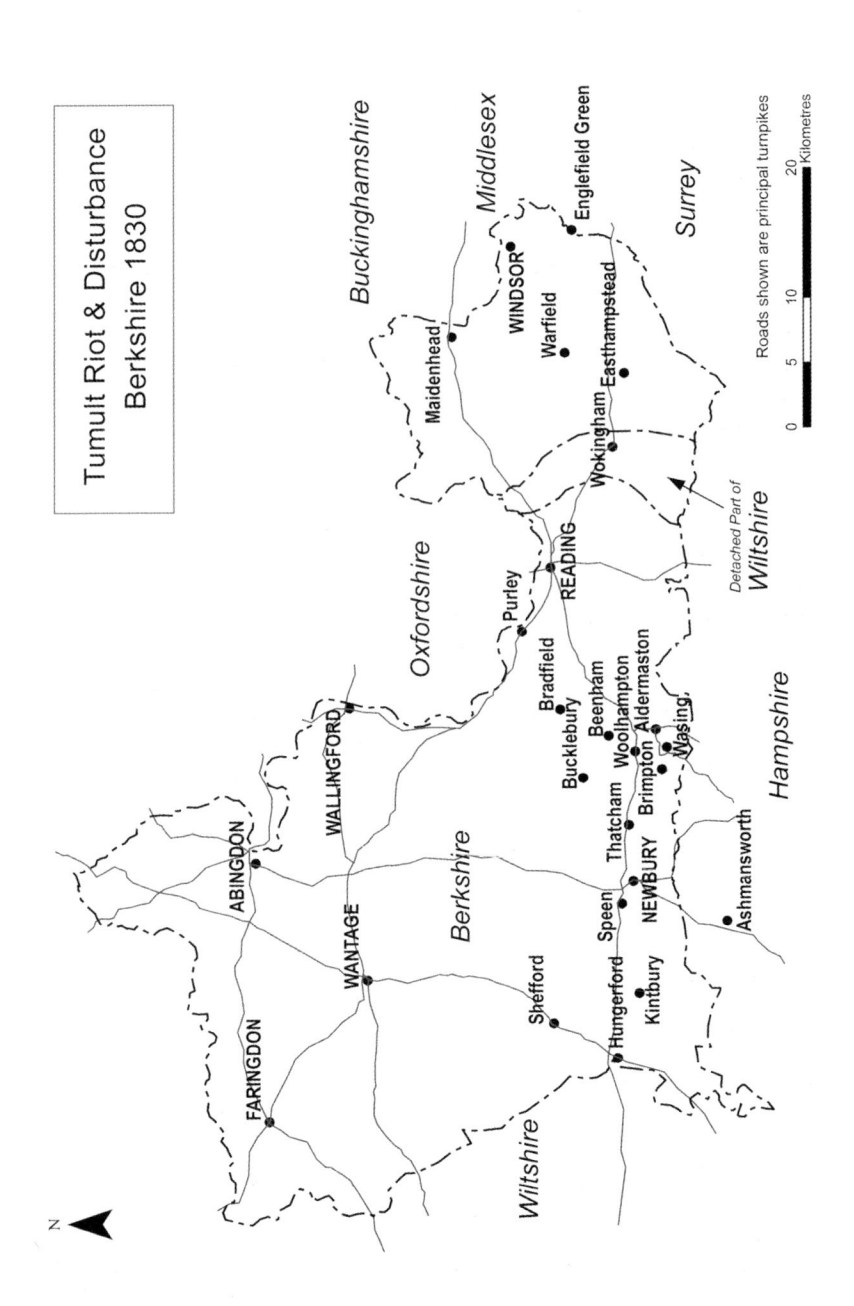

administrative centre for a detached part of Wiltshire, where the clerk of the peace John Swayne (acting on advice from Charles Ashe A'Court of Heytesbury) ensured that the magistrates' clerks for the fourteen divisions communicated directly with and assisted each other.[18]

II The Berkshire Riots and their Suppression

Between 10 November, when farmers in Colnbrook and Holyport near Maidenhead received threatening letters, and mid December 1830, when a handful of pre-trial arson incidents occurred in Cumnor and the Reading area, we now know that there were approximately 200 'Swing incidents' in Berkshire, roughly 40 more than Hobsbawm and Rudé estimated. They were preceded by a seditious meeting at Shefford and comprised over 80 episodes of threshing machine destruction, wage riots accompanied by clamouring for better parochial relief, and marches, most of them nocturnal, by organized bands of men to collect fees, food and beer money for ridding the countryside of threshing machines – at 25 pence to £2 each. Trouble erupted first in the east, where an arson attack on 11 November at Sir William Fremantle's Englefield Green estate prompted alarm and a rush to insure or re-insure property. Landowners in this locality were within easy travelling distance of the capital and some helped to provide a protective yeoman cavalry cordon around London, where King William IV's official visit to the city on the 9th had been cancelled for security reasons.[19] Probably acting on A'Court's advice, on 14 November the Tory M.P. for Sudbury Sir John Walsh, Bt. of Warfield Park:

> determined to sound the opinions of Garth[20] and Leveson Gower[21] etc. upon the project of taking active measures for putting ourselves in an attitude to stem the torrent setting against us on all sides. I mean the gathering force of the mob. There has been so much supineness among the gentry & middling orders in Kent & Sussex, that it has run very much a head. I went first to Garth, whom I found at home with Mrs G. I detailed all my news, my conversations with the secretary of the Phoenix Fire Office, the burning at Egham etc. & I proposed a liberal subscription, the establishment of a patrol, & if possible, the calling out the yeomanry. Garth seemed quite alive to the importance of such a

---

18 BRO, D/EPG/01/04/3, 10, 20, 21, 27.
19 This paragraph draws on my account of the Swing Riots in the *Berkshire Historical Atlas* (2010 edition).
20 Captain Thomas Garth, RN (d. 1841) of Haines Hill, Ruscombe.
21 General John Leveson Gower (1802–1883) of Bill Hill, near Wokingham.

course & expressed himself ready to assist me in any way. I went on to Leveson Gower, who was still warmer on the subject, & breathed nothing but war against the incendiaries. He took me to Mr Walters the sheriff,[22] proprietor of the *Times*. I told my story again to him. Walters is a democratic radical sort of fellow, & like all radicals, much taken by attention. He seemed willing to follow up my views.[23]

As Walsh intended, in east Berkshire where 'Captain Swing' was responsible for threats, robberies and warnings of arson, the wage demands of the poor were quickly quelled. Arthur Blundell Sandys Trumbull Hill (1788–1845), 3rd Marquess of Downshire of Easthampstead Park, the former Home Office undersecretary Henry Clive of Barkham and others promptly established the Wokingham based Forest Association for the Apprehension of Felons to organize nightly 'watches' and district patrols.[24] The mayors, magistrates and town clerks of the market towns of Abingdon, Hungerford, Maidenhead, Newbury, Wallingford, Wantage and Windsor also applied for assistance and similar schemes eventually provided patrols on the Buckinghamshire, Hampshire, Oxfordshire, Middlesex and Wiltshire borders, 'upon the plan of the Yeomanry lately disbanded'.[25] Yet, as the Hungerford riots revealed,[26] it was not always possible, even on receipt of prior information sworn before magistrates, to act before considerable damage had been wrought.[27] Trouble spread with a 'rapidity that defied all calculation'.[28] On 20 November the sheriff issued notices 'at the request of ten magistrates' requiring all [men] 'above age of fifteen years and able to travel, to be in readiness to aid and assist me in the preservation of the King's Peace within the said County, upon pain of imprisonment'. He had already summoned the county magistrates to what turned out to be a futile meeting at Reading on 24 November to authorize wage increases.[29] During the week-long changeover before Lord Melbourne replaced him as Home Secretary, Sir Robert Peel responded to a request from Lord Abingdon and the Berkshire M.P. Robert Palmer (1793–1872) for

22 John Walter (1776–1847) of Bearwood Park.
23 National Library of Wales, Aberystwyth, [hereafter NLW] Ormathwaite MSS, F/G 1/5, pp. 131–33.
24 TNA, HO52/6, ff. 81–85, 106; NLW, Ormathwaite MSS, F/G 1/5, pp. 136–39.
25 TNA, HO52/6, ff. 10–13, 18–24, 36, 58, 64, 85, 89.
26 On 22 November 1830 at Anning's foundry and the town hall (Hobsbawn and Rudé, *Captain Swing*, pp. 137–38).
27 BRO, D/EPG/01/4/7, 'The Information and Complaint of 5 Inhabitants of Hungerford of their Apprehension of a Riot'; TNA, HO52/6, ff. 6, 22, 27–30, 111–17.
28 *Berkshire Chronicle*, 27 November 1830.
29 BRO, D/EPG/01/4/2, 69; NLW, Ormathwaite MSS, F/G 1/5, p. 138.

military assistance. Troops were sent to protect the county town of Reading, where the postmistress and magistrates reported that the watch was inadequate, and to Newbury, whose hinterland was in turmoil.[30] Concessions announced on 15 November by the parish vestry of Thatcham had not, as expected, quelled winter wage riots. Observers noticed 'some unseen influence' exciting the men.[31] Many failed to return to work and during the next week machine breaking bands from Aldermaston, Beenham, Bradfield, Bucklebury, Wasing, Woolhampton & Brimpton joined others on the Englefield estate of Richard Benyon De Beauvoir (1769–1854), whence, 'pressing' men as they went, some trudged northwards to Wallingford and Abingdon and others returned to Thatcham and the countryside between Newbury and Hungerford. On Brimpton Common on the 22nd they encountered the vicar the Rev. Edward Cove with a large body of tradesmen and constables, who tried to apprehend them while Cove read out the Riot Act.[32] Cove and William Mount of Wasing had warned Peel on the 19th that magistrates in the Newbury division could not contain the disturbances. In another false 'quieting of the labourers' at Kintbury, a wage agreement brokered with the rector, the Rev. Fulwar Craven Fowle was breached and unruly bands of women went a-begging.[33] Fowle's parishioners, including the county M.P. Charles Dundas (1751–1832) of Barton Court, rallied to his defence when reports to the Home Office criticized his conduct.[34] The squarson Thomas Hodgson (1796–1884) informed his brother Christopher on 22 November:

> My whole parish of Ashmansworth rose yesterday. I went up and quieted them by assuring them of a redress of grievances by the farmers. Here all are in ferment today & many have joined the parties which have come from over the hills. Last evening we had a parish meeting by which I was compelled to give back 15 per cent from my tithes due this Michaelmas[35] ... The farmers agreed to increase the wages from 8s. to 12s. a week, a measure which I hoped would have kept our people quiet, but alas the whole frame of society is unhinged. Indeed, we are in a deplorable condition. If matters do not mend I must send my wife and children to London consigned to your care.[36]

30 TNA, HO43/39, p. 280, HO52/6, ff. 4, 27–30, 32–34.
31 *Berkshire Chronicle*, 27 November 1830.
32 Hobsbawn and Rudé, *Captain Swing*, pp. 136–40; TNA, HO52/6, ff. 2, 11.
33 TNA, HO52/6, ff. 28; 45–46, 51–54, 60–63; *Berkshire Chronicle*, 27 November, 4 December 1830. The Hungerford division was then a subdivision of the Newbury one.
34 TNA, HO52/6, ff. 77–80A, 99A.
35 So releasing funds for poor relief.
36 TNA, HO52/6, ff. 37, 38.

Gentry and farmers were loath to leave their families at home unprotected, especially in the west of the county;[37] and disrupted communications caused individuals to believe and claim erroneously that they were acting alone or because there was no or no other resident magistrate in the vicinity.[38] Divisional magistrates' meetings county-wide and the return to west Berkshire of Dundas, the former commander of the Berkshire yeomanry regiment, and his near neighbour the 2nd Earl Craven (1809–1866) of Ashdown House provided leadership for the farmers and constables trying to restore peace. Offenders were identified (Dundas knew all the Kintbury men), captured and, where possible, placed under military guard. Their ringleaders, some with prices on their heads, were hunted, arrested and brought before the magistrates for examination and committed, bailed or discharged as appropriate. Prison accommodation and character witnesses were sought.[39] Dundas informed Melbourne on behalf of the Newbury magistrates that when taking depositions, prisoners had been divided into three classes:

1st   Those who have extorted money
2nd   Those who have broken machinery
3rd   Those who were found with the rioters but who are not proved to have committed any outrage. Where it was so found and also that they were pressed into service & had a good character, I have discharged them.[40]

There were problems. Dundas, whose conduct Melbourne commended, had to justify his patrol's cross-border intervention in Hampshire, where he was not a magistrate.[41]

At Abingdon, where a mayoral election had been called under a writ of mandamus from King's Bench, control of the corporation and thereby the parliamentary constituency was at stake, and rioting persisted until the election was declared on 28 November in favour of the corporation and against the party of the sitting M.P. John Maberly. During it rioters 'committed from Wantage were rescued by a body of the Abingdon population at the gaol gates'; and magistrates required to escort prisoners there from Faringdon and Wantage informed the Home Office that they 'deemed it prudent to alter our course and lodge them in the gaol of

37   TNA, HO52/6, f. 25.
38   TNA, HO52/6, ff. 60–63.
39   TNA, HO52/6, ff. 43, 45–54, 91, 120.
40   TNA, HO52/6, f. 109.
41   TNA, HO52/6, f. 43. The personal, financial and legal implications of this decision are discussed in a letter of 15 December 1830 from Sir James Fellowes to Lord Melbourne (HO52/6, f. 163).

Oxford'.[42] 'Eighty sabres and belts' were sent overnight to Abingdon (26–27 November) with a lightly armed guard; but this was an exception.[43] Applications to lords lieutenant and the Home Office for warrants to swear in special constables and mounted patrols in the Thames valley region (south Oxfordshire, Berkshire and Buckinghamshire) continued to be granted but weapons were generally refused, even when applicants had contacts in high places.[44] Thus John Wilder of Purley Hall, one of the magistrates busy re-examining prisoners in Reading gaol ('I have hardly been in bed these two [days] and have nearly knocked up myself as well as my horses') failed to obtain guns for his men through the influence of his brother George, a senior Colonial Office clerk.[45]

III The Prosecutions

Most of the prisoners detained were indicted for multiple offences. This made referral by the grand jury for trial by a judge and petit jury more likely and could serve as plea bargaining ploy. Simple theft (larceny) instead of robbery (felony) for example would waive 'death' in favour of a lesser penalty.[46] Few of the recent reductions in capital offences introduced by Peel assisted the 'Swing' rioters; and although judges could commute sentences instantly, as Walsh informed Melbourne (28 November), the number of potential capital committals troubled the magistrates:[47]

> I have now to submit to your lordship an earnest wish from many of the magistrates & gentlemen of this part of the county, that in framing the indictments & conducting the proceedings against these persons, they may have the assistance of some legal gentlemen, particularly conversant with criminal law. They have doubts whether these persons

42 *Reading Mercury*, 6 September, 22 and 29 November, 6 December; *Berkshire Chronicle*, 11 September, 4 and 18 December 1830; TNA, HO52/6, ff. 39, 41, 56, 72, 95, 97, 118, 138A.
43 TNA, HO52/6, f. 74A.
44 TNA, HO52/6, ff. 58, 102, 109, HO52/12, f. 522 & endorsements; NLW, Ormathwaite MSS, F/G 1/5, p. 138.
45 TNA, HO52/6, f. 88.
46 N. Chester, *The English Administrative System, 1780–1870* (Oxford, 1981), pp. 52, 324; R. Burn, *The Justice of the Peace and Parish Officer* (23rd edition , 5 volumes 1820–23 revised by George Chetwynd), III, p. 29: 'where there are two counts in the indictment, as one for a riot, another for an assault; the same may be considered as two distinct indictments; and the jury may affirm the bill as to one of the counts, and reject it as to the other'.
47 See also V.A.C. Gatrell, *The Hanging Tree: Execution and the English people, 1770–1868* (Oxford, 1994), p. 497.

may not be indicted for capital offences, or whether their proceedings were merely riotous, & these doubts turn upon some nice constructions of the law of burglary & highway robbery, which eminent professional skill would readily solve.[48]

Dundas, writing to Melbourne the same day, requested a special commission specifically because of the high number of capital offences.[49] The Berkshire magistrates had already resolved (26 November) to try serious offenders at Reading on 7 December; but, as Budd informed the Home Secretary, there was a potential legal impediment.

There has been no adjournment of the last Quarter Sessions. I think it right therefore to refer your lordship to the opinion of the attorney and solicitor general which you will find in the 25th Ed. of Burn vol. 5 p. 194 as to the power of justices to hold an original general sessions, as that which is proposed to be held will be; in order that if there be any doubt as to the power of holding such general sessions notice may be given in time to countermand the holding of the same on the 7th Decr. At the same time, I beg to mention that I am quite at a loss to know what is to be done with the prisoners in case such general sessions cannot be held.[50]

Ministers had already decided that the worst Berkshire offenders would, as elsewhere, be tried in the county town by special commission. This would open in Reading and adjourn to Abingdon, 'as the assizes and county courts are held usually both at Reading and Abingdon'. To cut costs and reduce the risk of prisoners escaping, Newbury concurred in this arrangement and to the adjournment of their Epiphany quarter sessions to Reading to try any remaining cases promptly.[51] The twin-location of the special commission fuelled unsuccessful campaigns on behalf of Devizes, Marlborough and other towns with gaols and a history of hosting assizes, county courts and special commissions.[52] As elsewhere, Berkshire magistrates were expected to adhere to advice on security from

48 TNA, HO52/6, f. 106 (endorsed: 'Ld. M. hopes to be able to in compliance with the wish of the magistrates expressed in his letter, to direct a professional gentleman to assist the magistrates in Berkshire as to the charge[s] to be pressed with regard to the prosecutions under special commission').
49 TNA, HO52/6, f. 109.
50 TNA, HO52/6, f. 75.
51 TNA, HO52/6, ff.109 (Home Office endorsement), 137A, 176; BRO, D/EPG/01/4/29, 31, 38, 39, 41.
52 TNA, HO52/6, ff.109 (Home Office endorsement), 137A, 176, HO52/11, ff. 101, 122–23, 155–59, 167–69, 171, 190–94; *The Victoria History of Wiltshire* (London, 1953–), X, pp. 225–52.

lieutenant-colonel John Hastings Mair, a veteran of the 1827 Portuguese campaign and future governor of Grenada, who reported directly to the Home Secretary.[53]

Intense pressure of business and confusion over procedures and which cases the government would prosecute persisted until the special commission opened on 27 December. The petty sessions' clerks sent case calendars and depositions to clerk of assizes John Bellamy by mid-December at the judges' request, and at Reading on 11 December the clerk of the peace and eight magistrates met the principal steward and political agent of the Tory 4th Duke of Newcastle, William Edward Tallents (1780–1837), who had received a £1,500 retaining fee from the Treasury to supervise the special commissions in Berkshire, Hampshire and Wiltshire.[54] Where depositions were available, Tallents looked at 'nearly all the cases of the persons committed to [Reading] gaol ... who were concerned in the late disturbances' and informed Melbourne on 13 December:

> In this county as in Wiltshire not any preparations beyond the Depositions and binding over of the Prosecutors and Witnesses to give Evidence, have been taken towards the Trial of the Prisoners, and there seemed to be an impression upon the minds of the Magistrates that Government meant to take charge of the whole of the Prosecutions. I ventured, however, to assure them that the course pursued in Hampshire appeared to me to have received your Lordship's countenance and that although it was not at present decided in what cases or class of cases the Government would send counsel, that decision would shortly be made; and information should be given to the Justices how far such assistance might be expected in Berkshire as well as in Hampshire and Wiltshire.

Tallents declined to handle the Berkshire and Wiltshire commissions in tandem and concentrated on Wiltshire. However, he identified the Hungerford town hall case for special attention and recommended excluding it from multiple indictments: 'so flagrant an offence ought not to be permitted to pass without being made the subject of a separate Indictment'.[55] A magistrates' meeting at Newbury on 21 December revealed the extreme pressure on judicial process. No Treasury Solicitor could be spared to attend. A messenger Budd sent to the Home Office next day was told:

53   TNA, HO52/6, ff. 176 (Home Office endorsement), 189A; Hartley Library, University of Southampton, Special Collections, Wellington papers WP4/2/2/56.
54   TNA, HO40/27, f. 143, D/EPG/01/4/34.
55   TNA, HO40/27, f. 570.

each Sol[icito]r in the county should proceed with the cases which he has commenced as if he was to conduct them, & when Mr Maule[56] comes back [from Sussex assizes] he will communicate with those gentlemen who may have prepared or forwarded the cases which the government will take up.[57]

Within 24 hours of his return on 22 December, Maule had liaised with Henry John Shepherd of Hare Court, Inner Temple (originally one of the Berkshire counsel), John Campbell M.P., the future lord chancellor, and the short-hand writer and future judge John Gurney (1768–1845) as crown counsel; and John Patteson (1790–1861), the newly appointed Exchequer Court judge. He also wrote several letters to Budd and Grey at Newbury and magistrates' clerks at Hungerford, Reading and Wokingham. Letters despatched on 23 December, after Maule had received Tallents's Berkshire case papers, required the Hungerford, Newbury and Wokingham magistrates' clerks to arrange for 'new' witnesses, named in current depositions, to make sworn statements, to be brought to Reading on the 27th when the cases the government would prosecute would be finalized.[58] Maule also arranged a regular delivery of franks for postage, and cancelled rooms reserved by Tallents at the *Bear* in Reading favour of others at the *Crown*. On Boxing Day he informed the attorney general Sir Thomas Denman:

> The Berks. cases were put into my hands at the 11th hour, consequently I have been in the utmost confusion since my return from Lewes on Wednesday. The same course as to expenses etc is to be followed in Berks. as has been settled in Hants. and I found that the county had retained Stephens, Talfourd and Blackburne. Under these circumstances, Phillipps[59] was of opinion that Gurney and Campbell were sufficient on the part of the Crown and I hope that with this assistance matters will work as well as we can expect it.[60]

Dundas meanwhile informed Melbourne, following a private meeting with Phillips, that he had rejected the latter's suggestion that Tallents should attend the magistrates meeting on 23 December: '... we required no assistance as Mr. Gray who took the depositions, was fully competent to draw the Indictments, being in the constant practice of doing this at

---

56 Joint solicitor to the Treasury.
57 TNA, TS2/23, pp. 53–67, 72, HO52/6, ff. 163–83; BRO, D/EPG/01/5/22, 23, 27, 29, 30. The briefs can be found in TNA, ASSI/6/1 part 2, and with ancillary information in TNA, TS11/849–51.
58 TNA, TS2/23, pp. 59–66.
59 Home Office Under-secretary Samuel March Phillipps.
60 TNA, TS2/23, pp. 67, 71–72.

the General Quarter Sessions'.[61] Angry at the escalating costs of hosting the special commission, the magistrates resolved on the 23rd:

> That in regard to cases wherein the government counsel hold briefs the magistrates submit that drawing the briefs should be charged wholly to the government; upon which subject Mr Dundas has written to Lord Melbourne. That the county will pay the fees of their own counsel and also all the expenses of witnesses as at an ordinary assizes ... the government paying their own counsel and solicitor and for the copies of briefs delivered to them, and copies made for [their] use. The county to pay the clerks of petty sessions.[62]

They specifically endorsed Dundas's objection to paying for Tallents's services.[63] The Home Office's draft reply to Dundas reads:

> Attn. (for Ld M's sign[ature].)
> Beg to inform him that it was never the Intention of Govt. to put the county to any Expse. in conseqce. of the attendce. of Counsel ret[aine]d by Govt. and Ld. M. Has dir[ecte]d a letter to be written to Clks of Mag. for the Informn. of the Mags. upon this subject. Ld M. is persuaded there cannot be any difficulty upon the subject referred to, the only work of a Govt. being to act tow[ar]ds the county in the manner best calculated to give genl. Satisf[action]n to the Magistr.[64]

Directly the commission opened, the grand jury agreed to finance the civil police force Mair proposed. Reading remained quiet.[65]

IV The Trials

Defendants were expected to organise their own cases while awaiting trial and were rarely informed after committal whether and what new evidence would be presented against them. Most were in any case overawed by their plight and surroundings and ill-prepared to face the court or respond directly and coherently to charges and testimony against them. Some retained lawyers but, according to the prosecution lawyers, few of these were competent.[66] The Treasury Solicitors and their counsel, found the mass of briefs and the shortage of available precedents in print

---

61 TNA, HO52/6, f. 187.
62 TNA, HO52/6, f. 184. (Newbury magistrates resolution, 23 December 1830).
63 BRO, D/EPG 01/04/42; TNA, HO40/27 f. 570, HO52/6, ff. 184–88.
64 TNA, HO52/6, f. 189.
65 TNA, HO40/27, f. 465, HO52/6, ff. 189A.
66 M.S. Hardcastle (ed.), *Life of Lord Campbell* (2 vols, London, 1881), I, p. 497; Gatrell, *The Hanging Tree*, pp. 534–37.

to guide them frustrating, the travelling tiring and the repetitive nature of the cases boring.[67] Maule also criticized the 'unnecessary' adjournment to Abingdon, instead of completing the business at Reading or leaving the Abingdon cases to the next assizes.[68] Prosecution briefs held in the assize records and Treasury Solicitors' papers at the National Archives offer most detail, for they were the end-product of successive enhancements government lawyers requested that emphasized the threat posed by the mobs, the weapons they carried and their violent intent.[69] London dailies and the *Berkshire Chronicle* carry the fullest accounts of the court proceedings.[70] As a prosecutor and character witness, Dundas did not lead the grand jury as usual. Its composition is mentioned here and reviewed elsewhere.[71] Walsh's diary confirms the partisan divisions.

> Monday 27 Decr: I went to the court & met Sir M. Ximines, Lord Downshire etc. I walked with Lord D. to meet the judges. They came in about eleven, & after going to church, the special commission was opened. I was foreman of the grand jury. The judges were Sir [James] Al[l]an Park, Mr Justice [William] Bolland and Mr Justice [Patteson]. The grand jury had time to find three or four bills. We dined at the *Crown* with the sheriff. He made me take the top of the second table.

> Tuesday 28 Decr: We got to work about ten o'clock and were hard at it all day. There was a great similarity in all the cases. Riot, breaking threshing machines, extorting money were the principal offences. The most serious rioting was at Hungerford, where the mob had full

---

67 TNA, TS2/23, pp. 68–72, HO40/27, ff. 107–18; *Life of Lord Campbell*, I, pp. 497–98.
68 TNA, HO40/27, ff. 107, 115.
69 TNA, ASSI 6/1 (box 2), TS11/849, 850, 851; BRO D/EPG/01/5/40–46.
70 *The Times*, 26, 27, 28, 29 and 30 November, 2, 7 and 29 December 1830, 7, 8 and 9 January 1831; *Berkshire Chronicle*, 27 November, 4, 11, 18 and 25 December 1830, 1, 8 and 15 January 1831.
71 The grand jury at READING were Sir John Benn Walsh FOREMAN; Sir John Sewell; Sir Morris Ximenes; Robert Palmer; Charles Fyshe Palmer; Henry Clive; John Ramsbottom; John Berkeley Monck; Henry Russell; Major-Gen. Henry Willoughby Rooke; William Congreve; George Mitford; William Hallett; Thomas Hare Altabon Earle; George Henry Crutchley; James Wheble; John Blagrave; Edward Golding; Robert Harris; Edward Brice Bunny; Major Henry Court; Peter Green Crookham, Esq.; Philip Brown; & at ABINGDON, Sir Charles. Saxton of Circourt, FOREMAN; Philip Pusey; Thomas Goodlake; George Mitford; Thomas Duffield; Bartholomew Wroughton; Thomas Bowles; Robert George Throckmorton; Charles Eyston; William Bennett; John Hughes; William Morland sen; William Morland jun.; Aslam Blandy; William Bowles; Edward Waddelove; Edward Tull jun.; William Bowles; John Francis Spenlove; John Richard Barrett; George Butler. (H. Hodgkinson, *Assize Sermon*, Reading 27 December 1830; *The Times*, 7 January 1831). The Berkshire Record Society volume gives additional details.

possession of the town, and extorted money from the magistrates in the town hall. They likewise destroyed a large iron foundry. The grand jury invited the sheriff to dinner. I took the chair. Lord Abingdon, Ld. Downshire, Walter, the sheriff, Ld. Craven, Palmer, Dundas etc. I made some speeches after dinner and the thing went off extremely well.

Wednesday 29 Decr: Another hard day's work. There is a little set of radicals. Mr Monck, Whebble etc. who endeavour to spare every offender, and there is a tiresome pedantic old knight, Sir John Sewell, who delays the proceedings by raising doubts and points with which a grand jury have no business, and by cross-examining the witnesses at unnecessary length. I dined with a small party at the *Crown* ...

Friday 31 Decr: The same harassing work, which, however, we nearly got through ... We were dismissed by the judges ... This office of foreman of the grand jury has reflected some credit upon me, & made me known in our county. I had some difficulty in getting through the business, owing to the tiresome delays of Sir J. Sewell, & the radical dispositions of Messers Monck, & Whebble.[72]

From the Nisi Prius court, where the judge and petit jury sat, Maule notified Phillipps of the prisoners or cases 'disposed of' (24, 25, 24, 13 on 28–31 December 1830, 25 on 2 January 1831, 27, 17 on 6–7 January 1831), convictions and sentences. His last letter from Reading, on 2 January, stated:

We have convicted twenty five of capital offences, against four of whom there are double convictions. None of the cases of robbery have been attended with personal violence, but in two or three there have been menaces to the person, and violence done to the house. Fifty seven have been convicted of machine breaking of whom seventeen have been doubly convicted. I am not able to state whether any or how many will be left for execution. I should guess, judging from what has passed in court, that two or three will probably be in that unhappy condition. I mentioned to Park J. what you suggest respecting imprisonment ... but I thought he seemed to doubt whether these were the sort of convicts adapted to the penitentiary. We have but one or two felonies and a few riots for tomorrow, which will I hope drop the curtain on the proceedings here.[73]

---

72 NLW, Ormathwaite MSS, F/G 1/5, pp. 149–50. See also E. Foss, *The Judges of England: with Sketches of their Lives, and Miscellaneous Notices Connected with the Courts at Westminster, from the Time of the Conquest* (9vols, London, 1848–64); J. Grant, *The Bench and Bar* (2 vols, London, 1837) and the *Oxford Dictionary National of Biography*.
73 TNA, HO40/27, ff. 107–13.

When it proved almost impossible to make up petit juries on New Year's Day, the short-tempered Justice Park severely reprimanded the clerk of assizes and threatened to impose fines.[74] Yet, passing sentence on 4 January, he indicated that pleas for clemency, especially from juries, would be heeded.[75] Maule commended the Abingdon petit jurors:

> There seems to be a right feeling among the class of men from which the Petty Juries have been taken. They have acted firmly in all cases, and here, tho' in several instances some of them have been sworn as witnesses to the character of the rioters, it has not crossed their judgments in the conclusion they have come to.[76]

After pre-trial and post-trial plea bargaining 162 cases were heard, 41 were acquitted, 78 jailed, 27 sentenced to death (one executed), and 45 to transportation.[77]

V Rewards, Costs and Outcomes

Petitions for rewards for detaining felons were submitted to the Treasury once convictions were secured. None were considered without sworn affidavits and many were rejected or reduced. The Treasury Solicitors insisted that all information, payments and receipts be handled by magistrates' clerks.[78] At £2,035 the cost to Berkshire of the special commission was greater than anticipated despite the magistrates' efforts.[79] The petty sessions' clerks invoiced the county treasurer William Payn (who was latter accused of embezzlement) for £216 16s. 8d. for preparing 105 briefs. Payn estimated that the county had spent an additional £544 13s. 4d. by not prosecuting all cases themselves and asked the Treasury for reimbursement; but they declined to finance anything undertaken on the county's direction before Maule's return from Sussex on 22 December 1830. In other words, nothing; for Maule credited to himself all the work on the prosecution briefs:

> 'tho' I believe in a few cases, some additional evidence having been obtained, the briefs prepared for the counsel of the county were handed

74 *Berkshire Chronicle*, 8 January 1831.
75 Ibid.
76 TNA, HO40/27, f. 115.
77 Figures for pre- and post-1974 Berkshire. They do not tally with those calculated for M. Holland (ed.), *Swing Unmasked: The agricultural riots of 1830 to 1832 and their wider implications* (Milton Keynes, 2005).
78 TNA, T1/4193, TS2/23, pp. 164, 191–92, 239, 292–94, 336–37, 377, 453; TS24, 91–92, 109, 233.
79 BRO, Q/SO14, pp. 446–47.

to me in order that I might make the addition, or in one or two instances copies of the additional evidence might have been furnished, or the brief prepared for the county. Counsel might have even sent them to Mr Gurney.[80]

Government also kept the initiative by repeatedly refusing the magistrates' requests for assisted emigration for the families of men sentenced to transportation; and on the question of peace-keeping. On Mair's advice, the 'inefficient' district yeomanry troops were not reinstated despite the gentry's pleas. Instead, a Hungerford corps of yeomanry cavalry was established in 1831 as part of the 1st Yeomanry Cavalry Brigade.[81] The Reading gaolkeeper's achievement in accommodating 250 prisoners in premises adapted for 80–100 and problems so revealed served to justify county expenditure on a prison infirmary and store, but within a decade the whole had been condemned by government inspectors and a new gaol commissioned.[82]

By way of conclusion I should like to underline the evidence described in this article of self-seeking and manipulative behaviour by local and central government officials and others ready to utilize the Swing riots' crisis to bolster their own reputations and status. Ancillary to this were real concerns about the nature and limits of state power and its impact on individuals and on local government. That Berkshire was a small county under no overall political control may indeed have reduced the influence available to its M.P.s, officers and magistrates. However, an alternative interpretation, and my preferred one, is that the impact of centralization and government interference evident in the treatment of rioters and the selection of juries to try them was well-established and not part of a new 'socio-political' phenomenon of the 1830s attributable to 'Captain Swing'. The county bench and the communities involved remained susceptible to aristocratic domination; and 'landed gentlemen' still 'executed the limited responsibilities of the state in as effective a way as they could, in return for such rewards as would compensate them for their loss of leisure and enable them to sustain the necessary network of personal assistants and political clients'.[83]

---

80 BRO, Q/FZ/1; Q/SO14, pp. 453–69; TNA, HO40/27, ff. 155, 157. For Gurney's shorthand notes, see TNA ASSI/6/1 (parts 1 & 2).
81 BRO, Q/SO14, pp. 454–55, Q/SO15, pp. 138–41; TNA, HO40/27, f. 465.
82 BRO, Q/SO14, pp. 436–42.
83 P.J. Jupp, 'The Landed Elite and Political Authority in Britain, ca. 1760–1850', *Journal of British Studies* 29 (1990), 56.

Without looking beyond and beneath the portraits of communities treated in this article, many of the nuances that transformed mobbings and collective wage bargaining into 'Swing' riots may well remain lost.[84] Even so, the Berkshire evidence already reveals interesting and parallel trichotomies in parish and county management that eluded Hobsbawm and Rudé and which may be duplicated elsewhere. In local communities and parishes visited by 'Swing', clergy, vestries and occasionally divisional magistrates conceded wage demands under duress, which in Berkshire an indecisive county bench failed to sanction. After the semblance of peace was restored by coercion, promised wage increases were generally withdrawn; post-trial pleas for clemency or reduced sentences for rioters, and assisted emigration for their families as a means of reducing dependency and keeping down poor rates, were refused. When the county executive, gentry and magistrates sought assistance and additional powers from central government to put down 'Swing', ministers sent assistance, but only through personnel strictly accountable to themselves. Requests for additional powers for magistrates and former yeomanry commanders were refused. After rioting had ostensibly subsided and with judicial processes underway, the government took over the trials at a substantial cost to the county and denied the latter's claims that it had been misled over payments and wrongly charged. Nor did the magistrates in session succeed, when, from 1831–1833, they repeatedly and collectively addressed the underlying causes of 'Swing' by echoing the pleas of individual parishes and magistrates for assisted emigration – to remove surplus population and reduce the poor and thereby the county rates.[85] The only ministerial concession in this instance – a deliberate and superficial one – was that from January 1831 the refusals sent to the magistrates were handwritten versions of the usual standard printed replies.[86] This Berkshire study by and large confirms the Grey ministry's refusal to be perceived as lenient to offenders. Lord Melbourne determined, as Home Secretary, to make no major strategic or political changes in the way that popular insurrections were handled. The very

---

84 See also on this point, P. Jones, 'Finding Captain Swing: Protest, Parish Relations, and the State of the Public Mind in 1830', *International Review of Social History* 54 (2009), 429–58.
85 TNA, HO52/12, ff. 519–34; BRO, Q/SO14, pp. 453–55; Q/SO15, pp. 140–41. The county bench incidentally adopted a similar strategy and terminology in their petitions and complaints about Irish migrants.
86 TNA, PC1/79 (Lord Melbourne's instructions c. 10 January 1831).
87 On this point, which again eluded Hobsbawm and Rudé, see also Barry Reay, *Rural Englands: Labouring Lives in the Nineteenth Century* (Basingstoke, 2004), p. 149.

scale of the 'Swing' riots dictated otherwise.[87] What appear with hindsight to be well-intentioned and locally beneficial incentives proposed by parishes, magistrates and the county executive to bring offenders to justice and address the underlying causes of rural poverty and discontent manifest in 'Swing', were not perceived to be in the national interest.

'We do not come here ... to inquire into grievances; we come here to decide law': Prosecuting Swing in Norfolk and Somerset 1829–1832

Rose Wallis

By the end of 1830, approximately 1,900 prisoners awaited trial for their part in the Swing disturbances that had affected over twenty English counties throughout the autumn and winter. In five counties, where machine-breaking and damage to property had been most prevalent, the government appointed Special Commissions to try Swing offenders outside the usual court schedule.[1] The repressive sentences meted out by these centrally appointed, irregular courts, have somewhat eclipsed the prosecution of Swing offenders at county quarter sessions and regular Assize courts. Little comment has been made on the process of prosecution in general: how the cases were selected and how the charges were framed. In neglecting this avenue of research, we overlook the opportunity to address the actions and attitudes of the authorities at a more local level. Carl Griffin's analysis of the trial of the first machine-breakers at Elham in Kent has shown how the actions of the magistracy impacted on the movement of the disturbances and on the attitudes of central government; it also highlights how the county authorities tempered their responses according to their immediate social contexts.[2] Eric Hobsbawm and George Rudé noted that in some county courts a Swing offender 'might expect a more reasonable chance of acquittal than in others', however, the breadth of their study precluded the depth necessary to understand why the judiciary appeared more lenient in some counties.[3] This article investigates the ways in which the county

1 E.J. Hobsbawm and G. Rudé, *Captain Swing* (London, 2001), p. 258.
2 C. Griffin, '"Policy on the Hoof": Sir Robert Peel, Sir Edward Knatchbull and the Trial of the Elham Machine Breakers, 1830', *Rural History* 15 (2004), 127–28, 137.
3 Hobsbawm and Rudé, *Captain Swing*, p. 262.

commissions of the peace in Norfolk and Somerset structured the prosecution of Swing offenders at Assize and quarter sessions and contrasts them with the very different practice in Wiltshire.

Norfolk has been highlighted as one of those counties where, unlike Wiltshire, a Swing offender had a better than average chance of acquittal; indeed, the Home Secretary, Lord Melbourne, reproached the magistrates for the concessions they made to rioters during the disturbances.[4] Griffin's discussion of the sentences passed on the Elham machine-breakers reveals that what Sir Robert Peel (Melbourne's predecessor) described as, the 'unparalleled lenity' of the local judiciary, was due in part to an awareness of the general unpopularity of threshing machines and local economic conditions, but also due to fear of popular reprisals. The perceived betrayal of the labourers by one justice had already caused him to be the victim of an incendiary attack.[5] Similarly, in Norfolk, as we shall see, the magistracy's comparatively light handling was as much a consequence of a tactical decision to make examples than any expression of humanitarian leniency. Clearly we need to delve further into the local context of judicial decision-making to understand these discrepancies and how far they broke with the interests of central government. In stark contrast to Norfolk, Somerset remained largely undisturbed, but parallels can nevertheless be drawn between the two counties in the way prosecutions were structured and in the use made of exemplary justice. As well as grounding these trials within their immediate, local contexts, the practice of the courts in each county will be placed in the wider context of prosecutions for Swing offences elsewhere, and particularly with the Wiltshire Special Commission at Salisbury. First however, we should consider the incidence of related crimes and prosecutions over the broader period 1829–1832.

I

In the years immediately preceding the trials of 1831, the courts of Norfolk and Somerset, like those of Wiltshire, tried very few of those offences most closely associated with Swing: riot, machine breaking and arson. The counties' assize calendars for 1829 and 1830 contained just three cases of arson and one of riot, but in each case it appears that personal disputes, rather than social protest, underpinned the

4   Ibid, pp. 257–62.
5   Griffin, '"Policy on the Hoof"', 132–37.

prosecutions.[6] The vast majority of cases put through the courts in the period immediately before Swing were for varieties of theft. It is difficult to assess how far appropriative crime serves as an indicator of social protest, but the magistracy in all three counties saw a distinct correlation between poverty and crime. In the South-West, wages were declining, while petty theft and poaching were perceived to be on the increase. At the Somerset Easter Sessions of 1830, the Chairman Henry Hobhouse observed with regret the number of prisoners for trial, in particular the prevalence of convictions for hay and fowl stealing. But 'Poverty', he claimed, 'cannot be admitted as an excuse for such offences' and he called for examples to be made.[7]

At the Summer Assizes in Somerset in 1830, one case stands out, not for the motives of the perpetrators but for the mode of their punishment, for here, three incendiaries were hanged in what was probably one of the last scene of crime executions in England. This grizzly affair was staged at Kenn in the north west of the county with great pomp and circumstance, and only weeks before the outbreak of Swing.

The three labourers had fired Farmer Benjamin Poole's wheat mows in retaliation for the prosecution of an unlicensed alehouse.[8] At the behest of the High Sheriff, James Adam Gordon, the prisoners were executed on Kenn Moor, on 8 September 1830. They were not afforded the mercy of the drop-system, but suspended from a gallows and dropped from the back of a wagon in front of a crowd of over twelve thousand onlookers.[9]

Steve Poole has argued that the draconian response of the Somerset authorities had little to do with the circumstances of the crime, but more with the nature of the community in which it was committed. The punishment of the offenders was intended to 'create a lasting impression of judicial and hierarchical order on a poorly governed parish'.[10] Despite the proximity of this case, it is difficult to tie the Kenn fires to the Swing agenda. However, it was an event orchestrated to show the troublesome inhabitants of Kenn, and the county at large, that authority reigned.

In Norfolk, the long-term antagonisms between the grandee landowners, tenant farmers, and labourers created different social

---

6   Wiltshire and Swindon History Centre, Chippenham [hereafter WSHC], A1/125/55 Calendar Prisoners Quarter Sessions 1829, A1/125/55 Calendar Prisoners Quarter Sessions 1830; *Devizes and Wiltshire Gazette*, 1829–1830.
7   *Bath Journal*, 26 April 1830; *Devizes and Wiltshire Gazette*, 12 and 19 March 1829; Hobsbawm and Rudé, *Captain Swing*, pp. 76, 118.
8   S. Poole, '"A Lasting and Salutary Warning': Incendiarism, Rural Order and England's Last Scene of Crime Execution, *Rural History* 19 (2008), 1–15.
9   Ibid., 4, 10; *Bath Journal*, 13 September 1830.
10 Poole, '"A Lasting and Salutary Warning"', 10.

tensions. In more sympathetic tones than those expressed by Hobhouse in Somerset, Lord Suffield addressed the Norfolk grand jury, claiming the situation of the agricultural labourer 'has become so wretched from the extreme depression of wages. The demoralising consequences, in the increase in poaching and theft, have become so alarming, that it is of the utmost consequence to apply a speedy remedy'. The grand jury, comprised of the county's yeomen, took offence at the implication that the current state of distress rested with their failure to pay a proper wage. The jurymen retorted that all solutions lay in the hands of landholders (many of whom – like Suffield – were listening from the bench) in the reduction of rents and the provision of allotments.[11]

The business of the courts reveals some of the tensions between the county magistracy and the populace in the months before Swing; the distress of the agricultural poor and the incidence of crime was a pressing concern but the magistracy did not foresee the scale of the disturbances that would follow. If the 'salutary warning' from Kenn could be taken as an indicator, disorder in Somerset at least, would be met with sharp reprisals.

II

The Swing Special Commissions opened in mid-December 1830; by mid-January over 500 prisoners had been tried at Winchester and Salisbury. Leaving no doubt as to the purpose of the trials, Judge Alderson stated, '[w]e do not come here ... to inquire into grievances. We come here to decide law'.[12]

In ten days, the Special Commission at Salisbury tried 339 prisoners and convicted 206. Despite this being the largest group of prisoners to be tried in consequence of the disturbances, there is evidence to suggest that some cases were not selected for trial by the commission. Figures published in the press indicate that almost 400 people were held in Devizes and Fisherton, as well as 'several' more in the Bridewell at Marlborough.[13] It was expected that the commission would try all capital offences as exemplary cases, and the minor ones would be dealt with by the local judiciary at quarter sessions.[14] However, only five prisoners were scheduled for trial at the next quarter sessions, and four others were left

---

11 *Norwich Mercury*, 3 March 1830.
12 Hobsbawm and Rudé, *Captain Swing*, p. 259.
13 J. Chambers, *The Wiltshire Machine Breakers* (2 vols, Letchworth, 1993), I, p. 90.
14 Ibid., p. 83; The National Archives, London [hereafter TNA], HO 52/11, fol. 49–50, Colonel Muir to the Home Secretary, 26 November 1830.

for trial at the Lent Assizes.[15] The vast majority were tried, and tried by centrally appointed judges, either at the Special Commission or at the subsequent assizes.

The majority of cases tried by the Special Commission were for machine breaking or robbery. Due to the prevalence of the destruction of threshing machines – a non-capital offence – in the indictments, far fewer faced the death penalty than those tried at Winchester. However, the severity of the court can be seen in its unprecedented use of transportation. Over one hundred prisoners received the maximum penalty for breaking a threshing machine, seven years transportation.[16] In the ten cases regarding the destruction of non-agricultural machinery the penalties were greater still: nine of the prisoners were found guilty and sentenced to death but their sentences were commuted to transportation for life.[17] In all, 152 people were sentenced to be transported for terms of between seven years and life by the Special Commission, and all bar one reached Australia.[18]

The Wiltshire Commission appeared to be more sensitive to the age and circumstances of those brought before it than its predecessor in Hampshire; James Ford and Edward Looker, amongst others, both escaped the noose because of their 'tender years' and otherwise good character.[19] Nonetheless, the court made potent examples of those involved in some of the bloodiest disturbances during Swing.

The first case tried by the Salisbury Commission concerned the destruction of a threshing machine belonging to John Bennett, Member of Parliament and foreman of the Grand Jury at the Special Commission. According to Mr Bennett, approximately 400 labourers had assembled and approached his farm, Pyt House, threatening to destroy 'all the thrashing machines in the country, and that they would have two shillings a day'. The Hindon troop of Yeomanry arrived too late at Mr Bennett's to prevent the destruction of his threshing machine but engaged the rioters and a battle ensued; the troop met the stones of the crowd with bullets. In the fray, Mr Bennett had his hat knocked off and

---

15 WSHC, A1/125/57 Calendar of Prisoners 1831, Quarter Sessions February 15 1831.
16 TNA, ASSI 24/18/3 Special Commission minute book; Hobsbawm and Rudé, *Captain Swing*, p. 259.
17 TNA, ASSI 24/18/3 Special Commission minute book; Chambers, *The Wiltshire Machine Breakers*, I, pp. 104–211.
18 TNA, ASSI 24/18/3 Special Commission minute book; Hobsbawm and Rudé, *Captain Swing*, Appendix II, pp. 308–9.
19 Hobsbawm and Rudé, *Captain Swing*, p. 259; TNA, ASSI 24/18/3 Special Commission minute book; Chambers, *The Wiltshire Machine Breakers*, I, pp. 111–12, 196.

his nose bloodied; several of the rioters were wounded and one labourer, John Hardy, was shot dead.[20]

Lord Arundel, testifying to the character of James Mould of Hatch, one of the defendants, described Mould's wretched existence. Having struggled to maintain his family, his wife and six children were left wholly unsupported after his incarceration. Whilst awaiting trial, the family had been struck by typhus killing two of the children. Despite such pitiful circumstances and reports of a good character, Mould, along with twelve others received the maximum penalty of seven years transportation; two others were acquitted and two were sentenced to twelve months in prison at hard labour. James Blandford, singled out by Bennett as a recidivist, received consecutive maximum sentences and was transported for 14 years.[21]

Peter Withers and James Lush were the two prisoners left for execution by the Special Commission.[22] Their offences were marked additionally by accusations of violent conduct, in Withers' case throwing a hammer at a constable and speaking in terms 'to put down the Magistracy'. In passing sentence, Judge Vaughan commented on the 'lenity of Mr Bennett' without which those tried for the destruction of his threshing machine, might have found themselves in the same predicament as Withers. James Lush was capitally convicted for robbing Bartlett Pinnegar during a riot. When Pinnegar had drawn a pistol on the crowd and threatened to shoot, the crowd had rushed him, and a serious scuffle ensued. Both men were sentenced to hang on 25 January but the day before their execution, the sentence was reprieved and they were both transported for life.[23]

The cases against Peter Withers, James Lush and James Blandford and his co-defendants concerned outright, physical conflict, and at Pyt House and in the case of Withers, attacks on authority. Perhaps in punishing the actions of the labourers so severely the court not only made an example of the most sensational incidents of disorder, but also mitigated the use of violence by the 'victims', and the authorities, as a proportionate response.

---

20 TNA, ASSI 24/18/3 Special Commission minute book January 1 1831; *The Morning Chronicle*, 3 January 1831; Hobsbawm and Rudé, *Captain Swing*, p. 126; Chambers, *The Wiltshire Machine Breakers*, I, p. 104.
21 Hobsbawm and Rudé, *Captain Swing*, p. 126; TNA, ASSI 24/18/3 Special Commission minute book 1 January 1831; *The Morning Chronicle*, 3 January 1831.
22 TNA, ASSI 24/18/3 Special Commission minute book 6 and 7 January 1831; *The Morning Chronicle*, 12 January 1831; Chambers, *The Wiltshire Machine Breakers*, I, pp. 216–17.
23 *The Morning Chronicle*, 12 January 1831; Chambers, *The Wiltshire Machine Breakers*, I, pp. 229–31.

The Salisbury Special Commission dominated the prosecution of Swing offenders in Wiltshire. Although some of those apprehended during the disturbances may never have faced the bench, it is clear that the majority were tried by 'this extraordinary exercise of the Royal authority'. The scale of the disturbances, and their character, warranted the use of the highest courts, and perhaps the county judiciary were not deemed capable of managing the cases at quarter sessions. Certainly concessionary measures had been taken during the riots, and Colonel Brotherton's correspondence with the Home Office betrayed a lack of confidence in the local magistracy in their suppression of the disturbances.[24] Through the unprecedented use of transportation, the Commission clearly tended towards the punishment of all, exercising central, judicial authority with indiscriminate force.

III

At the request of the Lord Lieutenant, Colonel John Wodehouse, the Home Secretary organised a Special Commission for Norfolk, but of a rather different form to those at Winchester or Salisbury. As Colonel Wodehouse explained, 'yet many of the Persons here probably heretofore borne of good Characters ... were compelled either by open violence or threats to commit the felonies with which they stand charged'. The Magistrates wished to review all cases 'and only send those to trial, who were seen and known to be Ringleaders and Active Agents in perpetrating the Outrages' which 'might fully answer the ends of justice, and be a great saving of Expense to the Country'.[25] Wodehouse made the case for a system of exemplary punishment rather than the punishment of all, seeing the use of exemplars as both financially and socially expedient.

In Norfolk therefore, the majority of 'Swing' cases were tried not by Special Commission, but at the January quarter sessions in 1831. 158 people stood accused of machine breaking and riot; 68 of them were discharged on their own recognizance or acquitted. In Somerset, the county judiciary tried all of the cases associated with Swing. At the Epiphany sessions, eight were charged in relation to the destruction of threshing machines, six of whom were convicted, and thirteen men were indicted for riot: five were convicted, the other eight were still to be

---

24 Chambers, *The Wiltshire Machine Breakers*, I, p. 99; Hobsbawm and Rudé, *Captain Swing*, pp. 127: Col. Brotherton's letter suggests that the judiciary were not as active in suppressing the disturbances as central government would have wished; A. Randall and E. Newman, 'Protest, Proletarians and Paternalists: Social Conflict in Rural Wiltshire, 1830–1850', *Rural History* 6 (1995), 211.
25 TNA, HO 52/9 Wodehouse to Melbourne, 10 December 1830.

apprehended.[26] Very few Norfolk cases were 'reserved for the higher tribunal' of the Assize courts but three cases of machine-breaking at the paper mills at Lyng were tried at the Thetford Assize and the eight prisoners held for arson were remanded for trial by Special Commission at Norwich.[27] In Somerset, there was no Special Commission, only one case was referred to the Assizes, and even that was thrown out.[28]

The majority of cases heard at the Norfolk quarter sessions concerned machine breaking. In passing sentence on those accused, Sergeant Frere was clear in his purpose, 'to prevent a recurrence of such conduct, by the effects of example'. Those who received the most stringent sentence of transportation were a particularly necessary example. Having made a countywide recommendation for the disuse of threshing machines during the disturbances, the magistrates had been subjected to government criticism which placed the blame for ongoing disturbances with the over-conciliatory attitude of the bench.

The Home Secretary had 'sharply rebuked' all those who had 'approved uniform wage rates' or recommended the discontinuance of threshing machines, and instructed them to 'oppose a firm Resistance to all Demands' for wages and against agricultural machinery.[29] Stoically defending their conduct, Wodehouse however, was more inclined to blame poor wage rates:

> [w]e could not forbear to admit, that wages had been generally too low, and that we thought that, under the actual difficulty of finding employment for the Labouring Poor, which has too long existed, Threshing Machines ought to be discontinued.[30]

In court, more than one testimony claimed the prisoners' had said 'they had got an authority from the magistrates to break threshing machines'.[31] Accordingly then, in passing the maximum penalty on men such as William Dow – a prominent figure in the round of machine breaking at Cawston – the magistracy checked suggestions that they had tacitly sanctioned criminal behaviour.[32]

26 Norfolk Record Office, Norwich [hereafter NRO], C/S 1 MF 660 Quarter Sessions Minute Books, January 1831; *Norfolk Chronicle*, 22 January 1831; Somerset Record Office, Taunton [hereafter SRO], Q/SR/459 Quarter Sessions Rolls Epiphany 1831; *Bath Chronicle*, 6 and 13 January 1831.
27 *Norwich Mercury*, 22 January and March 12 1831; NRO, C/S 1 MF 660 January 1831; TNA, ASSI 94/ 2116, 94/2117
28 SRO, Q/SCS 60–86, January 1831, Q/SCA 1–30 Lent 1831; Hobsbawm and Rudé, *Captain Swing*, pp. 129–30.
29 Hobsbawm and Rudé, *Captain Swing*, pp. 257–58.
30 TNA, HO 52/9 ff. 14–15, Wodehouse to Melbourne 16 December 1830.
31 *Norwich Mercury*, 8 and 15 January 1831.
32 *Norwich Mercury*, 8 January 1831.

However, Sergeant Frere noted that the Norfolk disturbances lacked those 'flagrant acts of violence' that had accompanied other incidents of machine breaking; occasions, he continued, that 'imperiously call for much more severe examples than I am happy to say is requisite here'.[33] He attributed the more tempered response of Norfolk machine-breakers to the stringent example made of the Ely and Littleport rioters in 1816, whose violence had been met with severity. Of the 24 rioters sentenced to death by the Special Commission that sat at Ely in that year, five were executed and buried together with the epitaph 'May their awful fate be a warning to others'.[34] Only nine of the 65 prisoners charged with breaking threshing machines in 1830 received the maximum seven years transportation for it.[35]

Four cases of riot were focussed on as particular examples; all of which were characterised by attacks on figures of authority. At Haddiscoe, Southrepps, Docking and Attleborough, the labourers sought redress from clergymen or magistrates and in all cases a confrontation ensued. Frere reproached the Docking rioters for their physical attack on law enforcement officials claiming it 'approached the crime of high treason', and, had their case been referred to the Assizes 'their lives would have been justly forfeited'. Despite the heavy terms of imprisonment handed down, the Docking rioters sentences were framed as an act of clemency.[36]

The Attleborough rioters were also deemed an exceptional case. At a vestry meeting in the town, the Reverend Fairfax Franklin (also a member of the Commission of the Peace) had met with farmers to discuss a reduction in tithes and a concomitant advance of wages. When one farmer dissented from the proposed scheme the negotiations collapsed. The labourers gathered outside, clamoured for a greater reduction in the tithe, and the aged Reverend was held captive for several hours. Whilst escaping he was struck at by the crowd who eventually dispersed when the military arrived. The Reverend and his companion Mr Dover claimed they saw 'something like concert between some of the farmers and the labourers'.[37]

The perceived ringleaders, labourers Robert Smith, Samuel Smith and John Stacey, were imprisoned for two and a half years, two years, and 18

33 *Norwich Mercury*, 15 January 1831.
34 F. Knight, 'Did Anticlericalism exist in the English Countryside in the Early Nineteenth-Century?' in N. Aston and M. Cragoe, *Anticlericalism in Britain c. 1500–1914* (Stroud, 2000), p. 164; C. Johnson, *An Account of the Ely and Littleport riots in 1816* (Ely, 1893, repr. 1948), pp. 66, 77.
35 *Norwich Mercury*, 15 January 1831.
36 *Norwich Mercury*, 22 January 1831.
37 *Norwich Mercury*, 15 January 1831

months respectively.[38] Despite his ordeal, the Reverend Franklin appealed for the release of the Smith brothers, highlighting their previous good behaviour; but his petitions fell on deaf ears.[39] Sergeant Frere maintained that any farmers proved to have been complicit in the disturbances would be punished, sentiments which echoed those made by the Judges at the Salisbury Special Commission; however, little effort appeared to be made on this front by the Norfolk magistrates.[40]

Two separate indictments were brought against two farmers at the county sessions in April 1831. The Crown attempted to prosecute John Carman and David Roll for 'exciting riot' the previous winter. Carman was acquitted because there was 'no venue laid' of the alleged incident in the indictment. The chief witness for the prosecution against Roll, Mr E. Wodehouse (also a member of the Commission of the Peace), wished to 'withdraw all further prosecution, with a view to putting an end to these cases, and in the hope the defendant would see the impropriety of his conduct and desist from such a course of proceeding in the future'.[41]

In both literal and symbolic terms, the Attleborough riot presented the most awful consequence of an alliance between the labourers and the yeomanry in a co-ordinated attack upon authority, but it was the labourers that bore the brunt of the reprisals, while the farmers were taken back into the fold. This selection of exemplary cases would eventually culminate in the capital cases tried by the Special Commission at Norwich.

IV

Somerset by no means shared the same level of tumult as Norfolk, but punishment was nevertheless comparatively robust. The most severe sentences were passed on Isaac Wheeler and George Eavis. Wheeler had threatened to burn a threshing machine in a minor riot at South Brewham on the county boundary shared with Wiltshire,[42] and he received four months imprisonment for it. Only 21 of the prisoners tried at the equivalent court in Norfolk, for the actual destruction of threshing machines, received prison sentences of the same length or greater.[43]

38 R. Lee, *Unquiet Country: voices of the rural poor, 1820–1880* (Bollington, 2005), p. 20.
39 NRO, C/Saa 1/15 F. Franklin to the Visiting Justices of the County Gaol 25 July 1831and 22 September 1831.
40 *Norwich Mercury*, 8 January 1831; *Morning Chronicle*, 3 January 1831.
41 *Norwich Mercury*, 19 April 1831.
42 Hobsbawm and Rudé, *Captain Swing*, p. 129.
43 SRO, Q/SCS 60–86 January 1831; *Bath Journal*, 10 January 1831; NRO, C/S 1 MF 660 January 1831; *Norfolk Chronicle*, 22 January1831.

George Eavis was involved in both incidents of actual machine breaking to occur in the county, and he was also indicted for riot. He was sentenced to the maximum penalty of seven years transportation. The disturbances occurred at Yenston and Henstridge, on the same day, and in close proximity to the Stalbridge riot in Dorset.[44] Although there was little public discussion of the sentencing of Eavis and Wheeler, the comparative severity of their sentences reflects an intolerance to disorder, even on a small scale in Somerset, and the magistracy made their position perfectly clear.

The rioters indicted at the same sessions were uniformly convicted for a disturbance that appeared to stem more from opportunity and inebriation rather than considered grievances. The Reverend Moncrieffe had postponed a meeting to swear in special constables at Banwell, being apprehensive that the measure might cause alarm. The men that had assembled for the meeting 'having been regaled with beer, were accordingly dismissed'. They did not go home however but 'became themselves the originators of a serious disturbance'. They demanded money, beer, bread and tobacco, all of which was supplied by local shopkeepers; a loaf was then placed on a pole and carried aloft, 'and they swore they would have a larger sized loaf and two shillings a day wages'. When one man was arrested, other members of the crowd broke into the house where he was incarcerated and freed him, subsequently parading him 'in triumph around the village, in a chair'.[45] The press reported the incident with little concern, attributing the 'disposition to riot' to the 'effects of intoxication.' Although the men had initially assembled at Banwell to show their willingness to assist the magistracy in the maintenance of order, their drunken antics had made a mockery of the proceedings; consequently all of those 'deluded men' apprehended for the disturbance were toughly dealt with and sentenced to terms of imprisonment and hard labour.[46]

The only case reserved by Somerset's magistrates for the Assize was one regarding a threatening letter, and that was consequently dismissed as no true bill. In Wiltshire, a total of six cases relating to the disturbances were tried at the regular Assizes rather than by Special Commission.[47] Norfolk, as we have seen, removed very few cases to the higher courts but those cases that were, and the mode of their prosecution were orchestrated for

44   SRO, Q/SCS 60–86 January 1831; *Bath Journal*, 10 January 1831; Hobsbawm and Rudé, *Captain Swing*, p. 130.
45   *The Bath Weekly Chronicle*, 9 December 1830.
46   *The Bath Weekly Chronicle*, 9 and 13 January 1831.
47   WSHC, A1/125/57 Calendar of Prisoners 1831, Quarter Sessions February 15 1831; *Devizes and Wiltshire Gazette*, 10 March 1831.

maximum effect. The Assizes were usually held at Thetford but the Special Commission sat at Norwich to hear the cases of what the Assize judges described – in private correspondence – as a 'particular class of prisoner'.[48] Of the eight on trial for the destruction of various ricks and agricultural property by arson, Richard Nockolds was the only person executed for a Swing offence in Norfolk.[49]

Authority viewed arson with particular abhorrence: incendiaries worked in secrecy, with no other motive than injuring their victim through the destruction of property.[50] As Norfolk's landowners publicly exclaimed, 'It is for the honour of our country, it is for our credit as men, that we must find out and punish these cowardly miscreants. Englishmen were never assassins! Englishmen were never incendiaries ...'[51]

It was supposed by many at first that the disturbances were the work of foreign agents fomenting revolution. Justice Berney, writing to Lord Melbourne, was convinced that the fires were 'entirely occasioned by foreign influence ... a set of Hell Hounds who are carrying devastation through every part of [the country]'.[52] Nockolds was not a foreigner, but aspects of this xenophobic attitude permeated his case. In the words of Judge Alderson, he was 'not an agricultural labourer ... driven to extremities' but a weaver residing in Norwich. He had given up 'the restraints of religion' and been corrupted by Cobbett and Carlile; the Sunday reading-room he had established was seen as a nursery of dissent.[53] All legitimacy that could be derived from the plight of the labourers was denied Nockolds; the judge concluded, 'you therefore committed this act for the purpose of exciting general confusion and alarm throughout the country'.[54] Nockolds' trial and his execution were conducted in Norwich, his home and the county capital, as opposed to Thetford, where the assizes were usually held, to ensure maximum exposure. He was hanged in front of his family and a considerable crowd,

---

48 *Norwich Mercury*, 12 March 1831; TNA, HO44/ 52 4 and 8 March 1831
49 S. Evans, 'The Life and Death of Richard Nockolds Hand Loom Weaver of Norwich', in M. Holland (ed.) *Swing Unmasked: The Agricultural Riots of 1830 to 1832 and their Wider Implications* (Milton Keynes, 2005), pp. 170–84.
50 S. Poole, '"A Lasting and Salutary Warning"', 4–5. The only prisoner to be executed in Wiltshire was Henry Wilkins, charged with burning down a cottage, *Devizes and Wiltshire Gazette*, 10 March 1831.
51 Reproduced in J.E. Archer, *By a Flash and a Scare: Incendiarism, Animal Maiming, and Poaching in East Anglia 1815–1870* (Oxford, 1990), p. 91; R.M. Bacon, *A Memoir of the Life of Edward Third Baron Suffield* (Norwich, 1838), p. 324.
52 TNA, HO 52/9 Justice Berney to Lord Melbourne, 2 December 1830.
53 *Norwich Mercury*, 2 and 16 April 1831.
54 *Norwich Mercury*, 2 April 1831.

who watched in silence. There had been only one other execution in Norwich in the previous nine years.[55]

V

It is clear that Norfolk's magistrates dealt with Swing offenders in terms of exemplary cases. Their leniency must also be seen in the wider context of social conflict in Norfolk over a longer period, for local perceptions of Swing's relatively non-violent expression in the county were only so in comparison to the (by then) notorious Littleport and Ely riots of 1816. The magistracy of 1830 structured the prosecution of Swing offenders to restore a particular form of social peace. Their lenity does suggest they sympathised with the labourers' grievances, and this was betrayed by many in letters to the Home Secretary. Justice Berney, while convinced that foreign agitators perpetrated the fires, saw more overt disturbances as the result of genuine distress and 'that the demands of the labourers are but too just'.[56] Lord Suffield reported that the magistrates of North Walsham 'all avowed their disinclination to take severe measures against an oppressed class, until forced to do so for the preservation of life and property'.[57]

Such reports would have done little to inspire the government's confidence in the Norfolk judiciary, but the harsh examples they made served to counter their original concessions and their association with the escalation of machine breaking. The Bench also aimed to prevent any continued alliance between the labourers and farmers. In the disturbances of 1816 and 1822, the magistracy had had to contend with riots and machine-breaking perpetrated by labourers, and in 1823, the authorities faced an unprecedented meeting of disgruntled farmers at Norwich. In 1830, Swing saw the cooperation of the labourers and their employers – as was the case at Attleborough – with dangerous consequences. As John Archer has argued, Norfolk's gentry 'could perhaps live with an angry work-force but to withstand the verbal attacks of their natural allies, their tenants, in the rural war was unthinkable and beyond them'.[58] Perhaps to satisfy government, but also perhaps to paper over long-term structural

---

55 *Norwich Mercury*, 25 April 1829: Richard Everett was hanged in April 1829 for horse-stealing. The press claimed that only one other execution had taken place in Norwich in the previous six years. From a survey of two local newspapers between 1829 and Nockolds' execution in 1831, no other execution is reported to have taken place in Norwich during that period.
56 TNA, HO 52/9 Justice Berney to Lord Melbourne, 2 December 1830.
57 TNA, HO 52/9 fol. 110–13 Lord Suffield to Melbourne, 27 November 1831.
58 Archer, *By a Flash and a Scare*, pp. 85–86.

problems in Norfolk society, Richard Nockolds' execution was intended to terrify but also to tie the most 'heinous' Swing offences to elements outside the agricultural community.

The trials in Norfolk did little to resolve the long-standing differences between labourers, farmers and landowners; threatening letters were sent to prosecutors, and throughout the trials and for the greater part of 1831, fires blazed.[59] The alliance between farmers and the labourers however, was extinguished. Any new 'Swing' incidents put through the courts from 1831 were generally for arson and machine breaking; at Brampton Hall near Aylsham, a farmer was praised by the courts for arming himself and resisting the demands of labourers; an example the court thoroughly recommended.[60] In December 1831, Justice Hoseason writing to the Home Office cited the same issues plaguing Norfolk agricultural society.[61]

Having so few cases, the Somerset magistrates had greater scope for the punishment of every offender in 1831. But their consistent prosecution of those involved in the disturbance was intended to signal that any signs of insurrection would be nipped in the bud. The Assize judge praised the county for having none of those cases 'of that deep moral dye' which he had tried in other parts of the country, 'and even on the last time I visited this town' when he alluded to the Kenn incendiaries.[62] How far the terrifying spectacle of their execution impacted on the potential for conflict in Somerset cannot be accurately gauged; however, in an open letter to *The Times*, George Emery, deputy lieutenant of the county, recommended that terrible example as a means of successfully checking incendiarism.[63]

Despite the lack of serious and widespread disturbances in Somerset, the magistracy had remained on their guard throughout the winter of 1830, suggesting that while there were few incidents of overt protest, the judiciary still saw the potential for disturbance. In the New Year, writing to the Clerk of the Peace, the Lord Lieutenant, the Marquis of Bath, hoped the convictions at Quarter Sessions would stop incendiaries, but he had received reports of a recent attack in his neighbourhood on the property of a prosecution witness in the late trials.[64] Although we cannot always equate the motives of incendiaries with social protest, Somerset's judiciary had to consider arson attacks focussed on agricultural property

59 *Norwich Mercury*, 22 January 1831; Ibid, p. 95.
60 *Norwich Mercury*, July 1831.
61 TNA, HO 64/3 December 21 1831
62 *Bath Journal*, 4 April 1831.
63 *The Times*, 21 September 1830.
64 SRO, Q/JCP/7 Marquis of Bath to Edward Coles, 12 January 1831.

throughout the spring of 1831 and through the autumn and into the winter of 1832.[65]

In neighbouring Wiltshire, incendiarism also continued to concern the authorities; and issues surrounding wages persisted in ongoing labourers disputes and strikes.[66] Perhaps the legacy of Swing can also be discerned in some of the prosecutions made in the aftermath of the disturbances. At the summer Assizes, Sarah Wheeler was found guilty of arson despite the clearly domestic circumstances of the crime. Refusing to consider the pleas of the defendant or her witnesses, the judge 'told them that circumstances had nothing to do with a case like the present'. Wheeler was spared the noose but the judge warned her that she would be more than likely transported for life. In the same court, Job Hetherall was sentenced to be transported for life for sending a threatening letter. In his summation to the jury, the judge went to considerable lengths to stress that proof was only required that the prisoner had *caused* the letter to be written or sent. The jury returned their verdict immediately.[67] Such stringent examples failed as a deterrent: in the Spring of 1832, the Assizes had to rule again, in cases concerning anonymous threats to burn farms, and actual acts of agricultural incendiarism.[68]

VI

In his recent retrospective of the historiography on Swing, Adrian Randall stressed that 'close attention to the local is clearly essential if we are to really understand the social politics, normally hidden from the historian's sight, which was worked out in high relief only when riot or protest erupted'.[69] Studying the interactions of the local judiciary with those engaged in such phases of unrest is integral to reaching this understanding of social politics. Too frequently the repressive function of the magistracy and local justice systems are emphasised, neglecting to acknowledge fully that the administration of the law was a negotiated process. The supression of disorder was framed by local social and political contexts, and local history, as much as by statute law and the demands of central government. By viewing the trials of Swing offenders within a wider context of prosecution, this investigation has aimed to provide a

65 *Bath Journal*, 11 April, 14 November, 12 December 1831, and 2 January 1832; TNA, HO 64/2 17 January, 14 April and 31 December 1831.
66 Chambers, *The Wiltshire Machine Breakers*, I, pp. 243–45.
67 *Devizes and Wiltshire Gazette*, 21 July 1831.
68 *Devizes and Wiltshire Gazette*, 8 March 1832.
69 A. Randall, 'Captain Swing: A Retrospect', *International Review of Social History* 54 (2009), 427.

more nuanced understanding of the responses of local authorities to the disturbances, and what those responses tell us about the social relations within which they occurred.

Although their management and structuring of the prosecutions varied, some attitudes were shared by the judiciary at every level. Attacks on property have been highlighted as the trigger for more stringent sentencing; in trials considered for this study, the magistrates and judges also made potent examples of those who attacked or subverted the authorities. Concern for the maintenance of social order, and social hierarchy, is also evident in the judiciary's 'xenophobic' expressions: not only were incendiaries excluded from the legitimacy of the labourer's cause, but at the Salisbury Special Commission, it was considered 'more inexcusable' for craftsmen and non-agricultural labourers to be the perpetrators of depredations.[70] Rather than acknowledge the structural causes of unrest, the authorities could blame a foreign element for the destruction of 'that bond of mutual interest and goodwill which ought … to unite the higher and lower classes of the community'.[71]

The mass disturbances experienced in Wiltshire (and Hampshire) apparently warranted mass prosecutions in the centrally administered Special Commissions. Here, examples were made of the offenders on an unprecedented scale. Two-thirds of those tried were convicted, and more than half of those individuals were transported.[72] What is most striking is the almost total delegation of responsibility for the prosecutions to the Special Commission. The cost of prosecution would certainly have been lessened by the government defraying the expenses of the Commission nationally, and it is clear that the central authorities wished to ensure the suppression of tumult in Wiltshire; but it also points to inadequacies or concerns about the ability of the provincial judiciary. Further research is required to confirm this apparent dominance of the Special Commissions, most significantly in Hampshire where both the courts and the level of disturbance were comparable. In stark contrast, the Norfolk Special Commission provided little more than an opportunity to stage the execution of Richard Nockolds as a classic example of judicial terror. On

---

70 Hobsbawm and Rudé, *Captain Swing*, p. 259. For example see the case of William Hayter, TNA, ASSI 24/18/3 Special Commission minute book, 4 January 1831; Chambers, *The Wiltshire Machine Breakers*, I, pp. 138–39. See also discussion of Nockolds above.

71 Justice Parke addressing the Wiltshire Special Commission, 1 January 1831; Chambers, *The Wiltshire Machine Breakers*, I, pp. 101–2.

72 TNA, ASSI 24/18/3 Special Commission minute book, January 1831; Hobsbawm and Rudé, *Captain Swing*, pp. 259, 262–63.

the whole, in Somerset and Norfolk, the magistrates preferred to keep the trials within the purview of local authority at the quarter sessions.

Although Somerset produced few disturbances, the majority of the county's offenders were tried and convicted, and received robust punishment. Norfolk experienced considerable unrest and made carefully selected examples. In structuring these prosecutions the magistracy were comparatively lenient: the precedents of the previous disturbances of 1816 and 1822 caused the justices to reflect more favourably on the Swing rioters. The magistracy also took into consideration the complex relationship between landowners, tenants and labourers – ensuring the interests of the former at the expense of the latter. By engaging in regional studies of the actions of the magistracy, it becomes clear that 'repression' by 'authority' as an abstract entity over-simplifies the ways in which crime and protest were dealt with. In examining the discrepancies in the prosecutions of offenders at a local level, we can see how both national contexts and local contingencies tempered the administration of the law.[73]

---

73 This approach echoes Carl Griffin's call (with reference to Andrew Charlesworth) for the need to 'embed local and national administrative history within the local contexts in which they actually operated and gave shape to local events'. Griffin, '"Policy on the Hoof"', 131.

The Immediate Reaction to the Swing Riots in Surrey 1832–1834

Judith Hill

In the opinion of at least one historian of Swing, the riots 'rocked the foundation of English landed society', put the 'fear of revolution into the hearts of the English governing class' and, to many, posed a threat to social stability.[1] Of course, the agitation did not stop in 1830 and sporadic attacks on property continued into the winter of 1832, proving Hobsbawm and Rudé's assertion that 'not all the labourers had been demoralised by the terror of the special commission'.[2] Although as Figure 1 demonstrates the extent of the incidents should be revised upwards, the disturbances were neither as widespread nor marked with the same intensity of discontent as those which took place in Kent and Sussex. Nonetheless, the trauma and sense of insecurity produced by the riots affected both central and local government. This case study therefore focuses on the efforts that were made by the Surrey parish vestries to resolve or respond to the underlying problems that were responsible for the agricultural unrest of the early 1830s.

In many cases, the immediate reaction of parish authorities remains undiscovered within the parish records of villages and towns directly affected. It is only through a detailed study of these records that a comprehensive understanding of how the parishes responded to the disturbances can be established. This essay will focus on one aspect of these local records, poor relief accounts, to examine what they reveal about parochial reaction to events in the early 1830s. All of the available poor law records for the 107 rural parishes in Surrey have been consulted

---

1 R. Wells, 'Historical Trajectories: English Social Welfare Systems, Rural Riots, Popular Politics, Agrarian Trade Unions and Allotment Provision 1793–1896', *Southern History* 25 (2003), 99; S. Webb and B. Webb, *English Poor Law History Part II: The Last Hundred Years* (London, 1929), p. 45.
2 E. Hobsbawm and G. Rudé, *Captain Swing* (London, 1969), p. 283.

Figure 1: Protest Incidents in Surrey 3 August 1830 to the end of 1832

	Hobsbawm and Rudé	Revised Number
Incendiarism	23	44
Threshing-machine breaking	0	0
Strikes/wages/poor relief assemblages/assaults	6	8
Swing Letters	0	8

Source: E. Hobsbawm and G. Rudé, *Captain Swing* (London, 1969), pp.308–309; J.Hill, 'Poverty Unrest and the Response in Surrey 1815–1834'(unpublished Ph.D. thesis, University of Surrey, 2006) pp. 297–306.

for the period 1815–34.[3] By adopting an exhaustive method rather than merely sampling records it is possible to gain a more comprehensive picture of the administration of poor relief and to understand the range of individual and parish responses to the Swing disturbances in one county.

Recent literature and research has extended our understanding of protest and the demands made by labourers for assistance from the parish. Hobsbawm and Rudé argued that many of the Swing protests had the objectives of 'defence of the customary rights'.[4] E.P. Thompson addressed the issue of the 'rights' of the poor and developed the concept of the 'moral economy of the poor'.[5] Roger Wells and Peter Jones have both shown the moral economic model continued into the nineteenth century and 'was very much alive in 1830'.[6] David Eastwood has noted that the emphasis on providing work and wages after 1815 represented a continuing belief in both the importance and efficacy of local obligations on the part of parish officials.[7] Increasingly after 1815 rural population growth and demobilization met with economic decline and agricultural depression and as a result confidence in the poor law system faltered.

3   J. Hill, 'Poverty Unrest and the Response in Surrey 1815–1834', (unpublished Ph.D. thesis, University of Surrey, 2006).
4   Hobsbawm and Rudé, *Captain Swing*, p. 16.
5   E.P. Thompson, 'The Moral Economy of the English Crowd in the Eighteenth Century', *Past & Present*, 50 (1971), 76–136.
6   R. Wells, 'The Moral Economy of the English Countryside' in A. Randall and A. Charlesworth (eds), *Moral Economy and Popular Protest Crowds, Conflict and Authority* (Basingstoke,2000), pp. 209–72; P. Jones, 'Swing, Speenhamland and Rural Social Relations: the 'Moral Economy' of the English Crowd in the Nineteenth Century', *Social History* 32 (2007), 273.
7   D. Eastwood, 'Rethinking the Debates on Poor Law in Early Nineteenth England', *Utilitas* 6 (1994), 106.

Ratepayers increasingly complained to the vestries about the rising level of poor rates and for the need of overseers to maintain or even reduce expenditure on poor relief.[8] There is a clear awareness amongst historians of the importance of uncovering the realities of poverty as well as the practices that accounted for the labourers' experience of justice and inequality. Recent local studies have focused on the lives and strategies used by the poor to survive in such difficult circumstances and have shown that the poor adopted many strategies to cope with the fragility and sparseness of their material world.[9] Immediately after the protests it is evident parish officials were anxious to contain social tensions and concerted efforts were made to combat poverty by increasing poor relief payments and providing more worthwhile labour. It was at the vestry table where 'the relationships between employer and employed and between the vestry and the labouring poor' were shaped and where parishes sought solutions to the problems of increasing poverty.[10] This assessment of rural Surrey examines the labourer's increasing poverty in the context of their parish experience and the response of the parish officials immediately after the Swing protests of 1830.

I The Poor Relief System

The significance of the poor relief system in supporting the agricultural population is not always easy to determine. Recent research on the economy of makeshifts has portrayed poor relief as one element in the wider strategies deployed by individuals and families to survive.[11] What is evident is that the continued population growth, in conjunction with high prices, the decline of some domestic industries, the abandonment of living-in and yearly hiring practices in favour of day-labour, were significant factors in increasing the hardship of the poor. In addition, the loss of 'makeshift activities', including grazing rights, cow, pig and geese keeping, as well as fuel collection, had a detrimental effect on the

---

8   S. King, *Poverty and Welfare in England 1700–1850. A Regional Perspective* (Manchester, 2000), pp. 91–93.
9   S. King and A. Tomkins (eds), *The Poor in England 1700–1850: An Economy of Makeshifts* (Manchester, 2003); K.D.M. Snell, *Annals of the Labouring Poor Social Change and Agrarian England 1660–1900*, (Cambridge, 1985); T. Hitchcock, P. King and P. Sharpe, *Chronicling Poverty Voices and Strategies of the English Poor, 1640–1840* (Basingstoke, 1997), pp. 1–18.
10 P. Jones, 'Finding Captain Swing; Protest, Parish Relations, and the State of the Public Mind in 1830', *International Review of Social History*, 54 (2009), 453.
11 King and Tomkins (eds), *The Poor in England*; Hitchcock, King and Sharpe, *Chronicling Poverty*, pp. 1–18.

independence of the poor.[12] By the 1830s, the weakening of the economy of makeshifts led to more substantial life-cycle and point-in-time poverty than had previously been experienced. These changes inevitably led to a substantial increase in the proportion of labouring families dependent on poor relief. Research undertaken for Surrey supports Broad's and Steven King's argument that assistance from the parish at the beginning of the nineteenth century was increasingly important for the sheer survival of the poor.[13]

The poor laws 'were shaped by local communities' and enacted locally, 'where face-to-face negotiations determined their impact'.[14] As there was considerable leeway in the interpretation of the poor laws, it was common for its implementation to vary between parishes in the same locality, as was the case in Surrey. Of course, depending both on the demand for relief and the available resources, eligibility was policed by the parishes. Broad refers to this as 'the local autonomy of need', where each parish dealt with the problems of providing for relief on a local basis.[15] Hindle has commented on the 'highly localised nature of the social welfare provision'.[16] Parish overseers and vestries were clearly well acquainted with the problems arising from, and dealing with, local poverty.

Many contemporaries, including William Cobbett, regarded the old poor law as embodying traditional rights and social obligations, including 'the right in case we fall into distress to have our want sufficiently relieved out of this produce of the land'.[17] Historians have observed that perhaps the poor's greatest strength was the 'depth and emotional power of their own belief in their right to relief'.[18] Roger Wells and Peter Jones have both noted the importance of the moral economy that was very much alive in 1830 when the issue of a 'right to subsistence' became increasingly a contentious matter.[19] At the time in rural Surrey, as in

12 P. King, 'Gleaners, Farmers and the Failure of Legal Sanctions in England 1750–1850', *Past & Present* 125 (1989), 116–50; S. Williams, 'Earnings Poor Relief and the Economy of makeshifts in Bedfordshire in the Early Years of the New Poor Law', *Rural History* 16 (2005), 22–53.
13 Hill, 'Poverty Unrest and the Response in Surrey 1815–1834'; J. Broad, 'Parish Economies of Welfare 1650–1834', *The Historical Journal* 42 (1999), 1002–05; King, *Poverty and Welfare*, p. 229.
14 L. Hollen Lees, *The Solidarities of Strangers the English Poor laws and the People 1700–1948* (Cambridge, 1989), p. 7.
15 Broad, 'Parish Economies', 1002.
16 S. Hindle, *On the Parish? The Micro-Politics of Poor Relief in Rural England c. 1550–1750* (Oxford, 2004), p. 285.
17 W. Reitzel(ed), *The Autobiography William Cobbett* (London, 1967), pp. 224–5.
18 Hitchcock, King and Sharpe, *Chronicling Poverty*, p. 10.
19 Wells, 'The Moral Economy', pp. 209–71; Jones, 'Swing, Speenhamland', 274.

other southern counties, there was seasonal unemployment, together with an expanding, casual day-labour force, which directly resulted in endemic underemployment at low wages. Parish authorities as a result came under increasing pressure to provide relief. At the same time the increased problems of managing the poor forced vestries to inaugurate policy reforms. Parish officials and magistrates in southern England tried to reduce per capita spending on relief.[20] As the numbers needing help increased, growing tensions can be identified between the ability of the ratepayers to pay rates and the scale of allowances provided. For example, in 1821 the overseers in the parish of Cranleigh had to report that the collection of poor rates was deficient by 'upwards of £250'.[21] In addition many rural parishes had to revert to borrowing funds. The parish of Horley in 1824 borrowed £200 to pay the outstanding county rate and for 'the continued support of the poor'.[22] Parish officials had the difficult task of treading 'a fine line between the demand of the poor for welfare and the ability and willingness of ratepayers to supply the funds to meet the demand'.[23]

The appointment of paid assistant overseers and select vestries were measures introduced to achieve greater efficiency in the management of parish affairs. In rural Surrey the number of assistant overseers increased from 19 in 1819 to 40 in 1830. Charles Maclean in his report on Surrey to the Royal Commission on Poor Laws, supported the appointment of assistant overseers, finding them, 'very intelligent, zealous ... and economical to a parish'.[24] The appointment of select vestries also had the desired effect of reducing poor relief bills. For example in its first year of operation in 1819 the Frimley select vestry saved the parish 46 per cent in poor relief costs. The five select vestries of Abinger, Dorking, Epsom, Chertsey and Pirbright made, on average, a reduction of 33 per cent on the amount spent per head on poor relief between 1821 and 1831.[25] As a consequence many day labourers found themselves socially segregated

20 M. Blaug, 'The Myth of the Old Poor Law and the Making of the New', *Journal of Economic History* 23 (1963),164–5; D.A. Baugh, 'The Cost of Poor Relief in South-East England 1790–1834', *Economic History Review* 28 (1975), 57; K. Snell, *Parish and Belonging: Community, Identity and Welfare in England and Wales 1700–1950* (Cambridge, 2006), pp. 213–14.
21 Surrey History Centre, Woking [hereafter SHC], P58/1/1, Cranleigh Vestry Minute Book, 21 April 1821
22 SHC P58/1/1, Horley Vestry Minute Book, 26 July 1824
23 King, *Poverty and Welfare*, p.52.
24 Report of the Poor Law Commission on Poor Laws 1834, Appendix A part XXVIII Assistant Commissioners' Report for Surrey C.H. Maclean p.556A.
25 Expenditure on Poor Relief for Surrey, Abstract of the Poor 1818 xix (82), 1833, xxxii (32); Brayley *History of Surrey* Appendix 2 Population Figures.

and unprotected against unemployment and price fluctuations. The rural labour force became increasingly demoralized becoming dependent on parish work, and resentful of the farmers who were not only their employers but were those who 'controlled the vestry, made poor laws policy and took decisions respecting individual claimants'.[26] This resentment is clearly reflected in the emigrant letters written by poor, rural agricultural labourers and provide valuable insights of the changing quality of life experienced by labourers in southern England.[27] The Swing disturbances also clearly demonstrate rural labourers' demands for the 'right of subsistence' which included the provision of work, adequate relief payments or charity from wealthy neighbours.[28] The reaction of parish authorities to the unrest of 1830–2 confirms that the demands of Swing crowds were not only heard but acted upon by parish officials with the support of ratepayers. The labourers' demands for work, minimum wages, bread, poor relief and charity were met for a short time.

II Change of Attitude

Hobsbawm and Rudé noted that 'what shocked farmers and landlords painfully was not the feebleness but the strength of the labourers' activities in 1830, and therefore the continued necessity to conciliate them'.[29] More recently historians have also observed that the strength and resolve of the labourers' activities' unnerved farmers and landlords.[30] In examining reactions to the Swing disturbances, Knott and Daunton have noted that 'the initial response to the Swing riots was to offer more generous relief ... with the expectation that it would purchase order and deference'.[31] Newby concluded that 'many landowners acknowledged some degree of culpability and began to repair their authority by applying an analgesic to the problems of rural distress'.[32] This is a view shared by Dunkley, who has stressed that landowners recognised the need to show

---

26 Wells, 'Historical Trajectories', 89.
27 J. Hill, 'Letters Home: Reflections from Canada on the Plight of the Poor from Rural Southern England in the Years 1832–1837', *Southern History* 30 (2008), 24–42.
28 Jones, 'Swing, Speenhamland', 277.
29 Hobsbawm and Rudé, *Captain Swing*, p. 282.
30 D. Eastwood, *Governing Rural England. Tradition and Transformation in Local Government 1780–1840* (Oxford, 1994), pp. 161–62; J. Burchardt, *The Allotment Movement in England 1793–1873* (Woodbridge, 2002), pp. 70–97.
31 J. Knott, *Popular Opposition to the 1834 Poor Law* (London, 1985), p. 51; M.J. Daunton, *Progress and Poverty: An Economic and Social History of Britain 1700 –1850* (Oxford, 1995), p. 492.
32 H. Newby, *Country Life: a Social History of England* (London, 1987), p. 46.

interest in the welfare of labourers in southern England.[33] This greater interest and concern for the welfare of parish labourers, produced immediate wage concessions from employers and more generous relief from parish overseers.[34] Whether this was due to altruism or enlightened self-interest on the part of landowners, or to protect their property from attack is difficult to ascertain, but it is possible to identify a change in attitude among this sector of society. Neumann has observed that in Berkshire during the winter of 1830 'some parishes retained, or even enhanced, indiscriminate allowances which they would otherwise have discarded'.[35] A similar picture is evident in Surrey. In 1828 for example, Henry Drummond had reportedly stopped his own poor tenants from cutting juniper, hollies or furze on the wastes; he had intended to drive non-tenant stock off the downs and had enclosed eight acres of common land.[36] His attitude mellowed after the insurrections of 1830, as illustrated in a letter he wrote to William Bray of Shere in 1832:

> The rising of the labourers that is taking place throughout the southern counties of England threatens the destruction of all property. They are maddened by oppression and, chiefly, from the high price of cottage rents, they are determined to take the law into their own hands and say that they prefer being hanged or shot to continuing as they are. In these circumstances it is our duty, as well as our interest, to do what we can to obviate their distemper. It is very well known that it is not profitable to build cottages to pay any interest for the money so employed and therefore that whoever does build must build at a loss. I am willing to view this loss, and if you will grant me a copyhold lease of 20 acres on Shere Heath I will build twenty cottages, which I will undertake to let only to the labourers of your parish. As it is a great point to take some step before they shall be able to say that we do this from intimidation.[37]

The post-Swing period was a time of high social tension, with increasing unemployment and underemployment of agricultural labourers in the rural southeast. Within the parish vestries, landowners and farmers were now clearly prepared to listen and comply with labourers demands of 'bread work wages relief and charity'.[38] Surrey ratepayers now made fewer

33 P. Dunkley, *The Crisis of the Old Poor Law in England 1795–1834* (New York and London, 1982), p. 57.
34 A. Digby, *The Poor Law in Nineteenth Century England* (London, 1982), p. 10.
35 M. Neumann, *The Speenhamland County Poverty and Poor Laws in Berkshire 1792–1834* (New York, 1982), p. 191.
36 SHC, 1191/2, A. Brown, *Notes on the Parish of Albury 1662–1891*.
37 SHC, G52/3/4 H. Drummond Letter to William Bray, Private Papers Sir Jocelyn Bray 1820.
38 Jones, 'Swing, Speenhamland', 281.

complaints in vestry meetings about their rating bills, as they were more concerned to restore domestic tranquillity. In the short-term, ratepayers' hostility towards the rising cost of poor relief gave way to the more pressing concern to provide work and to alleviate the hardship of the poor. In his report on Surrey in 1835, Charles Mott Poor Law Commissioner for Surrey commented on the increasing burden of providing for the able-bodied poor. He noted that in Caterham, Mr Moore, the assistant overseer, grumbled that as a result of incendiary fires the rates had increased and 'the officers cannot control the money actually expended on the poor'.[39] In the winter of 1831 the Thames Ditton vestry established a committee of fifteen ratepayers, which organised a collection 'for the purpose of adding to the comforts of the poor'.[40]

This change of attitude is also evident in the Egham vestry, which, in the winter of 1832, told the parish officials that:

> although the wages should be kept down to induce these men to look out for work elsewhere, they should on no account be treated as paupers merely because they cannot find work and are therefore employed by the parish.[41]

The Chobham vestry made a similar statement in the winter of 1832–33, proposing to set up a subscription scheme to provide help for the many poor families in the parish. The overseers collected £13 to provide loaves of bread to 'deserving characters'. They added that others in distress who could not be considered by the overseers as deserving persons, in 'extreme cases' should be allowed small allowances.[42] The tone of these statements is interesting. Before 1830, overseers were anxious to discriminate between the 'deserving and idle extravagant or profligate poor' when distributing relief, but now many parishes were willing to consider all claimants.[43] After the disturbances, many vestries recognised the need to consider the welfare of all labourers in order to avoid further trouble, although the reaction in the parishes to Swing was 'uneven and short lived'.[44] This was the case in Surrey where, immediately after the unrest,

---

39 British Parliamentary Papers [hereafter BBP], *First Annual Report of the Poor Law Commissioners for England and Wales* XXIX 1836 [hereafter PLCR], Evidence C. Mott Poor Law Commissioner for Surrey Report Appendix B No.8 p. 312.
40 SHC, 2568/6/1 Thames Ditton Vestry Minutes 22 December 1831.
41 SHC, 2516/2/10 Egham Vestry Minutes 2 January 1832.
42 SHC, P34/box 2 Chobham Parish Records Winter 1832–1833.
43 1819 59 Geo.3, c.12.
44 Neumann, *The Speenhamland*, p. 191.

Figure 2: Surrey Total Expenditure and Per Capita Spending for the Years 1828-34

Year Ending 25 March	Total Expenditure on Poor Relief in Surrey (£000)	Per Capita (£)
1828–29	£243.4	0.52
1829–30	£265.5	0.56
1830–31	£265.4	0.55
1831–32	£283.3	0.57
1832–33	£278.4	0.55
1833–34	£261.5	0.51

Source: BPP, Abstract of Returns for Surrey 1834 xxxii (32) 349–350; 1834 xliii (355) pp. 402–3.

relief costs did rise, and for a short time ratepayers agreed to pay increased poor rates in return for domestic tranquillity.

In 1831 the new Whig government made it clear that they thought the protesters of 1830 had held the agrarian counties to ransom. Under threat of further violence, ratepayers, employers and parish officials had to a certain extent given way to labourers' demands by raising wages and relief allowances.[45] The Home Secretary, Lord Melbourne, had issued a series of memoranda to magistrates in 1830, warning them against setting wage rates and the use of threshing machines.[46] He expressed his concern that acquiescence by the parish authorities had 'a permanently bad effect upon the character of the agricultural population and compromised the ability of the rural leadership to govern in the localities'.[47] The economist and New Poor Law architect, Nassau Senior, also remarked that he believed agricultural property could not support indefinitely the higher wages: 'sooner or later these promises [of higher wages] must be broken and the peasantry will rise again'.[48]

Question 53 which was addressed to parishes by the 'Rural Queries of the Poor Law Commission', in 1833, asked: 'Can you give the commissioners any information respecting the causes and consequences of the agricultural riots and burnings of 1830 and 1832'. Their replies clearly reveal what they believed were the reasons behind the popular

45 Royal Archives, Windsor [hereafter RA], Box 5/9 Melbourne Papers, Lord Grey/Lord Melbourne 29 August 1832.
46 HRO 10M57.03, Lord Melbourne 'Circular to Magistrates', 8 December 1830.
47 Lord Melbourne/Duke of Wellington 10 November 1832 in L.C. Sanders (ed.), Lord Melbourne Papers (London, 1899), p. 152.
48 S.L. Levy, Nassau W. Senior 1790–1834 (London, 1970), p. 70.

disturbances.[49] Most of the twenty answers received from Surrey parishes mirrored national responses, namely that 'unemployment and wage levels were the real trigger for protest'.[50] Peter Jones has noted that the emphasis made at the time on work and wages is nowhere near as straightforward as it first appears. Instead the protesters 'expressed a series of interrelated demands', the end of threshing machines, a minimum wage, increase in poor relief and the payment of some kind of dole to the protestors.[51] At the time, recognition that these positive measures needed to be taken to alleviate the suffering of the poor was surprisingly consensual. The magistrate and Wiltshire landowner, George Poulett Scrope, for example, recognised that 'labourers have received too little wages, and parish allowance must be immediately raised'.[52] This was an opinion that placed him quite in line with the radical William Cobbett, whose Rotunda lecture on the condition of agricultural labourers argued that 'no body of the people except the Irish had ever been so ill used as English labourers' and the 'struggle between labour and employment would never cease until the labourer got the worth of his toil'.[53]

III The Government's Response: Support of Allotments

After 1830, there was a marked increase in the provision of allotments. Although the idea of providing land for labourers had been mooted at the end of the eighteenth century, it had declined after 1805 and has left few traces in the archives before 1830.[54] Hobsbawm and Rudé identified direct links between the introduction of the Allotment Acts of 1831 and 1832 and the Swing outbreak.[55] This has also been recognised by Jeremy Burchardt who concluded that 'there is little doubt that the immediate cause of the dramatic upsurge in the number of allotments was the Captain Swing riots of 1830'.[56] The incentive to increase the 'well-being, industriousness and contentment' of the agricultural labourer, and the need to decrease the poor rate burden resulted in a resurgence of interest.[57]

49 BPP, *PLCR*, Extracts from information received by Poor Law Commissioners Rural Queries for Surrey Appendix B Part I XXX Question 53, pp. 474e–88e.
50 M. Holland, 'The Captain Swing Project' in M. Holland (ed.), *Swing Unmasked the Agricultural Riots of 1830 to 1832 and their Wider Implications* (Milton Keynes, 2005), p. 20.
51 Jones, 'Swing, Speenhamland', 275.
52 G. Poulett Scrope, *County Chronicle*, 14 December 1830.
53 W. Cobbett, *Brighton Herald*, 18 December 1830.
54 Burchardt, *The Allotment Movement*, p. 51.
55 Hobsbawm and Rudé, *Captain Swing*, p. 296.
56 Burchardt, *The Allotment Movement*, p. 70.
57 Ibid., p. 46.

Speaking in the House of Lords on 11 November 1830, Lord Sheffield emphasised the effectiveness of allotments in keeping down poor rates while in the other chamber, an M.P. for Surrey, John Briscoe also advocated the provision of allotments.[58] Later in the month (22 November) the Marquis of Salisbury moved for the appointment of a Select Committee to inquire into the present state of the Poor Laws. He complained of the break up of small farms and the enclosure of wastelands, as well as the lack of sedentary employment for the wives and children of the peasantry. In doing so, he 'appeared to attribute to those causes much of the deterioration which the class of labouring population hourly exhibit'. His recommendation was that 'the hopes of the labouring poor should be raised and the original intention of the Poor Laws should be carried into effect'.[59] The government responded to this Tory initiative, with the establishment of a select committee to investigate social welfare.[60] The committee considered the plight of the agricultural labourer, and in his report on Surrey, Thomas Chapman, a land agent and surveyor, commented that if labourers were given between two and four acres of land to cultivate, it would enable them to feed their families and decrease their dependence on the poor rates.[61] The published report supported both allotments and the parochial resort to labour rates.

In the summer of 1831, Parliament expressed concern that high levels of rural unemployment could result in further discontent during the coming winter. The response was the passing of three separate Acts relating to allotment provision and parochial employment by spade husbandry. The first of these amended the 1819 Sturges-Bourne Select Vestries Act, and extended the enclosure limit from twenty to fifty acres. Overseers and churchwardens could now rent or hire land not exceeding fifty acres for cultivation by the poor or for leasing to them as allotments. They could also enclose for the same purpose (with consent of the lord of the manor, or other persons) any portions of waste or common land (in or near the parish) 'to any poor and industrious inhabitant or inhabitants of the parish' with the proviso that the latter could not gain settlement by leasing the land.[62] The second allowed parish authorities to enclose crown land up to 50 acres (with the consent of the Treasury) for the

58 BPP, Lord Suffield Parliamentary Debates, 11 November 1830 3rd Series i col 375 and J. Briscoe 19 November 1830 3rd Series I col 600.
59 BPP, Marquis of Salisbury 1830 House Lords Proceedings 22nd November 1830.
60 BPP, Select Committee of the House of Lords on the Poor Laws VIII [hereafter SC] 1830–1.
61 BPP, SC of the House of Lords on the Poor Laws VIII 1830–1, Evidence for Surrey T. Chapman p.338.
62 59 George III Cap xii 1819; 1 and 2 William IV C 42 1831

benefit of the settled poor of the parish.[63] In 1832 a further act authorised parishes to let such land (at a fair rent and in small allotments) to 'industrious cottagers of good character'. These were portions of land made over in trust to the poor collectively to compensate for lost rights of fuel gathering as a result of enclosure.[64] In Surrey, the only two early allotments directly linked to this legislation appear to be those in Walton-on-Thames, where between one quarter of an acre to one acre were rented out on a yearly basis to 'industrious cottagers of good character, being day labourers or journeymen legally settled in the parish'.[65] At Chobham, the vestry converted thirty-two acres of wasteland, partly into a parish farm or allotments, to be let out to poor labourers of the parish.[66] The churchwardens and overseers 'set out for the said poor labourers who applied for the same and were found proper persons, to have such parcels of waste land, most of half an acre, at an annual rent 1s. per rod'.[67] In his report, Maclean noted that about fifty labourers worked these allotments of half an acre of wasteland.[68] The committee set up to manage the Chobham allotments, aware that in the first season the labourers had 'no funds in hand to crop it', proposed to raise a sum of approximately £30 by voluntary subscription to manure and plant the land.[69]

IV Co-operative Action

Burchardt has identified this upsurge of interest in co-operative activity after 1830, which resulted in the formation of the Labourers' Friend Society to promote allotment provision, and the founding of the Agricultural Employment Institute.[70] The aim of the Agricultural Employment Institute was to purchase land and let it to labourers, while the Labourers' Friend Society was 'instituted in hope of improving

63 1 and 2 William IV c 59 1831
64 2 William IV c 42 1832
65 SHC, 605/1/1 Walton on Thames Allotments Orders 1 June 1832 also confirmed R. Ruegg work on FACHRS Allotment project 10th May 2004; Onslow, *Landlords and Allotments* (London, 1886).
66 Act 59 George III Cap xii 1819; 1 and 2 William IV C 42 1831; SHC, P34/box 2 Chobham Poor Land 6 January 1832; SHC, P34/box 2 32 acres enclosed 1832 and 10 acres 1842.
67 BPP, *PLCR*, Extracts from information received by Poor Law Commissioners Rural Queries for Surrey Appendix B Part I XXX, Reply to Question 20 Chobham p. 477c.
68 BPP, *PLCR*, Appendix A part 1 XXVIII Assistant Commissioners' Report for Surrey C.H. Maclean p. 577A.
69 SHC, P34/box 2 Chobham Poor Land 6 January 1832.
70 Burchardt, *The Allotment Movement*, pp. 51–52.

conditions of labourers generally, and of providing those in agricultural districts with small allotments of land'.[71] It sought to persuade landowners to let land to labourers for spade husbandry, with the intention of reducing or eradicating poor law dependency. Although the Institute failed in 1834, the Labourers' Friend Society, which held their first public meeting on 18 February 1832, continued to prosper, and obtained royal patronage and support from the landed elite. The Labourers' Friend Society published a monthly magazine that contained detailed information about allotments, and this was directed at landowners and clergymen.[72] They also employed G.W. Perry as an agent, to contact potential supporters, lecture on the benefits of allotments, form local societies and gain new subscribers. He travelled extensively on behalf of the society, visiting Surrey, Sussex, Hampshire and Wiltshire in 1832.[73] The 1834 report recorded visits to Berkshire, Oxfordshire, Gloucestershire, Buckinghamshire, Essex, Suffolk, Norfolk, Northamptonshire, Surrey and Sussex over the course of the year.[74]

Some Surrey landowners were closely involved with the society. In February 1832, two Surrey M.P.s, J.I. Briscoe and W.J. Denison, were appointed as vice presidents of the Labourers' Friend Society, and in August the Hon. Rev. Arthur Onslow from Clandon became a vice president. Briscoe commented that he believed the society 'is calculated to confer benefit on the landlord and tenant of the soil as well as the labourer'.[75] Landowners from across rural Surrey contributed to the association and local societies sprang up in the Guildford, Farnham, Godalming, Bagshot and Epsom areas, to promote and circulate information on the best methods of establishing allotments for the labouring classes. In Bagshot, Maclean reported that the 'liberality of His Royal Highness the Duke of Gloucester has enabled this society to commence its benevolent intentions'.[76] The society offered labourers between forty and fifty rods of land and advanced money to them to purchase manure and seed.[77] When the society was formed in Epsom in 1834, twenty-one large landowners met under the chairmanship of Henry Gosse to support the granting of allotments, 'a system by which the moral

71 London Metropolitan Archive, London [hereafter LMA], Acc/3445/SIC/01/05, Proceedings of the Labourers' Friend Society 1832–36, pp. 7–8.
72 LMA, *Facts and Illustrations* later *Labourers' Friend Magazine*.
73 Burchardt, *The Allotment Movement*, p. 88.
74 LMA, Acc/3445/SIC/01/05, 'Proceedings of the Labourers' Friend Society 1832–36'.
75 LMA, Acc/3445/SIC/01/05, 'Proceedings of the Labourers' Friend Society 1832–36', p. 19.
76 BPP, PLCR, Appendix A part 1 XXVIII Assistant Commissioners' Report for Surrey C.H. Maclean p.576A.
77 Ibid.

and physical condition of the labouring classes may be raised and ameliorated through the medium of their own exertions'.[78] In his report on Surrey, the Poor Law Commissioner Ashurst Majendie praised the acquisition of allotments by labourers as beneficial to 'their character and conduct' and warned 'the denial of land to them will constantly produce an increase of ill-feeling on their part'.[79]

V The Need for the Vestries to Provide Worthwhile Labour

In numerous parishes in Surrey, vestries also took positive action to try and alleviate the suffering among the unemployed poor and provide employment. Various minute books report on urgent parish discussions concerning the matter. After the unrest, many parishes realised that setting men to work on the roads and in the gravel pits to solve the problem of surplus labour only demoralized the rural workforce. In Majendie's view, the poor referred to such work as 'convict-labour'.[80] Instead of just providing work on the roads and in gravel pits, parishes increasingly considered the viability of offering more worthwhile work, such as spade labour, on parish land or on land leased by the parish.

It is possible to identify the existence of some grants of land, from the replies to the Rural Queries and from references in vestry minutes.[81] In Farnham, a 'considerable land is let to poor men in quantities of half an acre to two acres at £2 to £5 an acre' and a few farmers also gave permission for men to grow potatoes on their land.[82] In Godalming, the vestry set aside fifteen acres for rent by forty tenants, and the Mickleham vestry apportioned allotments on the church land which they offered to thirteen paupers to be 'cultivated with spade husbandry and cropped with potatoes'. In November 1831 the Caterham vestry agreed to employ the poor in digging and trenching ground for the planting of potatoes. Thomas Ellis, a farmer, declined to 'set out land without receiving £4 in addition to the rent', but the issue was resolved by Mr Pinder Simpson

---

78 Epsom meeting, 17 March 1834, *Labourers' Friend Magazine* (London, 1834), p. 81.
79 BPP, *PLCR*, Appendix A part 1 XXVIII Assistant Commissioners' Report for Surrey A. Majendie p.170A.
80 BPP, *PLCR*, Appendix A part 1 XXVIII Assistant Commissioners' Report for Surrey A. Majendie p. 170A.
81 BPP, *PLCR*, Extracts from information received by Poor Law Commissioners Labour Rate Schemes Poor Appendix D xxxviii Surrey pp. 55D–73 D.
82 BPP, *PLCR*, Extracts from information received by Poor Law Commissioners Rural Queries for Surrey Appendix B Part I XXX, Evidence Farnham Question 20 p.480c; BPP *PLCR*, Appendix A part 1 XXVIII Assistant Commissioners' Report for Surrey C.H. Maclean p. 576A.

who had been a victim of the Swing protests. During the disturbances at his farm 'two stacks of wheat, three barns, a large building, two or three stacks of barley and oats and a quantity of threshed wheat in the barns' were destroyed.[83] Simpson agreed to set apart one field for the employment of the poor and agreed to receive no rent.[84] Thomas Drewitt a Guildford farmer reported in 1833 that Guildford farmers were now 'more willing to grant land' to labourers, but he gave no further details, only stating that, as a proprietor, he allowed his labourers 'between 30 and 60 roods'.[85] Smallpiece reported three years later that in the Guildford area 'we have more spade husbandry and we have allotments of land for the poor in many instances, and the cultivation of potatoes has enabled them to keep a pig or two and that has increased their comfort'.[86] Figure 3 provides an indication of the land that was provided by the parish vestries of Banstead, Cranleigh, Dorking, Esher and Egham.

The same sense of urgency to provide work can also be seen in Godalming, where parish officials, anxious to find work for unemployed labourers during the ensuing winter, held a special vestry meeting in November 1830 to discuss the best methods of employing the poor. They also asked landowners to make jobs available and seven landowners offered work ranging from grubbing and digging to work in a stone pit.[87] In the large parish of Egham where several farmers had experienced a number of incendiary fires in May 1831 a committee was appointed with the task of finding land in the parish for the employment of the poor, while the overseers applied to certain landowners to rent small pieces of land to the parish. By the autumn of 1831, small pieces of ground had been obtained across the parish. Labourers grew potatoes for the use of the parish on some of this land and these were later sold at public auction.[88] The Egham vestry reported in December 1831 that wage rates for labour 'on the poor allotments was as low as possible' and only labourers with no other work were to be employed, an encouragement for labourers to find their own work before reverting to the parish for assistance. Owing to insufficient employment opportunities on the allotments, the overseers had to continue employing some men on the roads and in digging gravel.

83 BPP, HO 52/10, 5 November 1830.
84 Wells, 'Historical Trajectories', 103; SHC, MIC/9/2 Mickleham Vestry Minutes: 24 March 1832, LA2/2/21 Caterham Vestry Minutes: 28 November 1831.
85 BPP, SC on Agriculture V 1833, Evidence T. Drewitt Question 10249 p. 479.
86 BPP, SC on the Causes and Extent of Agricultural Distress VIII 1836, Evidence of G. Smallpiece Question 3075 p.150.
87 SHC, 2253/11/1 Godalming Special Vestry Minutes: 24 November 1830.
88 SHC, 2516/2/10 Egham Vestry Minutes: 16 May 1831, 3 October 1831, 5 December 1831 and 2 January 1832.

Figure 3: The Provision of Spade Labour by Surrey Parishes 1830–1834

Parish	Date	Provision
Banstead	1834	3 acres set aside attached to workhouse
Cranleigh	1833	150 acres of wasteland
Dorking	1829	Discussed the possibility of providing land
Esher	1832	Completed a parish survey of wasteland
Egham	1831	In the Autumn: Pieces of waste ground obtained across the parish, 4 acres in Knowle Hill area, Egham Field, 8 acres at Shrubs Hill

Source: SHC 2375/2/1 October 1834 Banstead Vestry Minutes, P58/1/1 16 September 1833 Cranleigh Vestry Minutes, DOM/9/3 27 October Dorking Special Vestry Meeting 1829, 238/ES/9/3 12 April 1832 Esher Vestry Minutes, 2516/2/10 16 May 1831, 3 October 1831, 5 December 1831, 2 January 1832 Egham Vestry Minutes.

Even after this concerted effort, the overseers nonetheless reported to the vestry in February 1832 that there still remained a 'large body of labourers out of employ'.[89] With the greater availability of summer farm work, parish officers informed labourers in June that they now had to find their own employment. In the autumn of 1832, the vestry again discussed the employment of labourers for the coming winter. It not only decided to use the same three sites as the previous year but also tried to obtain land in the Englefield Green area to employ men of that district. The vestry also confirmed they would follow the policy of the previous winter 'of finding work for all able-bodied labourers instead of giving parochial relief' as they believed such a system deterred the idle from applying for parochial assistance 'when they found they must work for it'.[90]

Unfortunately, although it appears that many parishes did introduce some type of land provision immediately after the Swing protests, they did not all survive for long. In 1843 Henry H. Vaughan Assistant Commissioner of the Poor Law Commission reported that land grants had been tried in most parts of Sussex, Surrey and Kent but now 'few [districts] in which they can be said to be general'.[91]

89 Ibid., 6 February 1832.
90 Ibid., 5 December 1831, 6 February 1832, 4 June 1832 and 16 November 1832.
91 BPP, SC on the Employment of Women and Children in Agriculture XII 1843, Evidence H. H. Vaughan for Surrey p.143.

VI The Labour Rate

The introduction of the labour rate was another method used to employ surplus labour.[92] Although variations of this device were in use before 1832, it was not until August of that year that Parliament gave parishes the statutory power to levy a labour rate. The scheme, introduced for the better employment of labourers in agricultural parishes, was to run until 25 March 1834. Roger Wells has seen this as 'one of the few measures directly addressing Swing's grievances' and a stop-gap measure by the Whig government before the reform of the poor law system.[93] The Labourers' Employment Act of 1832 provided a statutory framework for vestry adoption of labour rates, although on a temporary basis. In order for a parish to adopt the labour rate, three quarters of ratepayers in a parish had to agree to the introduction of the measure 'solely for the purpose of employing or relieving the poor of the parish'.[94] The act stated that 'whereas in many parishes ... it has been the custom to pay to labourers and others less than the common rate of wages for their labour and to make up the deficiency from the poor rates', the authorities now viewed this practice as unacceptable.[95] Parish officers calculated the labour rate, estimating the cost of relieving the able-bodied unemployed for a period of time set by the vestry. Each ratepayer then had the option of paying the rate or employing men at the specified wage. At the end of the period the wage bill was compared to his assessment, and if he had paid in full his assessment for the labour rate in wages, he was excused payment of the rate. If there was a shortfall, he was required to pay the balance to the overseer.

J.P. Huzel points out that in 1832 the labour rate was more prevalent than either the Speenhamland or roundsman systems, and 'especially in rural southern counties'.[96] Approximately twenty per cent of the grain producing parishes that responded to the Rural Queries acknowledged that they had used labour rates during the winter.[97] The Surrey poor law commissioners reported the full details of some schemes, as at Albury, Great Bookham, Bletchingley, Cranleigh, Elstead, Farnham, Frensham,

---

92 J.P. Huzel, 'The Labourer and the Poor Law 1750–1850' in G.E. Mingay (ed.), *The Agrarian History of England and Wales 1750–1850* 6 (Cambridge, 1989) p. 782.
93 R. Wells, 'Migration, the Law and Parochial Policy in Eighteenth and Nineteenth-century Southern England', *Southern History* 15 (1993), 117.
94 2nd and 3rd William IV 1832 c.96 for the better employment of labourers in agricultural parishes p. 2
95 Ibid.
96 Huzel, 'The Labourer', p. 782.
97 M. Blaug, 'The Poor Law Report Re-examined', *The Journal of Economic History* 24 (1964), 236–37.

West Horsley, Worplesdon, Woking, Send and Ripley.[98] There were many others operating in the county. Careful examination of vestry minutes and accounts indicates that the parishes of Abinger, Betchworth, Ewell, Godstone, Godalming, Horley and Shere also participated. Most schemes ran for periods of six weeks and, where necessary, continued sometimes on different terms. It has been possible to identify 19 labour schemes in Surrey, but there may have been more, for, as Maclean observed a 'great portion of the distressed agricultural parishes' had introduced the labour rate.[99]

The management of such schemes was extremely onerous and time consuming to administer; there were problems of enforcement and they were subject to considerable abuse. In agricultural parishes where large farmers relied on unskilled labour, they benefited both from a cut in their wages bill and a reduction in their poor rates. Some parishes, as at Cranleigh, made concessions to smaller farmers by allowing them to employ their sons as day labourers. However, small tradesmen, who used only family labour, did not benefit. Maclean recognised this point, commenting in his report that the labour rate 'created extreme dissatisfaction among the tradesmen, tithe-owners, householders, a class of ratepayers who have no opportunity, means or necessity to employ much labour'.[100] Although there was criticism of the scheme in the short term, it did possess many positive advantages. For example in Farnham in the winter of 1831–32, 196 men were being relieved by the parish. In January–February 1833, when the labour rate was operating, only twelve men were chargeable; a saving of £584 in eight weeks for the parish. In 1833, Thomas Drewitt reported that the poor rates in the Guildford area, hitherto increasing, were now in decline because of the introduction of the labour rate.[101] Similarly, Smallpiece observed that 'we have none unemployed now; it has relieved a great many of our worst parishes very much' and labourers are no longer 'lying about upon the roads; they are now employed to some purpose'.[102] Perhaps the reason for such widespread support was summed up by Maclean who observed that since

---

98 BPP, *PLCR*, Extracts from information received by Poor Law Commissioners Labour Rate Schemes Poor Appendix D xxxviii Surrey pp. 55D–73D.
99 BPP, *PLCR*, Appendix A part 1 XXVIII Assistant Commissioners' Report Maclean p. 554A.
100 BPP, *PLCR*, Appendix A part 1 XXVIII Assistant Commissioners' Report for Surrey C.H.Maclean p. 554A.
101 BPP, SC on Agriculture V 1833, Evidence T. Drewitt Question 10210-15 pp. 477–78.
102 BPP, SC on Agriculture V 1833, Evidence G. Smallpiece Question 12872, 12875, 12876, p. 616.

the introduction of the labour rate 'no fires, no depredations and no disturbances have occurred'.[103] This must have been a key factor for parish support.

Not all supported the scheme, and it was never renewed after 1834. The poor law commissioners thought the labour rate so pernicious that they issued the early publication of a report designed to secure the abandonment of the practice.[104] The commissioners viewed the scheme as supporting the tenant farmers (who controlled most vestries in rural Surrey):

> The country is now aware that the great motive to the maladministration of the poor laws is the desire of the farmers in the country to throw part of the wages of their workmen on those who are not direct employers of labour.[105]

They added that the poor now perceive their wages 'are not a matter of contract but a matter of right'.[106] In his report on Surrey, Majendie declared that it was 'decidedly wrong in principle as interfering with the market for labour and imposing the employment of labour on those who do not require it', but at the same time accepted it was useful as a 'temporary expedient'.[107]

In 1832 the percentage of labourers aided by their parishes in the south was far greater than in the industrial midlands and the north-west, as can be seen from Figure 4. This was because of the lack of employment opportunities, and for many parishes in the period after 1830 these responsibilities were overwhelmingly shouldered by local government.[108]

VII Emigration

After the turmoil of the Swing protests, more contemporaries favoured emigration as a solution to the unrest and a way to alleviate the problem of poverty, by removing surplus labour and the disorderly. The large market town of Dorking had one of the highest poor relief expenditures in rural Surrey.[109] By 1830, the town was experiencing considerable

---

103 BPP, *PLCR*, Appendix A part 1 XXVIII Assistant Commissioners' Report for Surrey C.H. Maclean p. 552A.
104 BPP, *PLCR*, Extracts from information received by Poor Law Commissioners Labour Rate Schemes Poor Appendix D XXXVIII including Surrey pp. 55D–73D.
105 BPP, *PLCR*, Concerning the Labour Rate XXXII p. 278.
106 *Ibid.*,
107 BPP, *PLCR*, Appendix A part 1 XXVIII Assistant Commissioners' Report for Surrey Evidence A. Majendie p. 166A.
108 Eastwood, *Governing Rural England*, pp. 171–73.
109 April 1830–March 1831 £3,835 per annum

Figure 4: Abstract of poor returns for five counties for 1831–32

Region	Per-capita Expenditure On Poor (£)	% of Poor Rate expended In Employing Poor On Roads	Total % of Poor Rate Spent On All Parish Work Schemes	Total % of Poor Rate Spent On Employing Poor	% of Population Occupied On Parish Work Schemes
Surrey	0.57	5.83	1.35	7.18	1.91
Oxfordshire	0.88	8.0	3.92	11.9	2.1
Buckinghamshire	0.97	6.5	4.28.	10.8	2.2
Nottinghamshire	0.33	3.8	0.22	4.1	0.25
Lancashire	0.22	1.0	0.68	1.7	0.08
Abstract of poor returns nationally for 1831–32					
England	0.50	3.6	1.31	5.2	0.52

Source: Abstract Poor Rates Returns year to 25 March 1832 and 1833 xxxii (32) pp.16–17

unemployment which was of great concern to the select vestry. The issue of pauper unemployment was discussed at numerous special vestry meetings between 1828 and 1830. In 1830 the Swing disturbances directly affected Dorking, for a crowd of eighty or more attacked the Red Lion Inn where magistrates were meeting. In addition several farmers in the vicinity were victims of incendiary attacks. As a result of increasing unemployment, a special vestry meeting held on 10 February 1832 decided 'to encourage emigration of persons receiving relief from the parish'.[110] The motion, proposed by Charles Barclay, chairman of the select vestry, and seconded by William Crawford, declared that:

> the number of labourers in this parish has for many years so far exceeded the number required for the cultivation of the land and for other purposes, that the overseers have been constantly under the necessity of employing a great many upon public works at a very considerable expense beyond the value of their labour.

Barclay also recognised that:

> there is no prospect of any improvement in the condition of these supernumerary labourers from any future increase of employment in this

110 SHC, Dom/9/3 Dorking Select Vestry: 10 February 1832.

parish, the only mode of affording them permanent relief is by giving encouragement to such of them as are willing to emigrate with their families to our colonies in North America.[111]

In 1832, emigrants were usually required not only to pay their fares but to provide clothing and provisions for the long sea journey, as well as the costs of transportation on arrival in the new country. People emigrating would have to forgo earnings for one to three months and so emigration of the poor agricultural labourer without assistance was extremely difficult. As Eric Richards has pointed out, the poor were not well placed to raise the costs: 'instead, the poor usually came last in the sequence of emigration'.[112] Therefore, typical self-financed emigrants tended to be substantial tenant farmers, skilled industrial workers or village craftsmen with some savings.

The scheme adopted by many parishes after 1830 was to encourage poor emigration by financing the journey of individuals or small family groups, although once at their destination, the emigrants were required to support themselves. For example in April 1832, the Esher vestry agreed to pay for the emigration to America of five single men and one family of six.[113] The parish of Thames Ditton assisted Henry Ratcliffe to leave for America.[114] All these schemes involved very small numbers and proved to be far less of a financial and administrative burden than organising large-scale emigration, although after 1830 there were agents, who wrote to parish overseers offering their services to organise parish emigration 'at the lowest possible rates'.[115] Nonetheless, large-scale emigration from Surrey was only organised from Dorking in 1832, the parish using the agent E.M. Mitchell of London. The Dorking scheme followed large-scale parish schemes such as those operating in the Kent parishes of Headcorn and Beneden. The Petworth Emigration Committee in Sussex from 1832 to 1837 assisted 1,800 men, women and children to leave England for Upper Canada on ships chartered by the committee, which sailed from Portsmouth every summer.[116] The Petworth emigrations took place under the patronage of the earl of Egremont who encouraged them by assuming the financial risk of chartering ships and other expenses. He also paid for

111 SHC, Dom/9/3 Dorking Select Vestry: 10 February 1832
112 E. Richards, 'How did Poor People Emigrate from the British Isles to Australia in the Nineteenth Century', *Journal of British Studies* 32 (1993), 250.
113 SHC, 238/ES/9/3 Esher Vestry Minutes: 12 April 1832.
114 SHC, 2568/6/1 Thames Ditton Vestry Minutes: 13 May 1832.
115 SHC, FP1/3/3 File 2 Farnham Vestry: Letter from William Canon 6 February 1833.
116 West Sussex Record Office, Chichester [hereafter WSRO], SRO PHA 137,140, Goodwood MS 1473, 1474; W. Cameron and M. McDougall Maude, *Assisting Emigration to Upper Canada: the Petworth Project 1832–1837* (Montreal, 2000).

the full passage of emigrants sent to Upper Canada from parishes where he owned all the land and part passage where he owned some of the land. The committee was also prepared to take people from neighbouring counties whose passage was paid by their own parish or by some other scheme, as was the case for the Dorking emigrants.[117]

An analysis of the records (Figure 5) reveals that in the short term, the Dorking emigration scheme of 1832 did alleviate the strain that had been put on ratepayers to provide for the poor. In 1833 Charles Barclay made clear reference to the problems of the winters of 1831 and 1832, when the parish had to find employment for between 70 and 80 persons, either upon the roads or in the gravel pits. 'This year', he wrote 'there have been only 40 or 50, showing a difference about equal to the number of the labourers who emigrated to Canada'. He further acknowledged that, 'by the assistance afforded to those who have emigrated we may also contemplate the improved situations of those who remain'.[118] If we compare the costs paid out in Dorking for employing the poor and providing casual relief before the emigration of 1832 and 1833, and the costs after those dates, there was a significant saving.

Figure 5: Dorking Poor Relief Payments 1830–1834

Date	Casual Relief	Employing Poor	Total
September 1830–March 1831	£316	£540	£856
March 1831–September 1831	£291	£338	£629
September 1831–February 1832	£285	£671	£956
February 1832–September 1832	£326	£384	£710
September 1832–March 1833	£343	£416	£759
March 1833–September 1833	£280	£164	£444
September 1833–March 1834	**	**	**
March 1834–September 1834	£269	£91	£360
September 1834–March 1835	£174	£195	£369
March 1835–October 1835	£225	£128	£353
October 1835–February 1836	£200	£211	£411

** Spoiled Record
Source: SHC, DOM9/3 part 3: Dorking Vestry minute Book 1830–1843.

117 Emigrants from Hampshire, Somerset, Hereford, Norfolk, Cambridgeshire, Wiltshire.
118 C. Barclay, *Address to the inhabitants of Dorking and Letters from Dorking Emigrants* (Dorking, 1833), p. 6.

Even so, in the short term, the emigration costs had to be considered. These amounted to £310 15s. from the poor rates and £415 17s. 6d. raised by subscription (which was not repaid). Members of the select vestry and subscribers accepted these immediate costs on the basis of the long-term saving and hoped more people would emigrate. The cynical approach would be to view emigration in the short term as being partially successfully in 'shovelling out paupers' as emigration was not considered in Dorking as a long-term solution to the problem of rural unemployment.[119] This may well have been because of the cost factor. As the Reverend Sockett commented to Charles Barclay, 'I am too well aware of the extreme difficulty that exists in some parishes in raising the money for sending out emigrants'.[120] To set up and administer such a scheme took considerable time and energy on the part of Charles Barclay and the select vestry. The immediate affects of the Swing disturbances in Dorking most definitely acted as a spur to encourage parishioners to contribute to the emigration scheme.

VIII Post Swing

Increasingly, after the disturbances of 1830, parish vestries found themselves providing the traditional allowances of pensions, clothing, sickness benefits and so on and, increasingly, wages for the unemployed poor labourers working on the roads and implemented labour schemes. At the same time vestrymen were now anxious to leave the business of administering poor relief, and supervising labour schemes to their paid officials. For example the assistant overseer in Godalming continually requested landowners to make jobs available to unemployed labourers and in Egham the assistant overseer continually applied to certain landowners to rent small pieces of ground.[121] Eastwood has noted, instituting a system of salaried officers changed the character of parish government. In parishes with assistant overseers, the routine financial management passed from elected overseers to appointed assistant overseers. After the unrest 'vestrymen were even more keen to leave the distasteful business of administering inadequate relief regimes, and supervising stringent make-work schemes, to their paid officials'.[122]

---

119 Hansard, C.Buller, 1843: col.522.
120 WSRO, Goodwood 1464, Letters from the Reverend Sockett to Charles Barclay.
121 SHC 2253/11/1,Godalming Special Vestry minutes November 1830;SHC 2516/2/10, Egham Vestry Minutes 16 May 1831,3 October 1831,5 December 1831 and 2 January 1832.
122 Jones, 'Swing, Speenhamland', 285.

Ameliorative action was not left exclusively to local authorities however, for central government too was now, as Dunkley puts it 'groping for some response'. For Peter Mandler this was as a 'quest for administrative solutions'.[123] By the end of 1830 the government believed that the administration of the present relief system was generating distress by promoting able-bodied pauperism, depressing wages and encouraging population growth.[124] It was now time for central government to intervene to reduce relief expenditures. The view that the poor law had destroyed the work ethic within the labouring classes had gained more general acceptance. Senior criticised the use of allowances in parishes as causing 'idleness and improvidence occasioned by making up wages out of rates'.[125] Furthermore, he agreed with Lord Holland that the present poor law system was responsible for much of the distress in the countryside.[126] Lord Holland also informed Grey in 1830 that the southern and midland counties 'cannot remain as they are and nothing can cure the evil but a speedy and effectual revision of the poor laws'.[127]

From its inception in 1830 the Whig government was also 'receiving advice that indicated a direct link between the administration of relief and social disruption in the South'.[128] Now there were those in government who believed that the present relief system was inadequate to safeguard society, and it was accepted that 'idleness, disaffection and dependent poverty were corroding the foundations of social stability'.[129] In parliamentary circles, the poor law was increasingly seen as a threat rather than a prop to social order. Lord Lansdowne directly attributed the unrest of 1830 to the precarious economic conditions of the agricultural labourer.[130] Many landowners viewed the popular protests as a signal that

123 P. Dunkley, 'Whig and Paupers: The Reform of the English Poor Laws 1830–1834', *The Journal of British Studies* 20 (1981), 127; P. Mandler, 'The Making of the New Poor Law Redivivus', *Past and Present* 117 (1987), 149.
124 University College, London [hereafter UCL], Brougham Papers, Lord Holland to Lord Grey 26 November 1830; University of Durham, Durham [hereafter UD], Lord Grey Papers Box34/File 2, Lansdowne to Lord Grey 2 January 1831 also Box 38/File 10, Lord Goderich to Lord Brougham 28 December 1830.
125 RA, Melbourne Papers Box 35/91, Memo by N.W. Senior 31 January 1831.
126 N.W. Senior, *Three Lectures on the rate of wages: delivered before the University of Oxford in Easter term 1830: with a preface on the causes and remedies of the Present disturbances* (London, 1831); UCL, Brougham papers, Lord Holland to Lord Brougham 31 December 1830.
127 UD, Grey Papers Box 34/File 2, Lord Holland to Lord Grey 26 November 1830.
128 Dunkley, 'Whigs and Paupers', 127.
129 Eastwood, *Governing Rural England*, p. 163.
130 The National Archives, London, Box 8/86 Melbourne Papers, Lord Landsdowne to Lord Melbourne 3 November 1830.

the parish administration of poor relief was badly mismanaged and no longer a guarantor of social stability.[131]

IX Conclusion

The 1820s was a period of deepening economic and agrarian crisis when parish officials 'began to pull back from many of the commitments they had made over the previous thirty years'.[132] The poor adopted many strategies to cope with the fragility and sparseness of their material world but found themselves more dependent on poor relief when the economy of makeshifts weakened. As a result the Swing disturbances may have been symptomatic of the widespread prevalence of low wages, unemployment and underemployment in southern England, deriving from adverse economic conditions. It is apparent that after the Swing protests the parish officials were anxious to contain social tensions. Local parish officers supported by ratepayers now tried to restore social equilibrium by making concessions. However this explanation alone is too simplistic. It is clear that in Surrey, as Peter Jones has also shown, the response of local vestries after 1830 shows the importance of the 'right to subsistence'. During the unrest the linkage made by labourers between the demands for work, wages and relief 'continued to be shared (or, at the very least acted upon in practice) by parish authorities' immediately after the agricultural protests.[133] Increased relief allowances, the introduction of the labour rate, the desire to provide more constructive outdoor employment such as spade husbandry, and sponsored emigration were just some of the immediate solutions introduced by parishes in rural Surrey. Of course these measures were not unique to this county, as numerous parishes across southern England attempted to resolve the underlying problems that had resulted in the Swing protests. However, beside the range of responses pursed by the vestries in Surrey, this analysis has also illustrated in some respects the changing attitudes towards the poor after Swing as well as how the increasingly complex arrangements that were put in place passed into the hands of paid officials. The response to Swing amongst the Surrey vestries therefore revealed not only the significance of the 'moral economy' but also the growing bureaucratisation of government within the parish.

---

131 G. Bowyer, *An Economic History of the English Poor Law 1750–1850* (Cambridge, 1990), p. 198; Knott, *Popular Opposition*, p. 51.
132 Jones, 'Swing, Speenhamland', 283.
133 Ibid, 280.

Select Bibliography

Archer, J.E., *By a Flash and a Scare: Incendiarism, Animal Maiming, and Poaching in East Anglia 1815–1870* (Oxford, 1990)
Archer, J.E., *Social Unrest and Popular Protest in England 1780–1840* (Cambridge 2000)
Bellamy, L., Snell, K.D.M. and Williamson, T., 'Rural history: the Prospect Before Us', *Rural History* 1 (1990), 1–4
Bushaway, B., *By Rite: Custom, Ceremony and Community in England 1700–1880* (London, 1983)
Chambers, J., *Wiltshire Machine Breakers: The Rioters* (Letchworth, 1993)
Charlesworth, A., 'An Agenda for Historical Studies of Rural Protest in Britain, 1750–1850, *Rural History* 2 (1991), 231–40
Charlesworth, A. (ed.), *An Atlas of Rural Protest in Britain, 1548–1900* (Beckenham, 1983)
Charlesworth, A., *Social Protest in a Rural Society: The Spatial Diffusion of the Captain Swing Disturbances of 1830–1831* (Historical Geography Research Series, 1, Liverpool 1979)
Charlesworth, A. and Randall, A.J. (eds), *Markets, Market Culture and Popular Protest in Eighteenth Century Britain and Ireland* (Liverpool, 1996)
Charlesworth, A., Gilbert, D., Randall, A., Southall, H., and Wrigley, Christopher, J., *An Atlas of Industrial Protest in Britain, 1750–1990* (Basingstoke, 1996)
Charlesworth, A. and Randall, A. (eds), *Moral Economy and Popular Protest: Crowds, Conflict and Authority* (London 1999)
Dyck, I., *William Cobbett and Rural Popular Culture* (Cambridge 1992)
Griffin, C.J., 'Knowable Geographies? The Reporting of Incendiarism in the Eighteenth and early Nineteenth-century English Provincial Press', *Journal of Historical Geography* 32 (2006), 38–56
Griffin, C.J., 'Policy on the Hoof: Sir Robert Peel, Sir Edward Knatchbull and the Trial of the Elham Machine Breakers, 1830', *Rural History* 15 (2004), 127–48
Griffin, C.J., '"There was No Law to Punish that Offence" Re-Assessing 'Captain Swing': Rural Luddism and Rebellion in East Kent, 1830–31', *Southern History* 22 (2000), 131–63
Griffin, C.J., 'Protest Practice and (tree) Cultures of Conflict: Understanding the Spaces of 'tree maiming' in Eighteenth- and early

Nineteenth-century England', *Transactions of the Institute of British Geographers* 40 (2008), 91–108

Griffin, C.J., 'Affecting Violence: Language, Gesture and Performance in early Nineteenth-century English Popular Protest', *Historical Geography* 36 (2008), 139–62

Griffin, C.J., '"Cut Down by Some Cowardly Miscreants": Plant Maiming, or the Malicious Cutting of Plants as an Act of Protest in Eighteenth- and Nineteenth Century Rural England', *Rural History* 19 (2008), 29–54

Griffin, C.J., 'Swing, Swing Redivivus, or Something after Swing? On the Death Throes of a Protest Movement, December 1830–December 1833, *International Review of Social History* 54 (2009), 459–97

Hammond, J.L. and Hammond, B., *The Village Labourer, 1760–1832: A Study in the Government of England before the Reform Bill* (London, 1911)

Himmelfarb, G., 'The Writing of Social History: Recent Studies of 19th Century England', *Journal of British Studies* 11 (1971), 148–70

Hobsbawm, E.J., 'History From Below – Some Reflections' in F. Kantz (ed.), *History from Below: Studies on Popular Protest and Popular Ideology* (Oxford, 1988), 13–27

Hobsbawm, E.J., 'The Machine Breakers', *Past & Present* 1 (1952), 57–70

Hobsbawm, E.J., and Rudé, G., *Captain Swing* (London 1969)

Hobsbawm, E.J., *Labouring Men: Studies in the History of Labour* (London 1964)

Holland, M. (ed.), *Swing Unmasked: The Agricultural Riots of 1830 to 1832 and their Wider Implications* (Milton Keynes, 2005)

Howkins, A., 'Labour History and the Rural Poor', *Rural History* 1 (1990), 113–22.

Howkins, A. and Dyck, I., 'The Time's Alteration: Popular Ballads, Rural Radicalism and William Cobbett', *History Workshop Journal* 23 (1987), 20–38

Jones, P., 'Swing, Speenhamland and Rural Social Relations: the 'Moral Economy' of the English Crowd in the Nineteenth Century', *Social History* 32 (2007), 271–90

Jones, P., 'Finding Captain Swing: Protest, Parish Relations and the State of the Public Mind in 1830', *International Review of Social History* 54 (2009), 429–58

Navickas, K., 'The Search for "General Ludd": the Mythology of Luddism', *Social History* 30 (2005), 281–95

Navickas, K., 'Moors, Fields, and Popular Protest in South Lancashire and the West Riding of Yorkshire, 1800–1848', *Northern History* 46 (2009), 93–111

Peacock, A.J., 'Village radicalism in East Anglia, 1800–1850', in J.P.D. Dunbabin (ed.), *Rural Discontent in Nineteenth Century Britain* (London 1974), 27–61

Pettitt, T., '"Here Comes I, Jack Straw": English Folk Drama and Social Revolt', *Folklore* 95 (1984), 3–20

Poole, S., '"A Lasting and Salutary Warning": Incendiarism, Rural Order and England's last Scene of Crime Execution', *Rural History* 19 (2008), 163–77.

Randall, A. and Newman, E., 'Protest, Proletarians and Paternalists: Social Conflict in Rural Wiltshire, 1830–1850', *Rural History* 6 (1995), 205–27

Randall, A., 'The Shearmen and the Wiltshire Outrages of 1802: Trade Unionism and Industrial Violence', *Social History*, 7 (1982), 283–304

Randall, A.J., *Before the Luddites: Custom, Community and Machinery in the English Woollen Industry, 1776–1809* (Cambridge, 1991)

Randall, A., *Riotous Assemblies: Popular Protest in Hanoverian England* (Oxford, 2006)

Randall, A., 'Captain Swing: A Retrospect', *International Review of Social History* 54 (2009) 419–27.

Reay, B., *Microhistories: Demography, Society and Culture in Rural England, 1800–1930* (Cambridge, 1996)

Reay, B., *The Last Rising of the Agricultural Labourers: Rural Life and Protest in Nineteenth Century England* (Oxford, 1990)

Reay, B., *Rural Englands: Labouring Lives in the Nineteenth Century* (Basingstoke, 2004)

Reed, M. and Wells, R. (eds), *Class, Conflict and Protest in the English Countryside 1770–1880* (London, 1990)

Rudé, G., 'English Rural and Urban disturbances on the eve of the first Reform Bill, 1830–1831', *Past & Present* 37 (1967), 87–102

Rudé, G., *Ideology and Popular Protest* (London, 1980)

Rudé, G., *The Crowd in History: a Study of Popular Disturbances in France and England, 1730–1848* (London, 1964)

Rule, J. and Wells, R., *Crime, Protest and Popular Politics in Southern England, 1740–1850* (London, 1997)

Stevenson, J., 'An Unbroken Wave?', *Historical Journal* 37 (1994), 683–95

Sutton, D., 'Radical Liberalism, Fabianism and Social History' in R. Johnson, G. McLennan, B. Schwarz and D. Sutton (eds), *Making Histories: Studies in History Writing and Politics* (Minnesota, 1982), 15–43

Tawney, R.H., *J.L. Hammond, 1872–1949* (London, 1961)

Thompson, E.P., *The Making of the English Working Class* (London, 1968)

Thompson, E.P., *Customs in Common* (London, 1991)

Tilly, C., *Popular Contention in Great Britain, 1758–1834* (Cambridge, Mass., 1995)

Walsh, D., 'The Lancashire 'rising' of 1826', *Albion*, 26 (1995), 601–21

Walter, J., 'Grain Riots and Popular Attitudes to the Law', in J. Brewer and J. Styles (eds), *An Ungovernable People,* (London, 1980), 47–84

Walter, J., 'Public Transcripts, Popular Agency and the Politics of Subsistence in Early Modern England' in M. Braddick and J. Walter (eds), *Negotiating Power in Early Modern England* (Cambridge, 2001), 123–48, 272–78

Wells, R., 'Crime and Protest in a Country Parish: Burwash, 1790–1850' in J. Rule and R. Wells (eds), *Crime, Protest and Popular Politics in Southern England* (London, 1997), 169–236

Wells, R., 'Mr William Cobbett, Captain Swing and King William IV', *Agricultural History Review* 45 (1997), 34–48

Wells, R., 'Rural Rebels in Southern England in the 1830s', in C. Emsley and J. Walvin (eds), *Artisans, Peasants and Proletarians, 1760–1860* (London, 1985), 124–65

Wells, R., 'The Development of the English Rural Proletariat and Social Protest, 1700–1850', *Journal of Peasant Studies*, 6 (1979), 115–39

Wells, R., 'Tolpuddle in the Context of English Agrarian Labour History, 1780–1850', in J. Rule (ed.), *British Trade Unionism 1750–1850: the Formative Years* (London, 1988), 98–142

Wrightson, K., 'The Enclosure of English Social History', *Rural History* 1 (1990), 73–81

Index

Abell, Mr (assistant overseer) 28
A'Court, Charles Ashe (Col.) 47, 49, 57, 144
Adams, William 121–2, 128–30, 135
Age, The 106–7, 109
Agricultural Employment Institute 187
America see United States
Andrews, Captain 134
Annales 5
Archer, E. 171
Archer, John 22, 35, 40
arson 10, 22–3, 35, 39, 42–4, 53–4, 58 n. 70, 63, 87–9, 91, 113, 116, 140, 144–5, 160, 166, 170, 172–3; see also incendiarism
artisans 35, 38, 139
Arundel, Lord 94, 164
Ashdown House 147
Avon valley 41

Bachelor, John 135
Baines, John 48
Baker, Thomas (farmer) 42
Baker, T. 113
Bakewell, Robert (geologist) 128
ballads 118–19; see also folk songs
Barclay, Charles 195, 197–8
Baring, Bingham (cousin of Francis) 126–8, 132–4, 136–8
Baring, Francis (cousin of Bingham) 132–4
Barnes, William (farmer) 29, 55
Barnes, William (carpenter) 122, 126, 129–30
Bartie, Thomas 135
Barton, Mr (investigating officer) 112
Baskerville, Justice 49, 57

Bawn, Kevin 38
Becker, Mr (overseer) 28
Bellamy, John 150
Benett, John 47, 50, 54
Berkshire 6, 15, 23, 32–3, 44, 90, 107, 112, 139–142, 143: map, 144–5, 147–51, 153, 155–7, 182, 188
Aldermaston 146
Barkham 145
Beenham 146
Bradfield 146
Brimpton 146
Bucklebury 146
Hungerford 142, 145–6, 150–1, 153, 156
Kintbury 146–7
Newbury 142, 145–7, 149–52
Reading 144–6, 148–54, 156
Ruscombe 144 n. 20
Speen 142
Thatcham 33, 146
Wasing 146
Wokingham 142, 144–5, 151
Woolhampton 146
Berkshire Chronicle 148, 153
Berriman, Thomas 39
Bertie, Montagu, 5th Earl of Abingdon, 142
Binfield, Kevin 19
Bishop, Mr (farmer) 29
Blackburne, Mr 151
Blake, Shadrack 55
Blunt, James (tithe holder) 31
Bohstedt, John 66, 75
Bowerton, Charles 53
Boyes, Faith (wife of John) 123
Boyes, John 121–4, 126–9, 132–8
Boyes, William 130–1

Brasher, John 51
Bray, William 182
Brewer, John 5
Briscoe, John 186, 188
Bristol 16, 134
  Corporation 16
Broad, J. 179
Brotherton, Col. 50–1, 165
Buckinghamshire (Bucks) 6, 107 n. 24, 142, 145, 148, 188
Budd, William 142, 149–51
Burchardt, Jeremy 185, 187
Burdett, Sir Francis Bt. 141
Burn, Richard
  Justice of the Peace and Parish Officer 141
Bushaway, B. 40
Butt, Mr (farmer) 25

Cambridgeshire 6, 38, 110, 197 n. 117
  Blundisham 112–13
  Cambridge 111
  Foulmere 38
  Gamlingay 110, 112
Campbell, John M.P. 151
Canada 181, 197
  Upper 196–7
Canning, Mr (farmer) 57
Canterbury 28 n. 30, 37, 137 n. 61
  Mount of Dane John 37
Carlile, Richard 14, 107–8, cf. 114, 116, 170
  The Life & History of Swing, the Kent Rick Burner, written by Himself 107–108, 118
Carlisle 6
Cartwright, Mr 46
Catholic Association 102
Catt, Mr (farmer) 35
Census
  (1831) 47
  (1841) 123 n. 19, 134–5
Champion (newspaper) 14
Chandler, Mrs 109

Chandos, Lord (M.P.) 142
Chapman, Thomas 186
Charlesworth, Andrew 2 n. 2, 13–15, 18–19, 22, 40, 59–60, 67–8, 87, 103, 175 n. 73
Chartism 14
Chumm, John 50
Clift, John 48
Clive, Henry 145, 153 n. 71
Cobb, Richard 7–8, 10, 13, 17
Cobbett, William 16, 37, 103, 108, 114, 123, 132–4, 137, 170, 179, 185
Codrington, Oliver 57
Coleman, S. 65
Coleridge, Henry Nelson 108
consciousness 4, 17, 63
  class 13, 15–16, 66
  collective 66–8
  common 82
  political 13–14, 63, 68
  proletarian 4
  radical 67
conservation 96–9
contagion 25, 33, 60, 64, 84
Corn Laws 115
Courtney, William (farmer) 30
Cove, Edward (Revd.) 146
Craven, 2nd Earl 147, 154
Crawford, William 195
crime 2, 114, 118, 136, 161–2, 167, 173, 175
  property 18
  social 92, 97–8, 140
croppers 44–6, 60
Cutler (Revd) 29

Dagle *see* Deacle, Thomas
Darnley, Lord 35
Daunton, M.J. 181
Davis, Mr Charles (farmer) 31, 47–8, 54–6, 60, 71
Dawson, Mr (farmer) 35
De Beauvoir, Richard Benyon 146

Deacle, Thomas (farmer) 121–34, 136–8
Deacle, Caroline 129, 131, 134
Debenalls, Mr 121; see also Dipnall
Denison, W.J. 188
Denman, Sir Thomas 50, 151
Devon 134
  Axminster 36
  Barton Court 146
  Newton Abbott 134
Devizes and Wiltshire Gazette 25
Diggles, see Deacle, Thomas
Dipnall, Mr 121, 125; see also Debenalls
dissent 8, 35, 167, 170
Dorset 6, 23–5, 31, 36, 39, 107, 169
  Bourton 26
  Silton Estate 36
  Bridport 24
  Dartford 35–6
  Dorchester 12
  Henstridge 31, 169
  Reigate 36
  Tolpuddle 11–12
    'Tolpuddle martyrs' 11
  Tomer 31
  Yenston 31, 169
Dorset County Chronicle 25
Dover 27, 31, 104, 113
Dover, Mr 167
Drewitt, Thomas (farmer) 190, 193
Drummond, Henry 182
Dublin 106
Duffie, Mr 115
Dundas, Charles M.P. 146–7, 149, 151–4
Dunkley, P. 181, 199
Durham 113
  Whitburn 113
Dyck, Ian 16, 127, 133

East Anglia 6, 9, 19, 35, 40
Easthampstead Park 145
Eastwood, David 139, 177, 198
ecology, moral 19, 86, 96–100
Egremont, earl of 32 n. 44, 196

Ellis, Thomas (farmer) 115, 189
Elver Wars, The 99
Emary, Mr (overseer) 28
emigration 156–7, 194–8, 200
enclosure 2–3, 8, 23, 94–5, 186–7
Era, The 134
Escott, Maggie 19, cf. 139–58
Essex 6, 112, 188
  Fyfield 29
  Lambridge 112
  Rochford 113
Estcourt, Mr 57
Examiner, The 104, 106, 109, 111

factories 46–7
Family and Community History
    Research Society (FACHRS)
    6–7, 10, 43 and n. 5, 44 and
    n. 7, 87, 187 n. 65
  Swing Research Project 76, 93
Ferris, William 41
Fire Office 25, 144
Fisher, Chris 95
Fitzgerald, John 104
Fitzwilliam, Mr 45
folk song 19, 116–17, 119; see also ballads
Fowle, Rev. Fulwar Craven 146
Fowler, Mr (farmer) 26, 54
France 109, 117 n. 2
Freeling, Sir Francis (Secretary to the
    Post Office) 35 n. 54, 142
Freeman's Journal 106
Freemantle, Nicolas 120–1, 124,
    129–30, 135
Fremantle, Sir William 144
Freud, Sigmund 64
Fulbrook, Mr (farmer) 55
Fussell, James 122, 124, 130–1
Fussell, John 135

Gardiner, George B. 117, 119
Garth, Captain Thomas, RN 144 and
    n. 20
Gash, N. 32

George III, king of Great Britain 3
George, St 19
George Inn 28
Gerrard, Charles 47
Gibbs, Mr 112
Gloucestershire 6, 21, 31, 43, 52, 85, 91, 100, 188
   Baverstone 31
   Bromsbarrow 43
   Chavenage 31
   Chipping Camden 21
   Dean, 95, 98, 100
      Forest of 85, 94–5, 98, 100
   Gloucester 91, 99, 188
   Newnton 31
   Tetbury 31
   Winchcombe 85, 91, 98–100
Goddard, Thomas 48, 60
Goderich, Lord 140
Goodman, Thomas 118–19
   The Confessions 118–19
Gosse, Henry 188
Gower, General John Leveson 144 n. 21, 145
graffiti 27
Great Reform Act 1
Grenada 150
Greve, H.R. 65, 71
Grey, Lord 141, 151, 157, 184, 199
Grey, Mr (farmer) 31
Griffin, Carl (C.J.) 9, 11, 19, 88, 90, 93–4, 141, 159–60, 175
Gurney, John 151, 156

Hammond, H.E.D. 117, 119
Hammond, J.L. and Barbara 2–3, 4 n. 4, 5 and n. 9, 6–7, 11, 17, 22, 59 n. 72, 123, 127, 136
   The Village Labourer (1911) 1, 123
Hampshire 6–7, 12, 14, 23–5, 29, 30–3, 44, 107 n. 24, 114, 117–18, 120–1, 127, 132, 135, 138, 143: map, 145, 147, 150, 163, 174, 188, 197 n. 117

Andover 30, 33
Ashmansworth 146
Barton Stacey 30, 33, 39
Baybridge 121, 125
Bishop Stoke 123
Bishops Waltham 122; see also Waltham
Broughton 29
Chilbolton 7
Colden Common 121, 123–4, 135
Corhampton 120, 124, 130
Dever Valley 33, 39
East Dean 29
East Tytherley 29
Fareham 35–6
Gosport 25, 32
Hannington 55
Havant 32–3
Kimpton 29
Leckford 29
Longparish 32
Michaelmersh 114
Nether Wallop 31
Newton Stacey 30
Owslebury 117–38
   Marwell Farm 121, 125–7
   Marwell Hall 121, 125–6, 131
Portsmouth 132, 135, 196
Romsey 29
Shoddesden 29
South Stoneham 123
Southampton 131
St. Mary Bourne 30
Strathfieldsaye 36
Sutton Scotney 136
Tasker 30
Test Valley 29
Upham 121
Upper Clatford 30
Waltham 121; see also Bishops Waltham
Weyhill 30
Whitchurch 30, 33

Winchester 117–18, 121–2, 130–1, 136, 162–3, 165
Hampshire Advertiser 36
Hampshire Chronicle 29
Hampshire Telegraph 123, 135, 138
Hannam, George (farmer) 30–1 and n. 38
Hare, Reverend 48, 50, 54–6
Hay, P. 98, 100,
Hayter, Benjamin 125, 136
Hawkins, George 48–9
Hawkins, Richard 7, 17
Hedström, P. 83
heritage
 sense of 99
 Swing's 104
Hetherington, Henry 106, 116
Hill, Arthur Blundell Sandys Trumbull, 3rd Marquess of Downshire 145
Hill, Judith 19, cf. 176–200
Himmelfarb, Gertrude 4, 7
Hoare, John 122, 125, 130–1, 136
Hobhouse, Henry 161–2
Hobsbawm, Eric 1–14, 17–18, 20–4, 31–2, 40, 42–5, 49, 53, 58, 61, 66–7, 76, 85–7, 93, 139, 144, 157, 159, 176–7, 181, 185; *see also* Rudé, George
Hodgson, Christopher (brother of Thomas) 146
Hodgson, Thomas 146
Holland, Lord 199
Holland, M. 122
Hollis, Patricia 4
Home Office 36–37, 112, 142, 145–8, 150–2, 165, 172
 papers 2–3
Horn, N. 75–6; *see also* Tilly, C. *Contentious Gatherings In Britain: 1758–1834* 75
Horsfall, William 46, 50
housing 39, 77
Howkins, Alun 4, 19, cf. 117–38

Howton, Caleb 123
Hull Packet 106, 110
hunger 39; *see also* riots, food
Hunt, Henry 37–9
Huntingdonshire 6
Hurst Farm 121, 123
Hutton (vicar) 29
Huzel, J.P. 192

incendiarism 8–12, 16, 19, 21–32, 34, 38–40, 53, 102, 137, 172–3, 177; *see also* arson
Informers Act 9
India 134
 Bombay 134
Inge, Cooper 62
Inskipp, Charles 103
Ireland 19, 103–6
Ireland, William (farmer) 91

Jacoby, Karl 96–7, 100
James, Warren 85, 94–5, 100
Jefferies, Thomas 55
Jennings, John 52
Jones, E.L. 4, 7, 14
Jones, Owain 94
Jones, Peter 13, 15, 18 and n. 53, 19, 23, 38, 40, 59 n. 73, 89–90, 93, 106, 108, 114, 116, 177, 179, 185, 200
Jones, Richard 108
Jordan, Richard 112
Journal of the Royal Statistical Society, The 2

Katz, E. 69
Kent 6, 8, 14, 17, 21–8, 30–5, 43–4, 62, 106–7, 111, 114, 135, 144, 159, 176, 191, 196
 Alland Grange 30
 Ash-next-Sandwich 28
 Beneden 196
 Birchington 33
 Borden 27

210   Index

Kent (*continued*)
  Chartham 35
  Cobham 35
  Elham 26–7, 34, 159–60
  Faversham 35
  Hartlip 27
  Headcorn 196
  Herne Hill 18
  Hernhill 33
  Hougham 27, 31
  Isle of Thanet 33
  Lower Hardres 8, 17–18, 43
  Lyminge 26–8
  Maidstone 34
    Weald, the 28
  Newington 27
  Sandwich 28
  Selling 35
  Stockbury 34–5
  Tunbridge-Wells 17
King, Steven 179
King's Bench 147
Knatchbull, Sir Edward 26
Knight (farmer, overseer) 27
Knight, James 121, 125
Knott, J. 181

labour 3, 38, 48, 52, 55–6, 59, 62, 110, 114, 141, 178, 185, 189–90, 194–5, 198
  day- 178, 180
  force 181
  hard 53, 164, 169
  history of 5
  Irish 18
  rates 186, 192–4, 200
  rural 18
  winter 18
Labourers' Friend Society 187–8
Lacy, Charles 45
Laincer, Mr (assistant overseer) 28
Lane, James 48
Langford, John 42, 47
Langford, Thomas 52–3

Lawrence, Thomas 53
leadership 56, 60, 136–7, 147
  military-style 50
  mythical 19
  rural 184
Le Bon, Gustave 64, 84
Leeds Mercury 45
Leicestershire
  Empingham 10
letters 128, 142, 151, 171
  anonymous 16, 76
  emigrant 181
  inflammatory 108, 110, 112
  Swing 27, 31–2, 43 and n. 5, 87, 106, 108–9, 111–12, 177
  threatening 8, 10, 19, 21, 31, 43, 48, 63, 104, 144, 172
Lincolnshire 6
  Bourne 113
  Marston 57
London 13, 15, 48, 68, 74–5, 77, 80, 84, 103–5, 107, 121, 123, 134, 137 and n. 62, 142, 144, 146, 153, 196
  Bedfont 111
  Blackfriars Road 108
  Egham 144, 183, 190–1, 198
  Hare Court, Inner Temple 151
  Kensington 113
  Orpington 21
  Rotunda 14, 108, 185
  Whitehall 113
Long, Lady Mary 121, 125, 131
Long, Mrs 129
Long, Walter 126
Longwood House 121–2, 125–6, 129
Lownde, Mr 121, 125
Ludd, Edward 45
Ludd, King (General) 19, 43, 88, 119
Luddism 19, 43–4 and n. 9, 45, 47–8, 50–1, 88, 120
  'the Luddism of the poor' 41, 45
Lyell, Charles 128
Lyne, Robert (farmer) 42, 48

Maberly, John M.P. 147
machinery 27, 43–5, 49, 48, 50–1, 57, 62, 79, 109, 114, 118, 121, 132, 143, 167
   agricultural 8, 62, 117, 163, 166
   anti–machinery disturbances 53
   machine-breaking 10, 22–8, 30–4, 38–40, 43, 46
   counties 54
   threshing 8, 10, 18, 23–33, 36, 41–9, 52–5, 57, 60–2, 106, 113, 144, 153, 160, 163–8, 177, 184–5
Maclean, Charles 180, 187–8, 193
Maidstone Journal 35
Maidenhead 144–5
   Colnbrook 144
   Holyport 144
maiming 140
   animal 76
   plant 94
Mair, John Hastings (Col.) 49, 150, 152, 156
Majendie, Ashurst (Poor Law Commissioner) 189, 194
Malford, Christian 11, 56
Malmesbury, Lord 102
Manchester Times, The 134
Mantell, Gideon 128, 134, 137
   Private Journal 128
Marwell Farm *see* Hampshire, Owslebury
Marwell Hall *see* Hampshire, Owslebury
Marxism 3–4, 66
Maule, Charles (Treasury Solicitor) 31, 37, 103, 151, 153–5
McCalman, Ian 137
Melbourne, Lord (Home Secretary) 12, 31, 102, 112, 140 n. 6, 147–52, 157, 160, 170, 184
Menzel, H. 69
Merrett, Mr (farmer) 35
Methuen, Paul 56
Middlesex 145
Middleton 45

Midlands 6, 46, 194
   Arnold 46
   Birmingham 11
   Chirton 46
Mildmay, Lady Caroline 135
Militia Acts 61
mills 21, 44–5, 47
   corn 52
   paper 166
miners 94
Minet, Mrs. (farmer) 35
Mingay, G.E. 6–8, 20
   The Unquiet Countryside (1989) 20
Mitchell, E.M. 196
mob 29, 34–5, 41–2, 46–7, 49–53, 55–60, 62, 64, 92, 112, 118–21, 123, 126–30, 135–8, 144, 153
mobbings 26, 29, 116, 142, 157
Montgomery, Mrs (magistrate's widow) 55
Mount, William 146
Moore, Mr (overseer) 183
Moore, Thomas
   Memoirs of Captain Rock, the Irish Chieftan, Written by Himself (1824) 105
More, Hannah 108
Morning Chronicle, The 110–11, 115
Mosyer, Mr (farmer) 21
Mott, Charles (Poor Law Commissioner for Surrey) 183
Myers, Dan 19, 65, 71, 80

Napoleonic War 3
Nash, William 51
Navickas, Katrina 19, 88–9, 120
Nelson, Admiral Horatio 121
Neumann, M. 182
New South Wales 135
   Williams River 135
Newcastle Courant 106
Newman, Edwina 15
Nolan, Emer 105, 107

nonconformists 13
Norfolk 6, 17, 44, 160–2, 165–172, 174–5, 188, 197
  the Wash 7, 12, 112
Northamptonshire 6, 188
Northesk, Lord 121, 129
North Wales Chronicle 109
Nott, Grace 121
Nottinghamshire 44, 51, 195
  Newark–on–Trent 130

O'Connell, Daniel 106
Old Posting House 122, 126, 129, 137
Onslow, Hon. Rev. Arthur 188
Orton, James 125, 135
Owenite Grand National Consolidated Trade Union 11
Oxfordshire 6, 106, 145, 148, 188, 195
  Abingdon 29 n. 33, 145–9, 153–5
  Faringdon 147
  Oxford
    Cumnor 144
    University of, Lincoln College 128
  Wallingford 145–6
  Wantage 145, 147

Packman, Brothers Henry and William 33–4
Page, Frederick (deputy lieutenant) 142
Palmer, Robert M.P. 145, 153 n. 71
Palmerstone, Lord 135
Paris 105
Park, Mr Justice 49, 154–5
Parliament 34, 113, 126, 132–3, 163, 186, 192, 199
Paters, Mr 113
Patient, Ambrose 47, 49, 57
Patteson, John 151, 153
Paven, Mr (farmer) 33
Payn, William (county treasurer) 155

Peacock, A.J. 9
Peel, Robert (Home Secretary) 36–7, 145–6, 148, 160
Pepper, Mr (farmer) 27
Pepper, Mrs. (widow) 71
Perry, G.W. 188
Peterloo [massacre, 1819] 119
Pettit, T. 40
Petty Sessions 57
Phillipps, Samuel March (Home Office Under-secretary) 151 and n. 59, 154
Pile, Mr Robert (farmer) 41–2, 46–50, 55–6, 58
Pleydell-Bouverie, William, 3rd Earl of Radnor 141
Political Register 133
Poole, Benjamin (farmer) 161
Poole, Steve 87, 161
Poor Laws 2–3, 33, 59–60, 106, 179, 181, 186, 194, 199
  Commission 38
  New Poor Law 11, 15, 57
Poore, Lady 56
Poore, Sir Richard 55–8
Poore Arms 56
Poor Man's Guardian 101, 106
Pope, Maurice (mob leader) 42, 48–9, 60
Price, Revd 27–8
Price, Robert (shoe maker) 34
prisoners 30, 52, 107, 131, 136, 147–9, 154, 156, 159, 161–4, 166–8
proletarianisation 4, 15
Prompter, The 108
Przybysz, Jamie 19, cf. 62–84
Purley Hall 148

Quaife, Thomas and James (farmers) 28, 29 n. 32, 36

radicalism 14–15, 67, 77, 103–4, 137–8
  Edwardian Liberal 3

London 137
rural 18
village 127
radicals 13–14, 37, 67–8, 74, 82–3, 87, 103, 145, 154
Randall, Adrian 15, 19, 85, 87–8, 173
Ratcliffe, Henry 196
Reay, Barry 6, 18
Reeves, John 47
reform 101, 114–15, 192
  Bill 2, 109
  parliamentary 14, 38
  policy 71, 180
Rest, Richard 120
Richards, Eric 196
Riot Act 146
riots 5–6, 12, 23, 41–3, 49, 51–3, 55–6, 58–61, 63, 72, 74, 76, 80, 85, 87, 89, 94–5, 119, 136
  enclosure see enclosure
  food riots 8, 52, 58–60
  grain 90
  James see James, Warren
  Swing 42–3, 51–2, 61, 74, 89, 127, 139–200
  urban 80
  wage see wages
Roach, E. (Revd.) 119–20, 129, 136
robbery 10, 43, 53, 87, 92, 122, 125, 130, 148–9, 154, 163; see also stealing
Robbins, William 46
Roberts, John 142
Robertson, Iain 19, 100
Rochester Gazette 34
Rock, Captain 19, 104–8
Rogers, Everett 65
Rolph, Mr 113–14
Rowley, John 26
Royal Commissions 109
Royal Forests 94
Rudé, George 1–14, 17–18, 20–25, 31–32, 40, 42–45, 49, 53, 58, 61, 66–67, 76, 85–7, 93, 139,
144, 157, 159, 177, 181; see also Hobsbawm, Eric
The Crowd in History (1964) 8
Rutland 10

Samuel, Raphael 5
Satirist, The 115
Saville, Joseph 110–13
Scrope, George Poulett 185
'Sevenoaks fires' 21–2
Severn, River 99
  Fisheries Board 99
  shearing frames 44–6
  machines 48
  mill 45–6
sheep fair 30
Shepherd, Henry John 151
Sherborne Journal 25
Sherwin, Master 111
Shewry, Mr 55
Simpson, Mr Pinder 189–90
Slasher, Captain 19
Smallbones, Jonathan 41
Smallpiece, G. 190, 193
Smith, John (farmer) 121–3, 131
Smith, Phoebe (wife of John Smith) 123, 125–6
Smith, Robert (brother of Samuel) 167–8
Smith, Samuel (brother of Robert) 167–8
Smith, William 46–7
Smoker, John 126, 129
Society for the Promotion of Christian Knowledge (SPCK) 108, 116
Somerset 9, 16, 23–6, 31, 36–7, 94, 127, 142, 159–75, 197
  Bridgwater 15
  Ilchester 94
  Kenn 9, 25, 161–2, 172
  Nether Stowey 15
  Otterhampton 15
  South Petherton 15
  Stogursey 15

Somerset (*continued*)
    Taunton 25, 37–8, 134
    Thurlbear 25
    Totterdown 16
    Uphill 127–8
    Whitelackington 36
Sondes, Lord 35
Soule, A. 71
Southampton Mercury 25
'Speenhamland' 2, 182, 192
Special Commissions 8 n. 17, 11, 19, 50, 52, 60, 107 and n. 24, 114, 131, 149–50, 162, 174
    Hampshire 39
    Swing 2, 162
Spicer, James 42, 53–4
Spilerman, S. 71
Stacey, Charlotte (wife of Courtney Stacey) 34
Stacey, Courtney 34
Stagg, James 117, 119
Stanbrook, Moses 121–2, 130
stealing 97; *see also* robbery
    fowl 161
    horse 171
    sheep 92, 100
    wood 95, 100
Stephens, Messrs T. and W. 36
Stephens, Talfourd and Blackburne 151
Stockport 45, 51
Stone, Laban 48
Strang, D. 65, 69, 71, 79, 83
Studdam, Elizabeth 33
Sturges–Bourne Select Vestries Act (1819) 186
Suffolk 6, 21, 110, 188
    Brandon 21
    Mildenhall 21
    Stradishall 110
    Sudbury 144
        Warfield Park 144
Surrey 6, 23–4, 143: map, 176–200
    Abinger 180, 193
    Albury 192

Bagshot 188
Banstead 190–1
Betchworth 193
Bletchingley 192
Caterham 183, 189
Chertsey 180
Chobham 183, 187
Clandon 188
Cranleigh 180, 190–3
Dorking 180, 190–1, 194–8
Edgeley 45
Elstead 192
Englefield
    Estate 146
    Green 144, 191
Epsom 180, 188
Esher 190–1, 196
Ewell 193
Farnham 188–9, 193
Frensham 192
Frimley 180
Godalming 188–90, 193, 198
Godstone 193
Great Bookham 192
Guildford 188, 190, 193
Horley 180, 193
Mickleham 189
Pirbright 180
Send 193
Shere 182, 193
Ripley 193
West Horsley 193
Woking 193
Worplesdon 193
Sussex 6, 17, 23–4, 31–2, 35, 103, 106, 111, 144, 151, 155, 176, 188, 191, 196
    Battle 28, 29 n. 32, 36, 103, 106, 111
    Brede 28
    Burwash 17
    Coldwaltham 32
    Hastings 28
    Icklesham 28
    Kirdford 32

Lewes 37, 128, 151
Mayfield 32
Petworth 196
Rye 21
Sydney, University of 128
Swallow, Samuel 46, 48
Swayne, John 144

Talfourd, Mr 151
Tallents, William Edward, 4th Duke of Newcastle 150–2
Tasmania 98, 100, 131
Tawney, R.H. 3
Taylor, Samuel 108
Taylor, Watson 57
Thames valley 148
  Ditton 183, 196
Thompson, E.P. 50, 58, 86, 90, 95–6, 110, 112, 177
  The Making of the English Working Class (1963) 1, 8
Thompson, William 46
Tilly, Charles 12, 68, 75–6, 81; see also Horn, N.
Timber Communities Australia 98
Times, The 27–8, 52, 110–11, 123, 127, 140, 145, 172
Times Literary Supplement 5
Tory 16, 26, 106, 144, 150, 186
Trafalgar 121
Tuma, N.B. 65, 69, 71, 79, 83

United States 71, 80, 96–7, 100, 134, 196
  Grand Canyon 96–7
  New York, 66 n. 12, 96, 105
    Adirondack Mountains 96
  Yellowstone 96

Van Diemen's Land *see* Tasmania
variation 141, 192
  local 8
  regional 17, 140
Vaughan, Baron 53

Vaughan, Henry H. (Assistant Commissioner of the Poor Law Commission) 191
Vaughan, Judge 164
Vendée 109
Vyse, Sir Richard Howard 142 and n. 13

wages 24, 27–9, 36, 40–1, 53, 55–7, 74, 77, 79, 127, 136, 166–7, 173, 177, 181–5, 192–4, 198–200
  bill 193
  day 169
  declining 161
  demonstrations 23, 30
  higher 28, 38, 40, 184
  inadequate 39, 114, 117–19
  increase in 146
  low 4, 53, 66, 162, 166, 180, 200
  plummeting 2
  improving 11, 31, 38
  winter 141
Wakefield, Edward Gibbon 114
Wakefield, John (bailiff) 27 n. 25
Wall, William 137
Wallis, Rose 19, cf. 159–75
Walsh, Sir John (Bt.) 144–5, 148, 153
Walters, Mr (sheriff) 145
Watts (farmer) 29
Wellington, duke of 36, 102, 107, 140–1
Wells, John 42, 53
Wells, Roger 4, 11, 13–15, 17, 22, 59, 87, 103–4, 127, 136, 141, 177, 179, 192
Wessex 135
Western Flying Post 25
Westmacott, Molloy 106, 109, 116
Westmore, Mr (farmer) 25, 32
White (farmer) 25
White, Charles (farmer and innkeeper) 123, 125
White, Edmund 49
White, Thomas 123
Whittet, Thomas 113

Wilde, Mr Serjeant 122, 130–2, 137–8
Wilder, George (brother of John) 148
Wilder, John 148
William IV, King 144
Williams, E.G. 12
Williams, D.E. 75
Wilson Croker, John 106
Wiltshire 6, 15, 25, 31–3, 41–2, 44, 46, 48–54, 58, 60–1, 109, 143: map, 144–5, 150, 160, 163–5, 168–70, 173–4, 185
   Aldbourne 60
   All Cannings 33
   Alton Barnes 41, 47, 50
   Amesbury 54
   Bedwyn 48, 57, 60
   Burbage 41, 47
   Charlton 56
   Christian Malford 11, 56
   Codford St. Peter 32
   Collingbourne 32
   Cricklade 46
   Devizes 41, 59, 141, 149, 162
      Division 56
   Enford 41, 47, 51, 56, 60
   Erlestoke 57
   Figheldean 51–2
   Fisherton 162
   Froxfield 54
   Heytesbury 47, 57, 144
   Hippenscombe 33, 55
   Horton 32
   Knook 25, 32
   Ludgershall 32
   Manningford Abbots 56
   Marden 47
   Market Lavington 11
   Marlborough 41–2, 49, 149, 162
   Oare 32, 54
   Ogbourne St Andrew 50, 57
   Pewsey 41, 54, 56
      Vale 59
   Potterne 59
   Pusey 109
   Quidhampton 51
   Ramsbury 11, 54, 142 n. 10
      'Ramsbury Ranter' 48
   Rockley 41, 49–50, 57
   Rushall 56
   Salisbury 160, 162–3, 165, 168, 174, 186
   Shalbourne 55
   South Savernack 42, 48
   Stanton St. Bernard 33
   Swindon 54
   Tisbury 47, 49–50
   Wanborough 42, 47, 53–4
   West Lavington 11
   Wilcot 41, 47
   Wilsford 47
   Wilton 33, 51–2
   Woodborough 56
   Wroughton 52
Windsor 145
   Castle 141
Withers, Peter 50, 57–8, 164
Worrall, David 14, 105, 108
Wraight, William 33
Wright Wilson Bt., Sir Henry 30, 39
Wrotham, George 114

Yeomanry 140–1, 156–7, 168
   Berkshire 140, 147
   Hindon troop 163
   Wiltshire 41, 42 n. 1, 58, 141 n. 6, 144
      Everley troop 41
      Marlborough troop 41, 49 n. 26
Yorkshire 44–6, 48, 50–1, 88, 112
   Marsden 50
   Holmfirth 46
Young, Henry (farmer) 121, 125

Zylan, Y. 71